WELFARE RIGHTS AND RESPONSIBILITIES

Contesting social citizenship

Peter Dwyer

The POLICY
P P
PRESS

First published in Great Britain in September 2000 by

The Policy Press
University of Bristol
34 Tyndall's Park Road
Bristol BS8 1PY
UK

Tel +44 (0)117 954 6800
Fax +44 (0)117 973 7308
E-mail tpp@bristol.ac.uk
www.policypress.org.uk

ISBN 1 86134 204 7

Peter Dwyer is Lecturer in Social Policy in the Department of Sociology and Social Policy at the University of Leeds, England.

Front cover: photograph supplied by kind permssion of Mark Simmons Photography, Bristol.
Cover design by Qube Design Associates, Bristol
Printed in Great Britain by Hobbs the Printers Ltd, Southampton

Contents

Acknowledgements

My thanks must go to a number of important people without whose help and cooperation the successful completion of this book would not have been possible. First, I would like to thank all the respondents who took part in the fieldwork which informs a significant part of this study. Additional thanks go to the individuals who helped to set up the focus group interviews at various organisations in Bradford. Second, many thanks to my good friend Richard Bednarek, whose work as an assistant moderator proved especially helpful. Third, thanks to Ian Law, Malcolm Harrison, Alan Deacon and Peter Beresford for their comments and input at various stages in the writing of this book.

On a more personal note thanks must go to my family and friends who supported me and put up with me boring them on numerous occasions over the past few years. Finally a particular mention must go to Linda, James and Anna for their patience, support and understanding throughout the whole process of finishing this work.

List of acronyms

AFDC	Aid to Families with Dependant Children
BCODP	British Council of Organisations of Disabled People
CI	Citizen's Income
COS	Charitable Organisation Society
CPAG	Child Poverty Action Group
CSJ	Commission for Social Justice
DfEE	Department for Education and Employment
DETR	Department of the Environment, Transport and the Regions
DPI	Disabled People's International
ERAS	Employment Rights Advice Service
IEA	Institute of Economic Affairs
IPPR	Institute of Public Policy Research
JRF	Joseph Rowntree Foundation
JSA	Jobseeker's Allowance
MAC	Mutual Aid Clause
NHF	National Housing Federation
NHS	National Health Service
NI	National Insurance
PI	Participation Income
PTP	Probationary Tenancy Period
PSI	Policy Studies Institute
UPIAS	Union of the Physically Impaired Against Segregation
WFTC	Working Families Tax credit
YTS	Youth Training Scheme

DEDICATION

This book is dedicated to my mother, Jean Dwyer, and also in loving memory of my father, James Dwyer (1936–98).

ONE

Introduction

This book explores some of the debates about citizenship and welfare. It is motivated by a desire to investigate and analyse competing accounts of citizenship's social element, at both social scientific and more specifically welfare service user levels. The latter is included in an attempt to allow some 'bottom-up' views into what is largely a debate dominated by social scientists and politicians. In order to do this the book draws heavily on a qualitative analysis of 10 different focus groups (see Appendix) that were purposively sampled according to a number of different criteria (eg ethnicity, gender, disability and age). It should be noted from the outset, however, that the book is not a comparative study which specifically highlights the impact that such criteria have on the varying accounts of citizenship and welfare given by the respondents. The inclusion of a number of different voices within the text is an attempt to carry out as inclusive a piece of research as possible. An important aim of the study is to move discussions about citizenship away from a purely theoretical level and allow the practical concerns of citizens (particularly those who are heavy users of public welfare services) to become an integral part of current debates concerning citizenship and welfare (compare Beresford and Croft, 1995). The term 'welfare service user' is used as a shorthand to denote ordinary citizens who are not normally involved in the formulation or implementation of welfare policies.

Although the empirical fieldwork that informs part of this book is largely (but not exclusively) focused on a body of respondents who have experience of having to rely on state-provided benefits and services for their day-to-day survival, the study recognises that 'welfare' is about more than that which Titmuss referred to as 'social welfare'. In his essay 'The social division of welfare' (1958), Titmuss argues that the state has a duty to meet the varying needs of its citizens. This it attempts to do, not with a single approach, but through three parallel systems of welfare, 'social,' 'fiscal' and 'occupational', each of which must be considered in any discussion of the welfare state[1]. By focusing their attention almost exclusively on Titmuss' 'social' component, it has been easy for certain politicians and commentators to set a narrow agenda when debating welfare reform. This agenda usually concentrates on both the pressing need to reduce the social security budget and the need to control and remoralise members of a welfare-dependant and deviant 'underclass'. This approach has had a negative effect on the welfare rights of many vulnerable groups in British society and has been increasingly challenged (Roseneil and Mann, 1994; Bagguley and Mann, 1992). Given this context, it is necessary to clarify from the outset that although this book is centred to a large extent on 'social welfare', and it seeks out the views of individuals who are often heavily reliant on publicly provided welfare services and benefits, it attempts to challenge the myopic approach outlined above; an approach that has at times dominated mainstream political and social policy debates about the reform of citizenship's social component.

As a counter to the above, there is a growing body of qualitative research that attempts to build an understanding of welfare and of social policy more generally by drawing heavily on service user accounts (eg Beresford et al, 1999; Beresford and Turner, 1997; Kempson, 1996; Law et al, 1994; Cohen et al, 1992; Croft and Beresford, 1989; Beresford and Croft, 1986). Similarly, the issue of citizenship and how ordinary citizens make sense of the concept is increasingly the subject of social research (Dean, 1999, 1997; Dean with Melrose, 1999; Dean and Melrose, 1998; Dwyer, 1998; MacKain, 1998; Beresford and Turner, 1997; Dean and Melrose, 1996; Conover et al, 1991; Croft and Beresford, 1989). It is intended that this book, by drawing extensively on service user accounts, will further our understanding of how ordinary citizens view citizenship and welfare in contemporary Britain. Simultaneously it is hoped that the research will in a small way enable the 'expert' perceptions and experiences of some of those at the sharp end of public welfare provision to inform social science perspectives and political debate about welfare citizenship.

Why citizenship, why welfare?

Citizenship remains a much discussed and highly contentious concept within social science, and as such any attempt to define it carries with it the possibility of challenge from those with a differing approach; indeed, in part this book is concerned with how ordinary citizens define the content and extent of citizenship. As Oliver and Heater (1994) point out, the word citizenship is used in a multitude of contexts and in so many different ways that a universal definition is virtually impossible. Faulks (1998), however, offers a salient insight when he notes that citizenship is usually defined by reference to three main criteria according to a legal definition, a philosophical definition or a socio-political definition.

> Legal definitions ... define the rights and duties of citizens in relation
> to the nation-state; philosophical definitions ... are concerned with
> normative questions such as which model of citizenship can best deliver
> a just society; and socio-political definitions emphasise citizenship as
> a status denoting membership of a society that involves a set of social
> practices. (Faulks, 1998, p 2)

There is of course no neat separation of these definitions; elements of the three dimensions that Faulks notes inform most perspectives. For the purpose of this book citizenship can be loosely defined as being concerned with a number of important interlocking relationships. It is fundamentally concerned with the relationship between individuals and the communities in which they reside, particularly the relationship between the individual citizen and the state[2]. It includes civil, political and social rights[3] and the ways in which they are connected. It also involves certain responsibilities; this in turn opens up important questions about the ways in which citizenship rights may be linked to those responsibilities. Indeed, Lister (1997a) characterises citizenship as a concept in which a key issue is the relationship between citizenship as a 'status', that brings with it enjoyment of civil, political and social rights, and citizenship as a 'practice', that involves responsibilities and duties. Having noted that citizenship is often defined in various ways and that a concrete definition remains elusive if not impossible, in terms of this book two initial questions need to be addressed: why utilise the concept of citizenship at all, and why focus specifically on the welfare element?

Citizenship is a valid concept for investigation for a number of important reasons. A notion of citizenship, however it is defined, has the potential to provide a benchmark against which it is possible to assess the status of certain individuals or groups in relation to access to the agreed rights and resources that are generally available to all those who are regarded as citizens within a specific community. Citizenship also offers the capacity for an exploration of the dynamics of social division to take in a number of important dimensions (eg class, gender, race, disability, age and so on) when assessing both the levels and causes of inequality within a society. A particular focus on the welfare element of citizenship can be defended in a number of important ways. As Harrison (1995) points out, in spite of the retrenchment that characterised the 1980s and early 1990s, the right to welfare continues to be regarded by many as a centrally important aspect of 'effective citizenship'.

> Citizenship is very much about relationships between individuals, groups, rights, duties and state institutions; it is also about relative degrees of incorporation and empowerment.... In any event, among its possible attributes effective citizenship certainly means being included in the systems of rights and welfare provisions that are mediated or managed by state agencies, and having one's needs met through mainstream political intermediation. (Harrison, 1995, pp 20-1)

The 'needs' referred to in the above quotation are, of course, not a straightforward issue; indeed a vast literature exists that offers competing discussions, constructions and definitions of need as it relates to welfare[4]. While it lies beyond the remit of this book to enter into these debates in any great detail, it is important to note that the way in which 'need' is defined and determined has a crucial effect on the type and extent of social rights enjoyed by different individuals and groups of citizens (Clarke and Langan, 1998). Claims to welfare rights are often underpinned by differing views on what constitutes a legitimate need and the role that the state or other agencies should play in meeting that need. As Marshall (1992) reminds us, there is no universal principle that legitimates the competing claims of citizens to welfare as a 'right', or the duty of the state to meet or refuse to meet specified welfare needs: both remain highly contested.

Three key themes, three elements of welfare

The linked concepts of citizenship and welfare open up the possibility of numerous themes for further investigation. This study, however, focuses on three key themes: that is, provision, conditionality and membership. In terms of citizenship and welfare they have an important relevance; indeed they are very much part of ongoing philosophical, social scientific and political debates about reform of the welfare state. Each of these themes also offers the possibility of asking welfare service users to share their views in relation to a number of fundamental questions that are of central importance when considering citizenship and welfare. In effect, the study is an attempt to consider answers and justifications to three main questions.

- Who/which institutions should provide welfare services and benefits to meet the needs of individual citizens? (provision)
- To what extent (if at all) should welfare rights first be conditional on individuals agreeing to meet communally (ie, in the modern context, state) defined responsibilities and duties? (conditionality)
- Who has a legitimate claim to welfare rights and who has not? (membership)

Such research can be further enhanced if these questions are considered in relation to differing elements of welfare provision. Accordingly three areas of welfare, that is, healthcare, housing and social security, have been selected for investigation. Focusing on more than one area of welfare in this way allows the book to explore pertinent issues in differing contexts, and offers the possibility of a more complex understanding of how citizens view the issues under investigation.

New Labour: a 'Third Way' for social citizenship?

In May 1997 a period of 18 consecutive years of Conservative government ended with New Labour's victory in the general election. It is clear that "the language of citizenship continues to lie at the heart of New Labour's project and in particular its proposals for welfare reform" (Dean, 1999, p 213). New Labour repeatedly focus on issues that are central to social citizenship: the role of the state and other agencies in meeting welfare needs, the relationship between rights and responsibilities, and issues of inclusion and exclusion (Blair, 1999a, 1998a, 1995b; Darling, 1999; DSS, 1998b; Harman, 1997; Mandelson, 1997).

Much of the rhetoric emanating from the Labour government emphasises a break with the past: 'out with the old, in with the new' (eg Darling, 1998; Blair, 1998b). For the government this notion of newness has a particular currency in legitimising the rejection of what it considers to be old outdated answers in favour of radical new answers. Labour is keen to package its policies as inherently different from those of its Conservative predecessors and sees its welfare reforms as the necessary corrective to two decades of inappropriate politics characterised by undesirable outcomes. Yet arguably the government's unease has less to do with principle and more to do with emphasis. Although Tony Blair has denounced the crude individualism and the market dogma of the New Right in the 1980s (Blair, 1998a, 1998b, 1995a), the government appears to be shifting its emphasis and accepting a more pragmatic role for the market, and combining this with a more sophisticated interpretation of the individualism that lay at the heart of the Conservative project rather than embarking on an inherently new programme for public welfare provision (Heron and Dwyer, 1999).

New Labour is, however, keen to present itself as new and radical with, for example, the Prime Minister especially enthusiastic to present the government's welfare reforms as part of a wider 'Third Way' endeavour (that moves beyond what he sees as the outdated concerns of the 'Old Left' and the 'New Right' politics), which he personally endorses as the new politics for a new century (Blair, 1999a, 1998a). It is important to look beyond the pronouncements of politicians and to assess the implications of current welfare reform in relation to citizenship; and also to explore the question of whether or not New Labour is engaged in something fundamentally new in relation to the welfare state.

The present New Labour government simultaneously rejects the outlook of the Old Left (typified by state control, high taxation and high public spending) and the New Right approach, with its hostility to public investment and collective forms of welfare, and seeks to replace them with a new Third Way politics positioned somewhere between the two (Powell, 1999; Hills, 1998). Debate about the ideological underpinnings, content and reality of a Third Way politics continues (Oppenheim, 1999; Powell, 1999; White, 1998), but both the Prime Minister (Blair, 1999a, 1998a) and the sociologist Giddens (1998) clearly believe that a Third Way politics, based on the core values of equal opportunity, rights being linked to responsibilities and individually autonomous subjects whose behaviour is regulated by wider communal rules, has something positive to offer social citizenship.

> The Third Way in welfare is clear: not to dismantle it [the welfare state]; or to protect it unchanged; but to reform it radically – taking its core values and applying them to the modern world. (Blair, 1999a, p 4)

In setting out its principles for welfare reform in the Green Paper *New ambitions for our country* (DSS, 1998b), the present government makes its message clear that they inherited an ineffectual and wasteful welfare state which failed to maximise its own potential and the potential of those who use it.

> The welfare system is a proud creation. But reform is essential if we are to realise our vision of a modern nation and a decent and fair society. Through our proposals we aim to break the cycle of

dependency and insecurity and empower all citizens to lead a dignified and fulfilling life. We need a new 'contract' between citizen and state, with rights matched by responsibilities. *We will rebuild the welfare state around a work ethic: work for those who can; security for those who cannot.* (DSS, 1998b, p 1; emphasis as in original text)

As the quote suggests, New Labour, unlike its Conservative predecessors, seeks to support state welfare, but in light of the social changes over the later half of the 20th century it sees the present welfare state as unsuitable for the next millennium. Labour therefore sees reform as essential if the welfare state is to meet the needs of citizens in this century. The above quotation is also useful in that it highlights the four linked themes that Powell (1999) identifies as central to Labour's Third Way future vision for welfare, that is, an active, preventative welfare state; the centrality of paid work; the distribution of opportunities rather than income; and the balancing of rights and responsibilities.

New Labour is adamant that it wants to fundamentally challenge all our attitudes in relation to the welfare state.

Our ambition is nothing less than a change of culture among benefit claimants, employers and public servants – with rights and responsibilities on all sides. Those making the shift from welfare into work will be provided with positive assistance, not just a welfare benefit. (DSS, 1998b, p 24)

In certain respects New Labour believes that the welfare state has encouraged a dependency culture among some individuals, with claimants passively relying on state welfare to meet their needs. Consequently the government now wants to encourage what they believe to be an active welfare system in which people are encouraged, persuaded or even compelled (Lund, 1999; Dwyer, 1998; Lister, 1998a, 1998b) to change their behaviour and attempt to improve themselves (and their chance of paid employment via training), rather than sitting passively by and expecting the state to meet their needs. According to New Labour, instigating policies that get people off welfare and into paid work is the best mechanism for tackling such passivity and dependency. The centrality of paid work within New Labour's welfare policies has been widely commented on (Lund, 1999; Powell, 1999; Stepney et al, 1999; Theodore and Peck, 1999; Tonge, 1999; Deacon, 1998; Dwyer, 1998; Jordan, 1998; Lister, 1998), and indeed the declaration that work offers the best route out of poverty for those who are able to engage with the paid labour market at first instance appears to be a common sense assertion. However, as Levitas (1998, 1996) has illustrated, employment in low paid, low status, insecure work does not necessarily guarantee that impoverishment is avoided.

The present administration also argues that a modern welfare state should provide opportunities for individual welfare recipients, but at the same time individuals have a duty to take up those opportunities. The state provision of welfare benefits, although seen as important for a minority who are unable to work, seems to have become an issue of secondary consideration, behind attempts to ensure the highest possible level of labour market participation. In terms of provision, therefore, New Labour accepts that the state has to assume a leading role in the provision of training and work opportunities, but in return it expects citizens to take up those opportunities and contribute to both their own and society's well-being. Alternatively individuals will have to get used to the idea that they have no right to expect support from the national community in the form of welfare rights.

The present government asks us to look beyond the narrow focus of welfare rights and emphasises a reciprocal relationship between welfare rights and responsibilities. Duty and responsibility rather than rights are now central to New Labour's approach. Pronouncements and policy documents on welfare regularly emphasise the importance of individual responsibility in all walks of life. In many areas New Labour now sees it as legitimate to link access to public welfare rights to individuals acting in a responsible manner, and it regards it as largely unproblematic to deny welfare rights to those who are deemed to be behaving irresponsibly. In certain sectors access to public welfare is becoming increasingly conditional (Dean, 1999; Lund, 1999; Dwyer, 1998; Lister, 1998) and this is a central theme of the book that will be developed in subsequent chapters.

Having highlighted the themes and values that Labour aspires to in its welfare reforms, it is useful to consider some specific key policies and legislation that have been introduced in the last two-and-a-half years. The initial point to note is that there has been a huge amount of activity with road shows, reviews, recommendations and new initiatives being introduced in many areas of welfare provision, for example social security, pensions, disability benefits, long-term care of older people and changes to the benefit system and tax system (see DoH, 1999; DSS, 1999a, 1999b, 1998a; Acheson, 1998; Hills, 1998). April 1998 saw the launch of Labour's 'New Deal' for welfare benefit claimants. Funded by a one-off windfall tax on the privatised utilities, this scheme, in which rights to benefit are linked explicitly to work and training responsibilities, was initially introduced for the young unemployed (for details see Chapter Three). The New Deal has since been gradually extended to cover other groups and under provisions in the newly ratified Welfare Reform and Pensions Act (DSS, 1999b) all new benefit claimants will have to attend compulsory job advice interviews with a case worker or face benefit sanctions. So in future lone parents will have to attend a meeting to discuss their job options once their youngest child is in school; new claimants for disability benefit will be treated in a similar fashion with medical examinations now emphasising an individual's ability to work rather than focusing on the levels of incapacity (DSS, 1999b).

In a concerted attempt to make work advantageous for the lower paid, the government has increasingly committed itself to using the tax system for the provision of welfare rather than paying out higher social security benefits. In October 1999 Family Credit was superseded by Working Families Tax Credit (WFTC) which provides a minimum income of £200 a week for a family with one child in which a parent is working (Inland Revenue, 1999). A disabled person's tax credit and a childcare tax credit that will pay up to £100 per week of the childcare costs for low-income families have also been introduced. The government has implemented a national minimum wage of £3.60 and it is committed to investing £300m in a national childcare strategy (Blair, 1999a; DSS,1999c). It is intended that these changes act as incentives for those on benefit to return to paid work if at all possible; such policies can be seen as consistent with the government's stated aim of moving people from welfare into work.

More generally New Labour is also concerned with combating social exclusion and poverty. Indeed, tackling social exclusion is seen by the government as one of its highest priorities, and in December 1997, it set up a social exclusion unit (SEU) which reports directly to the Prime Minister. Social exclusion is defined by the government,

> ... as a shorthand term for what can happen to people when people or areas suffer from a combination of linked problems such as unemployment, poor skills, low incomes, poor housing, high crime environments, bad health, poverty and family breakdown. (Cabinet Office, 1999, p1)

Leaving aside this catch-all definition, Dean (1999) has noted that the SEU has concentrated on producing reports which highlight specific problems (teenage pregnancy, truancy, rough sleeping, worst estates) rather than focusing on the negative effect that social inequality has on the citizenship status of many individuals. Other writers, most notably Levitas (1998, 1996), have argued that in terms of policy, New Labour defines social exclusion very narrowly as exclusion from paid work. She has argued that this is problematic for a number of important reasons. First, it marginalises other important causes of exclusion such as racism and sexism; second, it renders unpaid domestic and caring work invisible; and third, that it uncritically perpetuates a false underclass thesis that obscures the root cause of poverty, that is, capitalism.

In regard to tackling poverty the government has also made some bold statements, with the Prime Minister declaring that New Labour aims to eradicate child poverty within 20 years (White, 1999). The government has also recently published a report, *Opportunity for all* (DSS, 1999a), which combines a series of indicators to measure poverty with their strategy for tackling the causes of poverty. This approach is obviously different from its predecessors; it would be hard to imagine recent Conservative governments taking an interest in social exclusion and poverty in this way. Furthermore, the government remains willing to target public welfare provision, together with certain financial resources, at particular problem areas (Kemp, 1999; Hills, 1998). However, they also make clear that in return for state support it is expected that those who (potentially) benefit from such initiatives play their part by reacting positively to the opportunities offered; and it is opportunities rather than wealth that the government is most keen to redistribute. According to New Labour, a modern welfare state should offer a 'hand up' rather than a 'handout'. Merely increasing benefits is not seen as an option, because the government believes that such actions would encourage passive welfare dependency without tackling the root causes of poverty, that is, the unequal distribution of life chances and opportunities.

While the policies outlined above may be consistent with New Labour's stated approach, when considering social citizenship it is important to attempt to answer two questions. First, has New Labour gone about its welfare reform tasks in sufficiently new and innovative ways to be able to make grand claims about establishing a Third Way for welfare? Second, does the government's present approach promote inclusive outcomes for all of its citizens, or exacerbate certain forms of social division and social exclusion? A brief consideration of some recent and relevant policy developments in the three areas of welfare (health, housing and social security) that are the concern of this book may help to provide some answers.

When considering health policy Paton (1999) states that New Labour's overall strategy appears to be one of accepting and building on the approach of their predecessors. He notes that despite declarations to the contrary, the internal market introduced by the Conservatives in the 1990 NHS and Community Care Act remains, albeit in a somewhat altered state, with the terms 'commissioning' and 'service management' replacing 'purchaser' and 'provider' respectively. In future, the government has also made clear hospital building will be increasingly financed by private money; New Labour accepts and is looking to develop the private finance initiative, a policy that it had previously argued against in opposition (Powell, 1999). Such evidence suggests that it may be premature to talk of a Third Way in Labour's approach to health policy. In fact, as Paton (1999) notes, the government appears to be unable to decide between the (old red) devil of its rhetoric and the deep blue sea of its present practice.

> New Labour is more like Old Labour in terms of the goals it believes in for the NHS - a universal, comprehensive and egalitarian service. Yet in practice ... its approach is more in tune with the philosophy of the outgoing Conservative administration than in other areas of social policy: more old Labour in theory; more Tory in practice. (Paton, 1999, p 72)

Given that this book focuses on issues of provision, conditionality and membership (ie inclusion/exclusion), the ongoing debates concerning priority setting and rationing within the NHS are also of some relevance (see Walker, 1999; Langan, 1998a[5]). Increasing demands on the NHS, in terms of finance and new treatments, driven by advances in pharmaceutical and medical technology, combined with only limited increases in annual budget (and a government that is committed to low income tax rates and the control of public expenditure) indicate that the rationing debate may have an important impact on future rights to public healthcare. Exclusion from treatment on grounds of age, lifestyle/habit and nationality are already a reality for some (Langan, 1998a).

Kemp (1999) argues that housing was an area of social policy in which the Conservative administrations of the 1980s and 1990s had a profound impact. In terms of New Labour's response to the changes instigated by their predecessors, Kemp also notes that, "New Labour has accepted some of the analysis and many of the policy prescriptions of Conservatives" (Kemp, 1999, p 146). They are committed to their predecessor's vision of a quasi-market system of housing provision which sees housing associations as the main providers of social housing in the future. They have accepted and built on Conservative measures to curb anti-social behaviour (see Chapter Three), measures which potentially may exacerbate exclusion within social housing. Such outcomes run counter to stated wishes to promote inclusion via locally focused initiatives such as the 'New Deal for Communities' and other neighbourhood renewal projects aimed at deprived areas (Kemp, 1999; Hills, 1998). In terms of financial resources, while the amount of money spent on urban regeneration schemes and housing looks set to increase in the long-term analysis of the recent spending review figures indicates that capital investment in social housing by Labour in its first term of office will be significantly less than Tory spending in their last period of government (Shelter, 1998, p 10). In short, New Labour believes that the market is the best mechanism for providing housing, while simultaneously accepting that some government intervention may be necessary in order to ensure that those who do least well from the market system do not end up homeless (Kemp, 1999).

Previous discussion of the New Deal, the welfare reform Green Paper (DSS, 1998b), the Welfare Reform and Pensions Act (DSS, 1999b) and the recent cuts in lone parent benefit (see Smith, 1999) indicate that New Labour is committed to a less than generous system of social security benefits. The New Deal project to a certain extent accepts and builds on the New Right's premise of a welfare-dependant 'underclass' and the need to coerce or cajole passive welfare recipients into the paid labour market; indeed Stepney et al (1999) argue,

> ... that a simplistic and moralistic view of poverty and social exclusion was developed by the Conservatives in the 1980s and popularised in the media in the 1990s. Arguments about dependency, obligation and responsibility, first deployed against black 'welfare mothers' and young people in the USA (Mead, 1986) were imported to Britain in the Thatcher years, and have since exerted influence on both the Major and Blair administrations. (1999, p 123)

Today New Labour's reforms of social security largely build on the agendas of their Conservative predecessors. There is less emphasis on universal benefits being available as a right of citizenship and New Labour now looks to target benefits and wider social welfare spending via means testing.

It is reasonable to state that the policies outlined above are consistent with New Labour's stated goals in reforming the welfare state. Following the significant legislative changes of recent Conservative administrations (and their attempt to redefine the link between the individual citizen and the state), the role of the state continues to be renegotiated, particularly with regard to meeting the needs of its citizens through the provision of public welfare. The British postwar welfare settlement has always been subject to political debate, but against the backdrop of the New Labour government's substantial welfare reforms, research into the changing character of welfare citizenship in Britain, and the principles that underpin that change, is particularly valid.

Outline of chapters

The book is divided into two main parts. Part 1 explores some ongoing social science debates concerning welfare and citizenship. Following this introductory chapter, which defines the boundaries of the study, Chapter Two looks at the differing philosophical traditions of liberalism and communitarianism and explores how their conflicting views on the nature and importance of the 'individual' and 'community' affect their competing visions of citizenship. The individualism central to the liberal project is discussed and an important distinction is made between 'libertarian' liberals, who largely oppose collective welfare provisions, and their more 'egalitarian' counterparts, who envisage a citizenship that embraces a notion of 'social justice' and a system of recognised welfare rights. The communitarian approach is then highlighted and its concerns and criticisms of liberalism noted. Tonnies' work is then explored, as his *Gemeinschaft* and *Gesellschaft* offer insight into contrasting assumptions that underpin liberal and communitarian understandings of the concept of community. The chapter concludes by noting that philosophically, within both liberalism and communitarianism, the extent, and in some cases the legitimacy, of the welfare element of citizenship continues to be a source of much debate.

Although to some extent philosophical concerns inform Chapter Three, its primary purpose is to explore in more detail five perspectives on citizenship and welfare that are of relevance in the contemporary British setting. In each case a general introduction is offered, followed by a discussion of some salient issues. This in turn is succeeded by an analysis of each of the chosen perspectives in terms of the three key themes that are central to the study, that is, provision, conditionality and membership. The first standpoint to be considered is the one outlined by T.H. Marshall in *Citizenship and social class* (1992)[6]. His general theory of citizenship is discussed, with particular attention to the social rights element. A brief look at some of his many critics is also included in this section. The chapter then moves on to consider two very different approaches to citizenship and welfare, those of the New Right and the new communitarians. This is followed by an analysis of New Labour's outlook with regard to the welfare element of citizenship. Finally, an Islamic perspective on welfare is offered. This is included to provide some background information that is useful when considering the opinions of the Muslim respondents who took part in the research. Overall in this chapter, it is argued that the vision of citizenship which Marshall outlined, with its important social rights element, underpinned by extensive state guaranteed provisions, has been superseded by a new welfare orthodoxy that stresses a reduced role for the state in the provision of welfare and increasingly conditional social rights.

An important aim of Part 2 of the book is to move discussions about citizenship away from a purely theoretical level and allow the practical concerns of citizens (particularly those who are heavy users of public welfare services) to become an integral part of current debates concerning citizenship and welfare. Part 2, therefore, consider the perceptions, insights and opinions of the respondents who shared their views in the focus groups that formed the empirical fieldwork element that is central to this study. In order to present these views as accurately as possible, extensive use is made of the textual data generated by the respondents' discussions. Particular attention is given to the respondents' own justifications for their various points of view in order to generate a greater insight into how they experience and negotiate their status as 'citizens', particularly within the context of welfare provision. These empirical chapters relate directly to the three key themes that were chosen for investigation: provision, conditionality and membership.

The fourth chapter addresses a question central to social citizenship: the question of who/which agencies should be expected to provide welfare. The respondents' views on the role of the state, the market and other agencies in addressing their welfare needs are presented. Several related topics, including the adequacy/inadequacy of current state provisions, the problem of stigma and state welfare, and the issue of financing welfare rights, are also covered. Two key findings can also be drawn from this chapter: first, the respondents are unanimous in their agreement that social rights are a valid and valued part of the citizenship package; and second, the majority of respondents also believe it is important that the state continues to play a major role in providing to meet their welfare needs in the future.

Chapter Five analyses welfare service users' views on conditionality. Conditionality is concerned with the relationship between citizenship rights and responsibilities. The main feature of this chapter is an exploration of a 'principle of conditionality'[7] within the three areas of welfare that are under discussion. The related question of whether or not the respondents think that it is reasonable for the state to use means tests (a form of financial conditionality) in order to limit access to public welfare is then addressed by looking at two issues: the provision of long-term residential care for older citizens and the 'problem' of personal savings. Further sections in this chapter consider the issue of an unconditional citizen's income and also the possible extension of highly conditional welfare into the areas of fiscal and occupational benefits. The most significant finding of this chapter is that the degree to which the respondents see the imposition of a principle of conditionality as fair depends extensively on the area of welfare in which it is applied.

The final chapter that draws heavily on the empirical data is Chapter Six, which looks at membership. This chapter explores issues of inclusion and exclusion and highlights the ground rules which citizens see as being pertinent when assessing claims for inclusion in collective welfare arrangements. It is clear that many respondents view certain people as having legitimate claims to welfare, while the claims of others are often seen as invalid. A powerful discourse centred around a deserving/undeserving distinction was a recurrent feature of the respondents' conversations. Interestingly, a perceived lack of individual contribution and/or responsibility appears to be highly significant to those who seek to rationalise their decisions to exclude certain individuals from access to welfare rights; similar justifications were to the fore among those respondents who saw increasing conditionality as a positive step. This chapter clearly indicates that a substantial number of the respondents see exclusion as an acceptable part of any notion of citizenship.

In conclusion, Chapter Seven considers the key findings from the fieldwork presented in Chapters Four to Six. These findings are then reassessed in light of the previously discussed liberal and communitarian philosophies on citizenship. Finally, New Labour's recent reforms of welfare are reconsidered in terms of their impact on social citizenship. It is suggested that, although aspects of New Labour's reforms may attract popular support, nonetheless, New Labour will have to modify its present approach if it is serious about delivering a truly inclusive system of public welfare in the future.

Notes

[1] 'Social welfare' consists of the publicly provided funds and services (social security benefits, local authority housing, the NHS, personal social services and so on) that are often the single focus of dispute when the welfare state is discussed. In addition Titmuss emphasises the importance of 'fiscal welfare' (tax allowances and relief, mortgage relief) and also 'occupational welfare', the perks derived from advantageous employment in the labour market (pensions

and fringe benefits such as cars, meals, private health schemes and so on). The healthcare, education, social services and other wide ranging and significant benefits that the welfare state provides help to meet the varying needs of many different individuals and groups. By redefining welfare in a wider context Titmuss illustrates that differing welfare provisions, fully sanctioned by the state, are delivered to different groups within British society. The middle classes gain substantially from public welfare in the wider sense.

[2] An increasingly globalised economy and the emergence of supranational communities such as the European Union are issues that effect this relationship. Nonetheless, in spite of these changes, as Harrison (1995, pp 14-16) makes clear, to a great extent the nation state continues to have an important role in defining the backdrop against which individual citizenship is more generally experienced. This is particularly the case when considering many social rights.

[3] Other rights elements, environmental rights, are increasingly on the citizenship agenda; however, this book is concerned only with the three elements above and particularly the social element.

[4] See, for example, Langan, 1998b; Wetherly, 1996; Doyal and Gough, 1991; Croft and Beresford, 1989; Taylor, 1989.

[5] Langan (1998a) provides a particularly clear introduction to these debates.

[6] All page references for *Citizenship and social class* refer to a 1992 reprint of the 1949 lecture.

[7] Deacon (1994) describes such a principle as one where eligibility to certain basic, publicly provided, welfare entitlements becomes dependent on an individual first agreeing to meet particular compulsory duties or patterns of behaviour.

Part I
Social science accounts and debates

Philosophical underpinnings. Liberalism and communitarianism: the individual citizen and community

Introduction

In any analysis of contemporary citizenship it is necessary to consider two conflicting ontological views on the character and importance of both the individual and the social worlds (communities) that they inhabit[1]. The liberal position, with its emphasis on individual autonomy guaranteed by individually held rights, a universal conception of justice, and a 'neutral state', can be contrasted with that of its communitarian critics who stress the primacy of community and the social embeddedness of human actors. The philosophical debate between these two broad camps provides a backdrop against which it is possible to reconsider the differing notions of both community and state that liberals and communitarians hold, and any practical implications that this may have when developing ideal theories of citizenship. It should be noted that the aim here is not to set up two, over-simplistic, mutually opposed approaches and merely criticise. Indeed, it must be accepted that many conflicting opinions are held on both sides, and that away from the extremes of the debate it is possible to find some concessions across the divide. The primary purpose of the 'liberal' and 'communitarian' categories is to provide a starting point from which analysis may proceed. The use of such crude categories may also be defended because the taking of an essentially liberal or communitarian approach as an initial point of departure impacts upon the practice and scope of the citizenship later envisaged. Following on from this largely theoretical discussion of the individual subject citizen, the contested concept of community will be examined initially using Tonnies *Gemeinschaft* and *Gesellschaft* (1955) as a starting point. This chapter will also consider the extent to which the modern nation can be viewed as a community and the extent to which the modern state should intervene in the lives of its citizens.

The liberal individual

Liberal political theory covers a broad spectrum of ideas. A linear representation would probably have the libertarian liberalism of Nozick (1995), Hayek (1944) and Friedman (1962) at the opposite end of a line from the egalitarian approaches of Rawls (1995, 1971), Kymlicka (1995) and Dworkin (1995). However, all these approaches share one important common theme, that of the primacy of the individual actor when framing an understanding of the nature of social reality. Given this assertion of the primacy of the abstract individual in the liberal thesis, it is important to outline a basic understanding of the development and implications of such an approach.

Lukes (1973) identifies the central importance of individualism to the liberalism that developed in England in the latter half of the 19th century. It is an outlook in which four basic ideas find their expression: the dignity of man [sic], and individual rights to autonomy, to privacy and to self-development.

The acceptance of these central tenets leads to a morally situated way of conceiving the individual, one that draws heavily on Kantian a *priori* assumptions. The individual is seen as the 'natural' human condition: we each have individual wants, purposes and needs that are arrived at by personal rational thought and choice. Forms of social life, therefore, become means to personal ends. Society, or more specifically the communities that we inhabit at differing levels (from local neighbourhoods up to the nation state), are seen merely as sets of actual, or possible, social arrangements which respond to these individual requirements.

The political and economic implications of this liberal individual approach have a particular relevance to the citizenship debate. Government is based on the individually given consent of its citizens, its authority resting on consent gained at free elections. Citizens here are held to be independent, rational beings able to be the best judges of their own interests. The primary purpose of a government, therefore, is seen as the recognition and protection of limited individual rights. Political representation is limited theoretically to the representation of the interests of the individual and not those of classes or groups.

> Just as the free market was assumed to lead to the maximum benefit of all, so would the reformed political system (with electors and representatives all pursuing their individual interests) maximise the aggregate satisfaction of men's [sic] separate individual interests. The

'invisible hand' worked in politics just as in economics. (Lukes, 1973, p 83)

A 'neutral' and minimal state is assumed appropriate, with government seen as a referee of varying individual interests, while simultaneously stressing individual rights to liberty and property.

An economic individualism complements this view of the political world. It is a view underpinned by the belief that different individuals have differing abilities and each should be allowed to develop those abilities in open competition with other individuals. It is the market built on the institutions of free trade and private property that provides the arena for the contest. It is taken for granted that a minimal state will provide the conditions necessary for personal liberty, while a competitive market system will meet any requirements for efficiency and equity.

Libertarian liberals: anti-collectivists against an extensive welfare state

Nozick (1995), Friedman (1962) and Hayek (1944) all advance libertarian liberal arguments that envisage a limited role for the state. They believe the function of government is to ensure basic limited civil and political rights, but beyond this it should not intervene and attempt to promote or sustain any particular ideal of a just society. It is argued that beyond the random inequality of the market it is impossible to reach a consensus about a fair distribution of wealth, and any attempt to reach one would lead only to false definitions. The state action required to secure social justice merely interferes with market mechanisms, the key source of individual liberty. The rewards distributed by the market alone are held to be the only just ones, as they will reflect individual ability and effort.

Nozick (1995) asserts this approach. Preferring to speak of an individual's 'holdings', he regards even the term 'distributive justice' as ideologically loaded. Whether or not a distribution (holding) is seen as just depends on how it came about. Nozick maintains that in a wholly just world an entitlement theory based on two 'historical' principles would ensure a fair distribution.

(1) A person who acquires a holding in accordance with the principle of justice in acquisition is entitled to that holding. (2) A person who acquires a holding in accordance with the principle of justice in transfer from someone else entitled to that holding is entitled to the holding. (Nozick, 1995, p 138)

It follows from the above that nobody is entitled to a holding except by repeated applications of (1) and (2). A holding is deemed just dependant on its historical context, that is, how it came about in the first instance[2]. These two principles sit easily alongside an individualist free market approach. In contrast redistributive welfare economics are said by Nozick to be based on 'current time slice theories' that are primarily concerned with issues of who ends up with what. Justice in such approaches is based on 'end result' or 'end state' principles. This contrasts with his previously outlined theory, based on an historical principle of justice, which allows for the past circumstances and actions of individuals to create 'just' differential entitlements and deserts. In short, great inequalities in holdings can be justified. Nozick's notion of distributive justice has important implications for social rights. As an individual you may choose to be charitable in order to reduce the poverty of others, but state welfare policies funded by tax revenues are considered coercive of individual freedom and an unjust form of the redistribution of holdings. Socialist or social democratic redistributive schemes must therefore be abandoned in favour of what Nozick sees as the non-coercive distributions generated in market exchanges.

As King (1987) reminds us, latter day libertarian liberal economists draw heavily on Adam Smith's (1776) laissez-faire approach. Hayek's notion of 'catallaxy' is very similar to Smith's 'invisible hand' in that the workings of the market are said to produce a kind of spontaneous social order; a stance bearing a strong resemblance to Nozick (1995) who assumes that individuals in the pursuit of self-interest will produce a collective social prosperity. They also echo Smith's somewhat paradoxical approach in recognising areas where the state must intervene in order to ensure the continued operation of a free market system; a primary requirement being state support for a legal framework that guarantees the property rights necessary for such economic activity.

Smith (1766) similarly recognised that the state had to be responsible for the defence of its borders. Crucially he also believed that the state had a responsibility to provide some public goods for its citizens which the market alone would fail to produce. This last point brings us to the contested ground within the citizenship debate. The extent to which state intervention into the workings and outcomes of the market is accepted or rejected affects greatly the scope of social rights. The central issue here is whether or not a measure of material equality is to become as integral a part of the citizenship equation as the individual freedom that libertarian liberals hold to be of paramount importance.

Friedman (1962) outlines four legitimate areas for limited state intervention: defence, the judicial system, the meeting of 'externality' problems (ie addressing the consequences of unforeseen market failure), and a responsibility to meet the needs of those, such as children and disabled people, who through no fault of their own have a limited ability to engage with the market. There is a tentative acceptance "that the state has some responsibility for assisting the less well off but such efforts should be market based rather than paternalistic" (King, 1987, p 85); consequently the scope of government interventions must be carefully controlled to allow economic wealth and political freedoms to flourish. Today, given its dominance in the last two decades, this free market model of economic behaviour has a particular relevance. Its significance as a useful representation of the complex world of modern economic activity, in spite of its prominence, must, however, be seriously questioned. Monopolistic or oligopolistic enterprises are increasingly a characteristic in modern market economies and it is often such companies without opposition which continue to generate large profits. Consumer demand does not necessarily regulate supply either; the needs of the wealthy may indeed be met by the market but the needs of the poor are often ignored or undersupplied (King, 1987). A laissez-faire approach does not exist: it is doubtful if indeed it ever did. The policies that today challenge the principles of the welfare state have required the state to set up and maintain a particular framework in which competition and price mechanisms are protected and promoted, and companies have rights similar to individuals.

For 'libertarian' liberals the state recognises the extent of its responsibilities to its citizens by promoting such an economic framework while simultaneously upholding individual civil and political rights. The distribution of goods that then ensues from the efficient functioning of a market economy is regarded as just. Individuals are entitled to what they can get provided they do not cheat or violate another person's individual rights. This, however, is only one standpoint within the liberal tradition: egalitarian liberalism takes the issue of individual rights and distributive justice a significant step further.

Egalitarian liberalism

The egalitarian liberalism of Rawls (1995, 1971) pushes the ideals of liberal theory beyond traditional libertarian preoccupations with civil and political rights, and argues that liberalism needs to elaborate a notion of distributive justice which attempts to take into account the equality of claims of each individual in respect of basic needs and the means by which those needs will be met. He rejects the principle that the market will distribute goods fairly, pointing to a random distribution of both the talents and assets that help to define the end rewards under such a system. In doing so Rawls tacitly acknowledges the need for the state to recognise certain social rights. It is therefore seen as legitimate for the state to intervene in the lives of its citizens to ensure a redistribution of material resources so that all individuals can become free to pursue their own definition of the good life.

The basic question then becomes how (if the market cannot provide the foundational principles for a theory of distributive justice) can we come to agree on a basic format to ensure both liberty and a measure of equality? The two principles of justice that Rawls outlines to this end are, he suggests, those which would be chosen by any rational individual operating behind "a veil of ignorance" (Rawls, 1971, p 136). In effect, Rawls invites us to choose the principles with which we would define a just distribution of goods in an imaginary situation prior to knowing our own individual fit (such as class, status, conception of good, aims and so on) into that society for which we were attempting to define the principles. He then goes on to argue that any rational agent in such a situation would arrive at the same two principles in order to define a just distribution of goods.

> (1) Each person is to have an equal right to the most extensive total system of equal basic liberties compatible with a similar liberty for all.
> (2) Social and economic inequalities are to be arranged so that they are both (a) to the greatest benefit of the least advantaged, consistent with the joint savings principle (the joint savings principle provides for a fair investment for future generations), and (b) attached to offices and parties open to all under condition of fair equality of opportunity. (Rawls, 1971, p 302)

In such a society "all social primary goods – liberty and opportunity, income and wealth and the bases of self-respect – are to be equally distributed unless an unequal distribution of any or all of these goods is to the advantage of the least favoured" (Rawls, 1971, p 303).

Liberalism's dilemma: distributive justice beyond the market?

For the libertarian New Right (see Chapter Three), public welfare provision has become a central issue; it is an area where their ideological assertions that the market rather than the state is better suited to meeting the diverse social needs of modern society have had a practical impact on the social rights of many individuals. The essential difference within the welfare agendas of what may loosely be termed the libertarians and the egalitarians is the extent to which social rights should be universally guaranteed by the state or be provided on a selective basis by the market to those who can afford to purchase them.

A strong defence for limiting state-guaranteed social rights is made by Barry (1990). Outlining 'a classical liberal' (ie libertarian and anti-collectivist) approach to welfare, he argues that social (public) welfare can be seen as legitimate only if it maximises the choices available to all individuals to the same extent and helps to increase the provision of welfare generally available. Particular claims to welfare derived from membership of a defined community or any notion of shared citizenship are regarded as invalid in Barry's account. Indeed, he believes that an extensive welfare state is a causal factor in the perpetuation of social problems and a contributory factor in a failure to generate a 'good' citizenry, because easily available welfare has "a well documented tendency to encourage the preference of welfare over work" (Barry, 1990, p 39). Marshall's (1992) theorisation of citizenship is dismissed as fundamentally flawed on both an instrumental and moral level.

The basic problem here for Barry is the grounds on which the priority of needs over wants can be established. How, he asks, can need be objectively quantified when it is an infinitely contestable concept? Attempts by the state to do so which found their ultimate expression in the setting up of a comprehensive welfare state have, he maintains, established an inherently paternalistic system that precludes or limits individual choice and hands power over to bureaucratic officials and institutions. For Barry, 'classic Marshallian' citizenship theory and its many latter day disciples who emphasise universality do us all a disservice; the end result is not personal empowerment but a limit on individual choice and the waste of valuable resources. The welfare state, he argues, should be a minimal system to address the potential victims of governmental interventions. On a wider front, attempts to include social and economic rights within an agreed citizenship framework should be resisted on two grounds. First, such rights impinge on the liberty of individuals who should be free to make their own arrangements and not dependant on the coercive activities of the state; and second, they cannot promote wider equality within a society even if this is regarded as a legitimate aim because, according to Barry, "inequalities have as much to do with certain features of the human condition as they have with differing social and economic systems, if not more so" (Barry, 1990, p 72).

Barry's vision of citizenship, that sees the social element as legitimately limited to an expansion of market-led solutions to social and economic problems and an extension of the rights and importance of the consumer, does not go unchallenged. In opposition to such libertarianism, Plant (1990) essentially takes an egalitarian liberal stance and argues that social and economic rights must be part of the citizenship package if it is to retain a relevance; any distinction that privileges civil and political rights above and beyond the social element is seen as flawed. Plant (1990) believes that a citizenship which includes a substantial social element offers the possibility of developing a new politics of common identity that goes beyond old class or sectional interests.

The central aim of a social democratic state, according to Plant, should be to establish a set of citizenship rights to resources from outside the market. Critical of the stance taken by Barry (1990), he attacks libertarian approaches to freedom as defective. To hold a negative view of liberty, that is, to see freedom merely in terms of being free from intentional coercion, entails, according to Plant, a false distinction between ability and resources on the one hand, and the issue of freedom on the other. This philosophical dichotomy forms one of the bases of New Right (libertarian) opposition to redistributive policies and simultaneously endorses another: the idea that markets cannot infringe individual freedoms as their outcomes are unintended and non-enforceable therefore, "within the market all that matters is the consumer and his/her choices" (Plant, 1990, p 10). Given this outlook, the notion of a redistributive social justice is flawed as it leads to a false distribution of goods and rewards. Inequalities in income and poverty are believed to be more effectively dealt with by the 'trickle-down' effect of free market economics. Citizenship for libertarians, therefore, should not be concerned with an extensive publicly funded social element: this is seen as invalid. The state has a limited role of non-coercion; any empowerment of vulnerable groups, or more precisely improvement in their material conditions, is left to the mercy of economic theory or private charitable action.

Plant (1990) accepts that market outcomes are unintended but rejects the view that because their effects are unforeseeable we should bear no collective responsibility for the results of their operation. He believes that if citizenship is to become a positive basis for a common, inclusive national identity the needs of those who do less well from the continuing operation of a capitalist economy have to be met; that is, citizenship must include a package of social rights which are not tied directly to market outcomes if it is to have any future relevance. The content and extent of those rights may be open for negotiation and is an issue that is certainly linked to finite resources, but essentially decisions about need and how it

misconstrues our capacity for self–determination and neglects the social preconditions under which that capacity is established. The overtly individualistic liberal view of the 'unencumbered self' is held to be ontologically false. Communitarians believe that the individual central to liberalism is an impossibility; individuality, self-, identity, a notion of who we are is said to be socially embedded[3]. Self-determination is exercised within a social and communal setting. The only way to understand human behaviour is to refer to individuals in their social, cultural and historical contexts: we are first and foremost social beings (Avineri and de Shalit, 1995; Bell, 1995; Kymlicka, 1992; and more specifically Sandel, 1995; Taylor, 1995). Similarly communitarian thinking rejects the idea of liberal universalism, as overarching societal principles cannot be defended; objective standards of morality or justice are said not to exist as they take little account of the importance of community or social context when developing a political approach (Walzer, 1995; MacIntyre, 1995). It is only as members of a community that we can find and sustain deep moral beliefs. A strong sense of 'community,' defined here as "a body with some common values, norms and goals in which each member regards the common goal as her own" (Avineri and de Shalit, 1995, p 7) is, for communitarians, a basic need. Community makes individual autonomy possible by protecting and sustaining its members, and in return is able to demand and justify individual loyalty to communally defined obligations and practices that are particular and specific to a designated community.

Although some communitarian scholars do not believe that the concept of community can be stretched to encompass debate at a national level, Walzer (1995) sees the possibilities for modern nation states to embrace a communitarian approach. Miller's (1995) discussion also centres particularly on the idea of a national community bound together by a common citizenship that stresses obligations as the direct corollary of rights, but one in which the theoretical liberal stance of a neutral state must be abandoned for a politics of the 'common good'. A benchmark against which other people's preferences are viewed, this 'common good' "takes precedence over the claims of individuals to the resources and liberties needed to pursue their own conception of good" (Kymlicka, 1992, p 207). The way in which the communal life is lived will determine the relevant concept of the good life. An important attendant consequence of this idea is that if a national community is so radically divided that a single set of rules (as the basis for a common citizenship) cannot be agreed, then the nation must divide into smaller territories (Walzer, 1995).

Communitarians stress that the state cannot stand as referee to competing conceptions of the good but should actively intervene to promote specific ideas for the good of the national community. People must be bound together by shared ideas of what that good consists of, otherwise the continued drift towards the anomic individualism that liberalism promotes will pull society apart. Bell (1995) notes the paradox that underpins many modern liberal societies. The state intervenes to protect and promote civil and political liberties, and increasingly to ensure a particular interpretation of a 'just' distribution of material resources; but ironically the neutrality of state principle curtails governmental interventions that allow policies to be pursued that seek to ensure or revive a particular notion of community and communal living[4]. These criticisms of liberalism are the basis from which communitarian thinking moves forward; it is appropriate therefore to now examine them in more detail.

The constitutive community

Sandel (1995) outlines a powerful critique of 20th-century democratic liberalism and urges a political theory that acknowledges a plurality of answers rather than a universal vision as a way forward. The liberal approach, he contends, gives pride of place to the promotion of the universal notions of justice, fairness and individual rights. The just society envisaged by the liberal thinker does not at first appear to advance any particular perception of 'good' but attempts to provide for an ideal framework of a just society: one in which individual citizens can pursue their own values and ends consistent with a similar liberty for others. This liberal vision, as Sandel points out, has a deep and pervasive philosophical appeal that influences the way in which we live and think about the world. The communitarian sees this as being based on the flawed claim that 'right' must override specific notions of 'good'. Liberalism therefore becomes more than a set of regulative principles: it is also a view of how we can know our social world. These principles find their moral basis by assuming a Kantian *a priori*, transcendental view of the self, with the individual subject seen as prior to and independent of experience. The basis of moral law is found in the individual subject capable of autonomous will. As Sandel points out, this allows the possibility of freedom but also emphasises that individual rights must precede notions of common good.

Sandal holds that Rawls (1971) accepts such presuppositions when developing his ideal of the original position and the veil of ignorance. He invites us to choose the principles by which we would govern a society before we know what particular persons we are and before knowing our interests or ideas of good. Sandel is highly critical of this concept of the unencumbered self. A constitutive community which has a role in framing identity is clearly denied.

> Freed from the dictates of nature and the sanction of social roles, the human subject is installed as sovereign, cast as the author of the only moral meanings there are. (Sandel, 1995, p 20)

For Sandal, Rawls' liberal theory of justice is flawed because it is based on a concept of the individual that is meaningless to the communitarian. It is wrong to outline a speculative view of the individual actor that takes no account of the constitutive attachments of community, such as family, neighbourhood and nation. The end result is not a theory based on the ideal and free agent, but one based on individuals who are without real character and lacking in depth.

This traditional philosophical hostility of liberalism towards the idea of constitutive communities has privileged the ideal of the neutral nation state in liberal theory where it is viewed as the most (possibly only) valid form of political association. Sandel acknowledges the common liberal criticism that a large-scale national constitutive community echoes the darker politics of rule by a moral majority, but concludes that in making its peace with the concentrated power of the state 20th-century liberalism has become a failed project. For Sandel, the modern liberal procedural republic requires, indeed demands, a concentration of power which is intrinsically linked to the notions of universal rights and entitlements. This has led to a crowding out of other democratic possibilities and has undercut the kinds of community on which the nation state depends. Local preferences have been levelled out; as rights and entitlements have expanded the smaller forms of political association have been replaced by the universal form of the nation state. In public life "we are more entangled and less attached than ever before" (Sandel, 1995, p 28). Ironically, by placing universal rights at centre stage, Sandel argues that the liberal approach has made us less free; increasingly dependant on the nation state, we are individually disempowered and detached from the communities that enabled us to develop values.

The importance of obligation

The primacy of rights thesis that liberalism presupposes is further challenged by Taylor (1995) who attempts to counter its atomistic foundations by putting forward a view of humans as socially defined beings. He sees the political atomism of 17th-century social contract theory as being inherited by 20th-century liberalism which continues to view society as an aggregate of individuals joined together for the fulfilment of primarily individual ends. Unconditional individual rights play a central role, while an obligation to sustain society or to obey authority[5] is denied a similar status and, as it is dependant on individual consent, it is usually only granted when in some way it can be seen to be personally advantageous. Taylor argues that atomism has become ingrained in modern thinking and therefore allows the liberal view to appear plausible. If an anti-atomistic, social, view of humanity can be put forward and sustained, the primacy of individual rights can be seen as wrong and several criticisms of it become valid.

In asserting our individual rights before all other considerations, we stand in danger of destroying the society which we inhabit; not only do we deprive others of the right to exercise their rights but we also undermine our capacity to exercise our own rights in a social (communal) setting. He believes that it is important to recognise obligations wider than our own concerns; we must recognise the rules that a society needs in order to function (Taylor, 1995). Most primacy of rights theorists (Nozick, Hayek), according to Taylor, offer a limited perception of autonomy, usually an assertion of the freedom to choose one's life plans and to be free to act without constraint. Private property and the right to dispose of it is held to be an essential element of genuine independence. Taylor disputes such outlooks, believing that the 'free' individual of the West is only what s/he is by virtue of the whole society and civilisation that gave rise to and sustains them. The capacity for autonomy is developed in a social setting and this in turn creates significant obligations to reaffirm the value of this definition of freedom. Liberty is not individually defined; there are social conditions for freedom which is very much defined in association with others. Identity, a notion of who or what we are, according to Taylor, is centrally based on interaction with other members of 'our' society.

The problem of the liberal notion of social justice

A strong argument against the liberal concept of universally accepted values is presented by MacIntyre (1995). His account initially provides an insight on a practical level: two citizens, A and B, both inhabit a similar social world but each has differing ideas on the concept of social justice. A works hard and saves to send her children to school and chooses to pay for private medical care. When faced with the possibility of higher taxation she sees this as a threat to her chosen way of life and, regarding such interference as unjust, she intends to vote for a political party that shares a similar conception of justice and defends her right to accumulate property. In contrast, citizen B regards the present day distribution of goods as arbitrary and unjust and recognises that many poor and deprived people suffer from an inability to help improve their condition through no fault of their own. He is impressed, therefore, by a political party that promises progressive taxation to redistribute some of the material wealth and enable the funding of more comprehensive welfare and social services initiatives. A and B both make claims about what is 'just,' but in differing conceptual frameworks. A's notion of justice is grounded in an account of what and how an individual is entitled to by virtue of what they have acquired and earned. A assumes a legitimate entitlement to the goods that an individual actually holds. If the outcome of such a principle of just acquisition is a gross inequality in holdings, A has few misgivings. B, on the other hand, believes that such inequality is unacceptable, and thinks that a just society can only be achieved via a measure of state interference into individual citizens' lives. His idea of justice attempts to take into account the equality of the claims of each person in respect of basic needs and the means to meet such needs.

Although A's and B's views differ significantly, they mirror at a practical political level the views of Nozick (1995) and Rawls (1995, 1971) respectively and both take, according to MacIntyre, a liberal approach. Nozick's principle of distributive justice states simply that a distribution is just if everyone keeps the holdings that they are entitled to under free market distribution. Rawls' two principles outlined earlier go beyond this limited conception. Rawls' and B's position is a principle of equality with respect to needs, while Nozick's and A's approach is a principle of equality with respect to entitlements; only evidence about what was legitimately acquired in the past is relevant in the latter case, whereas future distribution is relevant to Rawls and citizen B. MacIntyre feels that A's and B's accounts are superior to Nozick's and Rawls' in that they stress an appreciation of the notion of desert. (A believes that s/he is entitled to his/her property because his/her efforts deserve to be rewarded; B believes that the poor do not deserve to be poor because the condition is largely not of their own making.) The positions of A and B reveal two rival concepts of justice emerging in a similar social context; however, both accounts stress that individual wishes play a primary role in framing them and any social factors of a secondary importance. MacIntyre (1995) maintains that the moral resources of culture allow us no way of rationally settling these differences of opinion and deciding which should be regarded as right or wrong. For MacIntyre, conflict and not consensus lies at the heart of modern society and it is pointless to make appeals to a unifying concept of justice. He is dismissive, therefore, of one of the central tenets of liberalism, that is, the liberal notion that society as a whole can hold universal values. For MacIntyre, there are no universal values, only many conflicting ones.

Interestingly Rawls (1995) denies that he makes any claims to universal truths, maintaining that within a democracy the public conception of justice that he outlines is political and not metaphysical. This political concept of justice is worked out for the specific practical reason of applying it to the political, social and economic institutions of a society. Justice as fairness for Rawls is intended to relate to the basic institutional structures of a modern constitutional democracy. The central question is, how does a society find a shared basis on which to achieve agreed and appropriate forms of liberty and equality? Rawls insists that the purpose of his two principles of justice is to provide such institutions with the means to realise liberty and equality in the face of strong disagreement as to how this can be achieved. His aim is an agreement by public reason; an attempt at a practical solution, not a metaphysical one.

Because Rawls starts from the tradition of democratic thought, society is to be conceived as a fair system of cooperation and individuals seen as people who have the ability to take part in social life and are as a result able to exercise and respect various rights and duties. Individual citizens are regarded as free and equal and holding the capacity for a sense of justice and a conception of the good. The 'original position' is merely a representative device to make us all free and equal, to remove us from our situated reality which would affect our conception of justice. It is appropriate, then, that we conclude and elaborate a political conception of justice from behind the veil of ignorance. It provides a way of theoretically removing oneself from a particular location in society (advantaged or disadvantaged) in order to work out the most appropriate paths to liberty and equality for all citizens. For Rawls, the original position is the best way to achieve this, but "the veil of ignorance does not imply that the self is ontologically prior" (Rawls, 1995, p 203). He does not presume a metaphysical conception of the person.

For the communitarian such an approach remains invalid. Individuals cannot become detached, theoretically or otherwise, from the communities that they in habit. Community is said to be constitutive of the individual and any notion of justice must emanate from the individual's particular social location and the traditions into which they are born. In challenging the central tenets of liberalism (individual autonomy, the possibility of universally held values, the neutrality of the state), and seeking to put forward a politics of the common good that emerges from the community, communitarians are open to criticism. If values and identity are realised or determined in a particular communal setting, then there appears to be limited reason and scope for self- criticism; only the possibility of criticising those whose views and lifestyles are different from your own. The communitarian approach is in danger of collapsing into moral relativism and becoming inherently conservative in its outlook. The politics of a common good may ultimately lead to intolerant and oppressive regimes. As Kymlicka notes, "the problem of the exclusion of historically marginalised groups is endemic to the communitarian project" (Kymlicka, 1992, p 227). In response, Avineri and de Shalit (1995) remind us that the egalitarianism of Walzer (1995), and the market socialism of Miller (1995), give a radical edge to the communitarian approach. Reflection and critical scrutiny can remain part of the communitarian agenda. Communitarian critics of liberalism believe that the roots of authoritarianism do not lie in a highly developed notion of community but rather emerge from the alienation of individuals from the public and political debate that liberalism encourages. "Liberalism in so far as it is individualistic is the politics of rights, while communitarianism is the politics of the common good" (Sandel, 1995, p 7). The communitarian goal is to encourage a participatory politics in which people recognise their social obligations as well as their individual rights. This they achieve actively within specific communities.

Having outlined some differing views on the importance of the individual subject, it now becomes relevant to further consider the importance of the 'community' to both liberal and communitarian schools of thought.

'Community'

Community, as Plant (1978) reminds us, is an often used but highly contentious concept that covers a complex range of descriptive and often incompatible meanings. A consensus that community is something worth discussing appears to exist but there is little agreement as to what should be talked about. Certainly liberal and communitarian scholars have differing understandings of the social relationships that community should embody, each basing their views on differing normative and philosophical assumptions. In spite of this confusion, 'community' cannot be dismissed because it retains an importance at many levels. Walzer (1995) argues that for the individual, membership of a community is of singular importance. Excluded non-members are liable to become vulnerable individuals, cut off from communally provided welfare and security. A particular concept of community is often central to wider policy initiatives and Dworkin (1995), in developing an outline for a theory of liberal community, obviously feels that the idea of a national political community remains important to liberal thinking.

Prior to a more detailed look at the notions of community that liberalism and communitarianism imply, a brief look at the work of Ferdinand Tonnies and his concepts of *Gemeinschaft* and *Gesellschaft* may prove useful.

Tonnies' approach to community

In distinguishing between *Gemeinschaft* and *Gesellschaft*, Tonnies (1955) outlined two ideal types of social interaction between individuals. The private exclusive world of *Gemeinschaft* (community) is contrasted with a legalistic conception of association in *Gesellschaft*. "If the theme of Gesellschaft is individuality, the theme of Gemeinschaft is commonality, shared enjoyments, shared possessions, shared friends and common enemies" (Adair-Toteff, 1995, p 61). The bonds of Tonnies' community cannot be easily broken and are based on three types of specific relationship: kinship, centred around the family home; neighbourhood, a community of local, usually rural dwellings linked via mutual contact and cooperation in labour and the management of order; and finally a friendship that has its roots in similar forms of work and attitude (Bell and Newby, 1974). This is a world characterised by *Wesenwille*, an underlying essence of community that is represented in traditional cultural practices and social bonds.

In contrast, the world of *Gesellschaft*, "conceived as mere co-existence of people independent of each other" (Tonnies, quoted in Bell and Newby, 1974, p 8), is the condition of the modern world: a place where each individual strives to achieve an advantage and affirms the actions of others only as far as they can further their own interests. A sense of *Kurwille*, the right to choose, motivates individual actors in their choice of personal means and ends. A sense of community is largely missing and people are essentially cut off from each other, finding a platform for interaction largely in the economic sphere.

Gesellschaft, the modern world of association, sits more comfortably with looser liberal views of the individual and the social bonds that are necessary for society. Tonnies, like many communitarian critics of today, appears to a greater extent to be at ease with the more concrete notion of community (*Gemeinschaft*), a world in which the individual is bound by the rules and traditions relevant to that particular person's historical and cultural location. Adair-Toteff (1995) maintains that Tonnies was not the backward looking pessimist he is often perceived as, but more of a utopian visionary who believed (given the anomic drift of modern society) that a rebuilding of the communal bonds of *Gemeinschaft* could become the foundations of future society which had the principle values of equality, liberty and ethical behaviour to the fore. This 'back to the future' approach mirrors that of many of the 'new' communitarian critics, for example Etzioni (1997, 1995) and Selbourne (1994), who urge a new recognition of the importance of an individual's obligations to the communities in which they are situated (see Chapter Three).

Communitarians and community: exclusive visions?

Walzer (1995) maintains that membership of various forms of community is one of the primary goods that human beings distribute to each other. Any notion of distributive justice presupposes a bounded world in which distribution takes place. Membership of a community is of great individual relevance as it determines many other important factors, such as who is included and who is excluded when it comes to making collective choices; who are required by members to pay obedience and taxes; and to whom services and goods are then allocated. Crucially it is members who are in charge of how they distribute the goods that the community generates; therefore it is they who dictate their relationship with strangers excluded from the community. This has an impact in modern states at a national level in the negotiation and enforcement of immigration and nationality policies. In an attempt to grasp the complexities of modern political associations, Walzer compares the state to the smaller communities of neighbourhood, private club and family. In the first instance Walzer maintains that the modern state appears as a random association of people not unlike a neighbourhood, a form of association that people are free to choose for themselves. Individuals and groups can, however, be welcomed or ignored within a neighbourhood; the power of choice lies with the community that is already in existence, not with the newcomer. In this respect the state also "appears like a perfect club with sovereign power over the selection process" (Walzer, 1995, p 17). Members decide freely on their future associates and the decisions they make are authoritative and binding. In deciding rights of entry, states also often operate on a 'kinship principle', only admitting newcomers who are in some way 'related' to the present citizenry and share common cultural, physical or ideological characteristics. It is only as members that individuals can hope to share security and social goods of the community. An appeal to 'community' presupposes a bounded world advantageous to its members but often problematic to those unable or unwilling to join or abide by the communal rules. Walzer is aware that "issues of admission and exclusion are at the core of communal independence" (Walzer, 1995, p 83). For the communitarian the existence of membership barriers is relatively unproblematic; communal integrity is maintained by admitting only those individuals who recognise their obligations to a particular way of life.

Community is a concept of central importance to communitarians, as their title implies. It is more than just an external place that we inhabit; the notion of 'constitutive community' is a view of the world in which individuals are communally embedded and simultaneously those communities are an important constituent part of personal identity. Bell (1995) provides an insight into the intensity that this definition of community implies. Constitutive communities are said to provide the meaningful ways of thinking and acting for the individual, as well as providing a basis from which to judge other people's behaviour. Bell distinguishes three types of community that are constitutive for Western individuals and central to how people define themselves, starting with 'community of place',

> The place we call home, the place we were born and bred and often the place where we would like to end our days, even if home is left for some time as an adult. (Bell, 1995, p 104)

Bell maintains that but for economic and political pressures most individuals would choose to remain in the community in which they found themselves by accident of birth. Implicit here is a longing for the closeness of family and kin, mixed with an almost nostalgic geographical attachment to birthplace. "A shared history going back several generations is the most salient characteristic of a community of memory", the second type of important constitutive community outlined by Bell. "Besides tying us to the past, such communities turn us towards the future as communities of hope" (Bell, 1995, p 125). The most salient example of this kind of community in the modern context is the nation. Here the communitarian asks us to envisage a group of associated strangers who share a common history that is tangibly expressed in their everyday life and outlook: a 'common good,' a nationalism that stresses a need for mutual obligation and service. Nationality can indeed be a positive element of identity, but the nationalism that accompanies it can also be a negative, intolerant force that seeks to perpetuate exclusive and dangerous ideals of righteousness based on dubious links to blood and soil. Bell (1995) appears to uncritically gloss over some strong lessons of history. Such appeals to history remain problematic; tradition, as Hobsbawm and Ranger (1983) note, is selective and invented. The third and final constitutive community that Bell defines is that of 'psychological communities'. This type of constitutive community, based as it is on personal interaction, is limited to a few hundred people at most, and typically made up of family members, church groups and long-standing civic associations.

This final concept of community appears to mirror the *Gemeinschaft* that Tonnies outlined, where individual interests are subjugated by those of the community. At one extreme of this version of community there is a vision of a wider society ordered by complementary and functional hierarchical inequalities bound together by an inherently conservative ethic. At the other, as Plant (1978) and Gutmann (1995) make clear, communitarianism can become a rallying call for radical action. An important strand of Marx's work was a powerful criticism of the individual isolation that capitalism can promote. For Marx, the liberal notion of the state as a universal community that attempts to reconcile differences in civil society is an illusion; the state merely represents the interests of the ruling capitalist class. 'Community' would only be achieved once the proletarian revolution had secured common ownership of the means of production. This Marxist view seeks to pursue a non-hierarchical vision of the common good that will ensure the autonomy of those neglected by capitalism. Plant (1978) suggests that, in spite of the radical differences between socialist and conservative approaches, both see the re-establishment of a strong sense of community as imperative. Today a communitarianism influenced by conservative considerations is evidently ascendant.

> Whereas the good society of the old critics was one of collective property ownership and equal political power, the good society of the new critics is one of settled traditions and established identities. (Gutmann, 1995, p 121)

The liberal view: communities of association

In contrast, liberal political thought is hostile to the communitarian approach and prefers to view society as the aggregate outcome of individual actions, a social world consisting of a loose association (rather than binding communities) of individuals connected by consent and contract. Coupled with this ideal, however, is a recognition that unlimited competitive individualism could soon reduce the world to chaos. This fear is manifested in liberal attempts to develop a thinner notion of community, one that preserves the gains in individuality and autonomy that have emerged as the ties of traditional community have weakened, but one which is also sufficiently supportive to ensure that individual isolation and social breakdown do not ensue. Community, in effect, would allow the priority of personal freedom to be maintained but also provide "an institutional framework within which individuals may experience a sense of solidarity and significance" (Plant, 1978, p 106). Tonnies in *Gesellschaft* recognises the possibilities for this approach when he notes,

> ... even competition carries with it, as do all forms of such war, the possibility of being ended. They (individuals) may even unite themselves together for a common purpose (or also – and this is most likely – against a common enemy). This competition is limited and abolished by coalition. (Tonnies, quoted in Bell and Newby, 1974, p 11)

This concept of community appears to be close to the liberal social democracy of Marshall (1992), Miller (1995) and Dworkin (1995), characterised by a national community of moral, cultural, political and economic pluralism but one in which the ideal of a binding and restrictive community has to be rejected.

A central question needs to be addressed: is liberalism as hostile to community as some communitarians believe? Dworkin (1995) identifies four arguments that each use the concept of community in an increasingly substantial manner. First, in democratic societies 'community' is often associated with the right of a majority to impose ethical rules. Second, a paternalistic approach envisages a community in which each citizen is responsible for the well-being of other citizens, and is accordingly a place where political power is, according to Dworkin, rightly used to improve the lives of all citizens through the reduction of 'defective' practices. A third argument would stress a need for community based on self-interest.

Here atomism is condemned and a belief that individuals need community to develop a sense of worth and well being is put forward; consequently, because of its individualistic foundations, this is seen as antagonistic to community. The fourth view, 'integration', supposes "a very different structure in which the community and not the individual is fundamental" (Dworkin, 1995, p 210); here an individual's values become subordinate to those of the community in which they live. Individual success is bound up in community success and vice versa. Importantly he rejects the communitarian premise that community has an overarching importance in all areas of life. This Dworkin labels the 'civic republican' approach to integration, a society where the individual success of its members is intrinsically bound up in and dependant on their fit with the surrounding community. In such an approach community assumes a metaphysical importance; it has a primacy over the individual in all areas of life. In the liberal 'practice view' of integration that Dworkin proposes, the collective unit of community is established in social practice; it does not precede the individual but rather is created and embedded via social interaction.

This liberal assessment of community stresses that integration into community has a relevance only at a limited political level, to include such acts as voting, lobbying, demonstrating and also more formal input into the adjudication and enforcement of legislation. As an unjust political community affects the personal autonomy of everyone within its borders, it is seen as being in each individual's own interests to participate in the life of the community and ensure that everyone is treated with equal concern. This 'practice view' defines the community's communal life in a much narrower way than the integration envisaged within a communitarian approach. Dworkin clearly believes that to extend the integration principle into other areas of individual life is inappropriate, but he stresses an egalitarian approach and the importance of a healthy political community open to the participation of every citizen. Each individual must recognise that "political community has ethical primacy over individual lives" (Dworkin, 1995, p 223). Concern must primarily be for all members within that community; issues of personal gain must be secondary considerations.

Clark's (1973) definition of community based on the identification of a sense of solidarity and significance between members appears useful, as it can be applied in different locations, for example when addressing a nation, a locality or an ethnic group. Beyond these two fundamentals, a further specification about the size of the grouping being referred to as a community is all that appears necessary. However, if the communitarian concept of 'constitutive community' (Bell, 1995) is contrasted with the liberal community that Dworkin (1995) sees as appropriate, it becomes clear that both commentators attach a sense of significance and solidarity to their respective approaches, but both differ greatly in the definition of the essence of community. In the political and philosophical discourse a precise definition without recourse to specific normative and ideological considerations appears to be an impossibility (Plant, 1978). Perhaps it is enough to be aware that 'community' is a loaded concept, its meaning dependant on usage and purpose. Consequently it is important to always be conscious of the particular assumptions that underpin its use.

Which way for citizenship?

The basic notions of the individual and community and the different ways in which they are conceived has a crucial impact within the citizenship debate. Should we take an essentially liberal stance and stress the primary importance of individually held rights, and if so should our citizenship theory move beyond the limited libertarian approach and embrace more egalitarian ideals? Alternatively, it is possible to take a communitarian approach and stress individual commitment to wider communal obligations. Each approach outlined above has elements that are problematic for the citizenship status of many individuals.

As Parry (1991) states, each separate path to citizenship leads us to a different promised land, and a minimalist libertarian theory demands little of citizenship. Citizens are related by recognition of rules which regulate their conduct. In order to pursue their own individual interests those citizens subscribe to the rule of law in a condition of civil association, usually within a defined territory in which they are situated either by chance or by choice[6]. Commonality grows from engagement in the same language of civil discourse; every individual is "equal to speak in the same terms, even if they do not use the language to utter the same belief" (Vogel and Moran, 1991, p 169). Citizens live in a commendable condition of 'watery fidelity', a civil association of equal basic civil and political rights that allows people with little in common to find a way of living together. Community, in the *Gemeinschaft* sense, is deemed inappropriate for the public sphere.

The egalitarian liberal approach is, for Parry, a universalist rights-based theory of citizenship that stems from the fundamental moral assumption that the rights of citizenship should ensure the possibility of agency for all citizens. Freedom here is not just a negative concept, limited to freedom from coercion: it also has a positive aspect. The role of a theory of distributive justice is to ensure that sufficient resources are available to give each individual the power to act. In this setting the modern democratic state and its institutions are able to fulfil a positive role and open up 'windows of opportunity' that allow citizens to realise their possibilities for individual agency and self-determination. "The ultimate test of a state would appear to be its success in contributing to the realisation of agency for those within its jurisdiction" (Vogel and Moran, 1991, p 176).

In contrast communitarian theories of citizenship stress a reciprocal relationship between the existence of community and citizenship. All individuals are regarded as members of some type of community; the autonomous individual is regarded as an impossibility. Location in a community and all that it entails, social bonds, allegiances, and commitments, provides the essence of individual identity. The unencumbered self of liberalism is seen as flawed; morality and regulation come from the communities in which the individual is located.

All three of the approaches outlined above seem problematic; important aspects of each need to be challenged if a theory of citizenship is to be proposed to meet the diverse needs of modern societies and the individuals that inhabit them. The libertarian ideal, in recognising civil rights, grudgingly accepting political rights and failing to endorse social rights, stops short of what many now consider citizenship should entail. A more egalitarian theory that stresses extensive and universally held rights is based on an understanding that each individual must recognise the rights of others to autonomy, that is, the ability to act for themselves. The problem of citizens holding contradictory aims and values may in fact limit such autonomy. The communitarian model of citizenship, stressing as it does that rights are conditionally linked to duties, can impact negatively on personal autonomy. The unproblematic acceptance of the community's right to exclude those individuals who choose a different way of life is a further problem. To exclusively endorse either a liberal or communitarian project would be to outline a defective theory of citizenship and also to misinterpret the present debate; such an either/or option is too simplistic, given the complexities of social relationships in modern Western capitalist nations like Britain.

Having outlined the negative aspects of each approach, it is now appropriate to consider the positive contributions that each can make to citizenship theory.

Sandel (1995) rejects liberal theory because it is based on mistaken metaphysical and metaethical views. Similarly MacIntrye (1995) urges that we give up a liberal politics of rights for a politics of community.

Indeed MacIntyre believes that the moral vocabulary surrounding the issues of rights and the common good is so distorted that individuals have lost both practically and theoretically a grasp of morality; everyone asserts their individual rights but nobody recognises their obligations. This, counters Gutmann (1995), is to misunderstand the major aim of liberal theories of justice, which is "to find principles appropriate for a society in which people disagree fundamentally over many questions, including such metaphysical questions as the nature of personal identity" (Gutmann, 1995, p 126). The aim of liberal justice is to regulate our social institutions, not our entire lives. For MacIntyre the doomed project of modern liberal political philosophy has been an attempt to convert egoists into altruists; but Gutmann again contradicts him and stresses that the central point of modern liberalism is not that individuals are either egotistical or altruistic, but that they disagree over the nature of the 'good' life. The moral universe does not exist in these dualistic terms; it is not a case of identity being either independent of our ends or simply constituted by our community, nor is it a simple case of individual rights alone or community obligations alone but a combination of the two. Gutmann (1995) advises us to reject what she refers to as the 'tyranny of dualisms' that many communitarian critics of liberalism expound. The real question that should be addressed is whether or not a communitarian politics has more to offer than rights–based liberalism. Sandel (1995), as already noted, extols the virtue of basing morality and a sense of justice on a particularly situated community's traditions and practices. However, history does not support Sandel's optimism; that same approach has traditionally excluded women and other groups from full citizenship status[7]. A great deal of intolerance has emerged from the communitarian scheme with its emphasis on identity and community rooted, often, in a self-righteous sense of the worth of particular values and a specific sense of justice. "The enforcement of liberal rights, not the absence of settled community, stands between the moral majority and the contemporary equivalent of witch hunting" (Gutmann, 1995, p 133).

In spite of its failings, Gutmann recognises the constructive potential of the communitarian project. It presents possibilities for a combination of 'community' and basic liberal values to forge a new kind of politics. Given the communitarian concern about the concentration of power within modern states, it may be possible to discover ways in which power can be devolved to a more local level, and democracy revitalised. Increased democratic participation and regulation may enhance rather than jeopardise individual rights. Communitarian thinking could be used to challenge universal liberal notions of justice and add a new dimension by emphasising the importance of local decision making. Similarly, the particular points of view of certain groups or communities may break through into mainstream discourses and then have an influence in renegotiating universally held values. Gutmann feels that communitarian thinkers should seek to improve the liberal vision, not to replace it.

Liberal theory largely assumes an individual approach to political relationships; it is the individual who holds rights and who strives to be free and on an equal footing to other individuals. Although the individual citizen remains a major player in the citizenship game, it is not necessary or productive to endorse the liberal abstract conception of the individual. For Lukes (1973) this approach is inadequate in two important ways. It is a primitive, pre-sociological view of the nature of the individual that denies the importance of any social conditions or attachments. It is feasible to take seriously some of the values that the individualistic approach bought to the fore (autonomy, respect, privacy and the right to self-development), while simultaneously abandoning the ontological view of the abstract individual and the political and economic doctrines that such an outlook seeks to perpetuate.

> There are crucial and indispensable gains but if we are to take liberty and equality seriously they must be transcended. And that can only be achieved on the basis of a view of un-abstracted individuals in their concrete, social setting, who, in virtue of being 'persons' all require to be treated and to live in dignity, as capable of exercising and increasing their autonomy, of engaging in valued activities with a private space and of developing their several potentials. (Lukes, 1973, p 153)

Clearly, here, there is agreement with the communitarian contention that individuals develop within their social locations: 'self' is not an *a priori* concept but defined by attachments to communities and historical contexts. Once this position is accepted, it may enable a theory of citizenship to be sensitive to the various needs of different communities within a wider national or even international framework. While rightly accepting that identity is to a great extent socially constructed, Lukes seeks communities that do not smother and suffocate the individuals within them. It is here that individually held rights assume an importance. Lukes believes that only a society which embraces a humane form of socialism can achieve a suitable balance between the diverse needs of its individual citizens and communities.

The relevance of Miller's (1995) socialist conception of a national community to such an approach should not be over looked. Miller (1995) first argues that markets alone cannot provide a sense of community; it is therefore necessary to develop a form of market socialism. Second he contends that the collective identities relevant to citizenship today are predominately national ones and consequently the 'nation' is the only form in which overall community can be achieved in modern societies.

It is the modern conjunction of nation and state that makes it possible for national communities to establish ideals of self-determination and distributive justice. Miller is aware that nationality is a manufactured item, with members often sharing a generally believed 'background story'. It is important that there is a common view about what the nation is, and how its members differ from members of other nations; but Miller is attempting to put forward a minimalist view of nationality, one that can serve as a basis of a wide community and nothing more. To this end he draws a necessary distinction between a common public culture and the various private cultures that may flourish within that 'thin' common bond. Nationality and citizenship can go together, especially for socialists looking for the right kind of political community. "Nationality gives people a common identity that makes it possible for them [people] to conceive of shaping their world together. Citizenship gives the practical means of doing so" (Miller, 1995, p 93). Citizenship here is defined beyond merely being subject to the laws of the state: it implies a basic status guaranteed to each individual independent of other inequalities. It further echoes Marshall's approach by outlining the importance of 'protective rights' (civil) to safeguard private freedoms; 'political rights' to enable people to take part in decision making; and 'welfare rights' (social) that guarantee a minimum of goods and services that allows each citizen to be a full member of the national community. The distinction between the different types of rights is intended to be analytical only; each is considered supportive of the others. It is a citizenship that requires the independent, rights–bearing citizens of liberal theory but it is also concerned with the belief and behaviour of those citizens who are required to act in the pursuit of the common good and not only private interests. Miller's theory, like Lukes' (1973), accepts that to some extent personal identity is constituted by membership of a collectivity, in this instance the nation; but it is important that members are able to critically scrutinise their relationship to the national community. The community is not able to ignore the needs of its citizens, as the moral assumptions that underpin such an egalitarian citizenship theory provide for individually held rights and the distribution of goods according to agreed levels of need.

Notes

[1] This discussion is largely concerned with what may be termed 'Western' debates around the notions of the individual and community. What follows is not an attempt to see such debates as superior to others, but an exploration of some of the issues relevant to a British setting.

[2] Such historical arguments are not without problems. The claims of aboriginal peoples (eg native Americans and Australians) against present 'landowners' have profound implications for Nozick's approach.

[3] It should be noted that support for this approach is not limited to communitarians. See, for example, Twine (1994) and Lukes (1973).

[4] This line of argument can be challenged. The French state has in the past been keen to promote a particular version of the family, and in many Islamic nations the state actively promotes a specific way of life.

[5] It should be noted that there is often a deeply authoritarian aspect to liberal thinking. In reality individuals in many 'liberal' nation states are not free to do just as they please.

[6] Parry draws heavily on Oakshott (1975) within his discussion.

[7] Liberalism is also obviously problematic when considering exclusion. Gender, ethnicity and disability remain three potentially problematic areas.

THREE

Five perspectives on citizenship and welfare

Introduction

This chapter looks at five approaches to citizenship and its welfare component that are relevant to the contemporary British setting: namely Marshall's view, the subsequent challenges of the 'New Right' and the 'new communitarians', New Labour's approach to welfare, and a Muslim view. What follows, therefore, is essentially an appraisal of various normative accounts that offer competing views about approaches to meeting welfare needs (provision), striking the correct balance between rights and responsibilities (conditionality), and legitimisations for including or excluding certain individuals or groups from collective welfare arrangements (membership). A principal task will be to explore the extent to which each of the following perspectives differ, or indeed exhibit similarities, in relation to the three themes specifically chosen for investigation in this book, that is, provision, conditionality and membership. Some of the concerns and criticisms of certain major perspectives (eg Marxism and feminism) are dealt with only briefly in this chapter. It should be noted, however, that this is not an attempt to marginalise important views; indeed issues that relate directly to class, gender, ethnicity and disability inform some of the discussions that follow, particularly the section on Marshall.

The key elements of T.H. Marshall's highly influential account of citizenship are first examined and the important 'third element' of social rights is explored in some detail. The views of some of Marshall's many critics are also considered. It is noted, however, that many such critics continue to believe that elements of Marshall's approach (with its emphasis on an extensive package of collectively funded universal, social rights) remain relevant in the contemporary social climate. Following on from this, the focus shifts to consider two challenges to Marshall's thinking on welfare, that arguably continue to be highly influential as the British post-war welfare settlement is re negotiated. First, aspects of the New Right's welfare agenda and how they were incorporated by successive Conservative administrations into a version of citizenship that attempted to reduce and redefine the state's welfare role are considered. Second, the emerging views of the self-styled 'new communitarian' movement are discussed and some of the potential effects that they may have on publicly provided welfare explored. New Labour's approach to welfare is then highlighted and claims about its inherent originality and inclusiveness are disputed. In the penultimate section some aspects of an Islamic approach to welfare are considered. Given the focus within the fieldwork that informs this book, where the views of some Muslim respondents were explored, such discussions are both necessary and pertinent. In conclusion, following this overview of differing perspectives on citizenship and welfare, it is argued that the citizenship ideal that Marshall outlined, with its emphasis on an important welfare rights element, underpinned by extensive state guaranteed provision, has now been superseded. A new welfare orthodoxy that stresses a reduction of the state's role as a provider of welfare, a stronger link between rights and responsibilities, and an increasingly 'moral' agenda, is now dominant (Heron and Dwyer, 1999; Lund, 1999; Dwyer, 1998; Lister, 1998b).

Civilising capitalism: Marshall's rights-based approach

> Citizenship is a status bestowed upon those who are full members of a community. All those who possess the status are equal with respect to the rights and duties with which that status is endowed. There is no universal principle that determines what those rights and duties shall be, but societies in which citizenship is a developing institution create an image of an ideal of citizenship against which achievement can be measured and towards which aspiration can be directed. The urge forward along the path thus plotted is an urge towards a fuller measure of equality, an enrichment of the stuff of which the status is made and an increase in the number of those on whom the status is bestowed. (Marshall, 1992, p 18)

Given the continuing interest in *Citizenship and social class* (1949/1992), Marshall's much discussed text (eg Lister, 1998a, 1997a-c; Bulmer and Rees, 1996; Dahrendorf, 1994; Oliver and Heater, 1994; Roche, 1992), although published over forty years ago, remains a valid starting point for any consideration of citizenship and welfare in contemporary Britain.

Essentially Marshall outlines a theory in which the three linked elements of civil, political and social rights assume a central importance.

> The civil element is composed of the rights necessary for individual freedom – liberty of the person, freedom of speech, thought and faith, the right to own property and to conclude valid contracts, and the right to justice. The last is of a different order from the others, because it is the right to defend and assert all one's rights on terms of equality with others and by due process of law.... By the political element I mean the right to participate in the exercise of political power, as a member of a body invested with political authority or as an elector of the members of such a body.... By the social element I mean the whole range from the right to a modicum of economic welfare and security, to the right to share to the full in the social heritage and to live civilised life according to the standards prevailing in society. (Marshall, 1992, p 8)

Marshall does not see these civil, political and social rights as abstract entities but as embedded in developing social institutions and material conditions; consequently, he argues that individual freedoms and the evolution of citizenship are linked to the ongoing development of British society. He therefore asserts that the demise of the feudal order and the onset of capitalism (which required the freeing up of labour and capital) ensured that the legal (civil) rights necessary for individual freedom within a market place were developed through the courts and the establishment of a legal system. This, he argues, was prior to the emergence of political rights tied as they were to the later establishment of parliamentary and local representation. According to Marshall, it is the founding of the welfare state in the late 1940s, and the establishment of the universal right of citizens to an extensive set of state-guaranteed social and economic provisions (the culmination of a long struggle), that gives rise to a citizenship in which civil, political and social rights become part of an integrated whole.

The rights outlined above are central to Marshall's approach, in which the status of citizen is explicitly linked to an enjoyment of those rights. Marshall recognised their importance by stressing that citizenship rights are to be regarded as universal, "not a proper matter for bargaining" (1992, p 40), and of particular significance to those individuals and groups that suffer because of their location within the market-generated system of social stratification. A fundamental focus of Marshall's work was centred on how, by developing the notion of citizenship on both a theoretical and practical level to include rights to welfare (the social element), it may be possible to remove some of the inequalities generated by the continuing operation of an essentially capitalist market system. The intention was to check the worst excesses of capitalism by the promotion of citizenship, to modify rather than destroy: "The inequality of the social class system may be acceptable provided the equality of citizenship is recognised" (Marshall, 1992, p 70). The equal rights that citizenship status implied could not, therefore, ensure equality of condition; the thorough reduction of merit-based inequalities was deemed undesirable. It is, as Marshall asserts, the addition of a comprehensive package of social rights that generates the conflict between citizenship and the market. Described by Marshall in the boldest terms as a 20th-century 'war' between citizenship and the capitalist class system, this conflict is inevitable, given his expansive description of the social element. A paradox exists, in that while the economic system that is the basis of modern British society continues to generate inequality, citizenship is organised around a struggle for greater equality (Barbalet, 1988; Turner, 1986). When writing *Citizenship and social class*, he was clearly aware of the limits of his theory, noting in a later work that the "hyphenated society" (Marshall, 1985, p 123) of modern democratic-welfare-capitalism combined an expansion of the progressive egalitarian rights of citizenship with the continuation of an economic system that generates inequality. As Turner (1986) points out, it would be wrong to attribute to Marshall a more radical agenda; Marshall's citizenship theory fits comfortably within the liberal democratic tradition which seeks to emphasise equality of opportunity and simultaneously make tolerable continuing inequality of outcome by the promotion of universally held rights.

According to Marshall, the 'equality of status' that existed between each individual citizen in terms of common rights and duties would ensure that citizenship as an institution reduced some of the inequalities of individual condition generated by the continuing operation of a class system within a capitalist market economy. The principle of a guaranteed minimum (which the establishment of social rights brings about) does not necessarily affect income differentials but does provide a 'real' income for all, in the form of state subsidised and funded essential goods and services, or even actual income in cases such as pensions and child benefit. In this way the right to social welfare is no longer solely dependent on the market; a provided and not a purchased service becomes the norm.

What matters is that there is a general enrichment of the concrete substance of civilised life, a general reduction of risk and insecurity, an equalisation between the more and less fortunate at all levels – between the healthy and the sick, the employed and the unemployed, the old and the active, the bachelor and the father of a large family. Equalisation is not so much between classes as between individuals within a population which is now treated for this purpose as though it were one class. Equality of status is more important than equality of income. (Marshall, 1992, p 33)

So the egalitarian real income of social citizenship lies side by side with an inegalitarian money income system. Marshall believed, however, that circa 1950 there was an ongoing 'double movement' to remove non legitimate inequalities within both the economic system and the citizenship arena, but that the measure of legitimacy in each of the spheres differed. In the latter notions of social justice prevail, in the former this is combined with the logic and needs of the market. The two may be in opposition but, as Marshall makes clear, "we are not aiming for absolute equality" (Marshall, 1992, p 45). Marshall's citizenship is clearly a vision of society in which the enrichment of the universal status of citizenship is combined with the recognition and stabilisation of certain status differentials, largely through educational training and achievement which are then consolidated by awarding different levels of monetary income tied to a stratified occupational hierarchy. In short, market-generated class-based inequalities are held in check by the promotion of citizenship. He believed that individuals will tolerate certain social inequalities provided that such inequalities are generally accepted as legitimate. This approach assumes that a universal system of values exists for all members of society, and that these values will continue to exist, and a certain level of inequality be regarded as fair provided rapid and open social mobility exists, or is at least seen to exist. As Turner (1986) reminds us, if open access to positions of importance, and the increased incomes that they often entail, are no longer generally perceived to be universally available to all with the correct technical training and qualifications, inequality may become a dynamic for resentment and the value of Marshall's citizenship theory be undermined. Citizenship could then no longer then be seen as a universal system of rights and resources that allowed all individuals to pursue their individual self-interest (Plant, 1988).

Marshall's approach may be fundamentally problematic. Much of Bottomore's (1992) criticism of Marshall is based around the view that the addition of a set of universally guaranteed social rights to the previously acknowledged civil and political elements of citizenship cannot successfully challenge inequality while they remain tied to an essentially capitalistic market system which in itself perpetuates inequality. Social rights are seen as purely ameliorative measures that do not tackle the root cause of economic divisions within society. Administrative and structural considerations often mean that welfare institutions mirror the inequalities that are already present within a society. Ferge (1979), like Bottomore (1992), believes that a more radical reconstruction of the economic and social structures on which capitalism is based is necessary to reduce class-based inequalities; only the development of more wide ranging 'societal policies' will curb the excesses of capitalism and ensure the extension of citizenship rights to all.

The social element

The importance that Marshall (1992) attributed to a substantive social rights element within his citizenship theory has attracted much discussion. Several commentators (Barbalet, 1988; Oliver and Heater, 1994; Roche, 1987) have pointed to a conflict of principle between civil and political rights as opposed to social rights; the former having their basis in individual freedoms while social rights are centred around notions of collective equality. Oliver and Heater (1994) view social rights as distinct and separate from civil and political rights, stating that social rights, with their emphasis on a redistribution of goods and services, stand in opposition to a market-based economy; while civil and political rights are viewed as necessary for the continued function of such a system. Civil and political rights are seen as 'first generation rights': they are residual in nature, have their basis in formal legal equality and law, and are central to the liberal tradition. As such as it is believed that they do not conflict with the values that underpin the capitalist system to the same degree as social rights may. Civil rights are seen as necessary to ensure the freedoms that are required for the successful operation of a market economy, and the ensuing extension of political rights as important in legitimating the continuation of a market approach by linking it to notions of democratic choice. Social rights and the economic commitments that they usually entail are viewed as 'second generation rights'. Often an entitlement to services, they are to be found in positive legislation that establishes such rights, and give the legal authority for governments to raise, via taxation, the funds necessary to finance public welfare provision. Consequently the level of funding required to guarantee social rights is apparently substantially greater than that required for either civil or political rights. Ensuring that the financial resources to meet the costs of social rights are available is largely a matter of political will. Social and economic rights cannot, therefore, be regarded as 'residual'; they are not rights or freedoms that remain once all legally established limitations on individual actions or freedoms are taken into account, but result from affirmative action by the state (Oliver and Heater, 1994).

Barbalet (1988) further questions whether social rights can be regarded as citizenship rights at all (see also Rees, 1995a). Although he accepts that social rights may facilitate the participation of some individuals as 'full members of the community', Barbalet believes that Marshall is wrong to make them an integral part of his citizenship theory, as they are at best only conditional opportunities. Barbalet argues that social rights are dependent on professional and bureaucratic infrastructures (and ultimately fiscal policy) and as such cannot be regarded intrinsically as rights. Such claims can be countered by pointing out that both the legal system and modern politics share the same essential financial features (Rees, 1995b; Plant, 1992). Barbalet also notes that social rights do not meet one of Marshall's main criteria for inclusion as citizenship rights *per se*, namely universality. Social policy is often directed at specific targets which means that benefits and provisions can only be enjoyed by particular individuals. Barbalet appears here to confuse the issues of universal availability and universal enjoyment of rights. Social rights are universal rights in the sense that once certain criteria of individual need, contingency or past contribution are met, access to the entitlements specific to that provision becomes available as a right[1]. A person may then enjoy the benefits (and it might be useful to add any potential drawbacks) associated with that provision. As Marshall states, there is no "universal principle" (1992, p 18) that determines rights; if there were, social policy and its associated costs would not be a central focus for political debate or disagreement. The criteria and conditions for provision are defined as a society develops and various groups and classes lay claim initially to 'their' rights, crucially often in conflict with one another. Social and economic rights and the struggle that surrounds them are, therefore, central to the citizenship issue (Lister, 1993).

Attempts to distinguish between civil/political and social rights have been further challenged. Turner (1986) and Twine (1994) point to a false dichotomy in such debates, arguing that individuals and society coexist in an interdependent relationship, with the human actor (very much a social being) achieving and maintaining personal satisfaction and fulfilment only within a cooperative social environment.

> Citizenship [which includes here a substantial social element] is the institutional framework by which individual agents can be developed

and cultivated in a modern capitalist environment. (Turner, 1986, p 93)

It can, therefore, be seen as enhancing rather than negating individual freedom. Lister (1990a) and Vogel and Moran (1991) similarly argue that social rights are necessary to ensure the individual freedoms implicit in civil and political rights. Marshall's conceptualisation of citizenship, by including social rights alongside civil and political rights, is thus viewed as making some measure of autonomy possible for a large number of individuals in modern society.

Provision

In terms of welfare provision Marshall clearly sees an extensive set of state-guaranteed social rights as a legitimate part of the citizenship package. Given the establishment of the welfare state (1948), the Labour government's promise of policies to support full male employment, and a belief that Keynsian economics would provide the means to sustain the social element, perhaps we should not be too surprised that the important question of funding social rights is largely omitted from his theory. The problem of finance, although regarded as vital by Marshall (1992, p 7), is left very much to the economists. Marshall's attempt to consider a theory of citizenship, especially the social element, in isolation from its economic and political context, although understandable given the time of his writing, weakens his entire approach. Given that social rights are a priority within Marshall's approach, the omission of a full consideration of their funding implications may seem odd to contemporary readers but Marshall's optimistic statement that the 'war' between citizenship and capitalism was being decided very much in citizenship's favour should be judged only in its specific historical context. An element of contradiction in his later work seems to suggest that Marshall never managed to quite resolve his own feelings on the important issue of funding provision. After initially stating that "social policy must be conceived as a part of a general economic policy and not a separate area of political action governed by principles peculiar to itself" (Marshall, 1965, p 71), a possible indication that all social policy is closely tied to (if not governed by) economic policy, he later notes that "nobody seriously proposes that the rate of expenditure should be fixed first and the standard of service adjusted accordingly" (1965, p 134). This would seem to imply that Marshall viewed social rights as important enough to be subject to funding principles that would at least ensure a reasonable level of service. Hindsight allows us the dubious luxury of pointing out that what is deemed reasonable by some is condemned as inadequate by others. Nonetheless, by endorsing such an approach Marshall indicates that he regards the funding and provision of a set of social rights by the state as an integral part of his citizenship theory.

Conditionality

Marshall saw citizenship as a status that entailed both rights and duties. His consideration of the duty component is, nonetheless, particularly brief. Compulsory duties, the duty to pay tax and national insurance contributions, to accept compulsory education and the now defunct military service, are seen as relatively unproblematic and it is taken for granted that if the citizen wishes to claim their rights then they must accept such attendant duties (Rees, 1995b). Paramount importance is attached to the duty to work. Marshall's emphasis on this 'essential duty' and more importantly "to put ones heart into one's job" (1992, p 46) clearly indicates that the individual citizen has a duty whenever possible to recognise a responsibility for themselves and the wider communities that they inhabit. This is a stance further emphasised when Marshall points to a general obligation to live the life of a good citizen (which may be assumed as a call for individuals to uphold the law) and appeals to individuals to give such voluntary service as they can to the wider community.

The duties that Marshall outlines are not as unproblematic as they may at first appear. A potential clash between citizenship duty and individual autonomy soon becomes apparent if we consider two examples offered by Oliver and Heater (1994). A legally imposed duty exists that demands we pay tax; however, many people would like to pay as little as possible. There exists a fine line between avoidance and evasion, but both are opposed to the tone of Marshall's argument. Second, Marshall implies a duty to obey and uphold the law. This is in essence an ethical obligation that we, as individuals, can choose to ignore by failing to assist the police or even engaging in a life of crime. What appear in the first instance to be two of the most straightforward of citizenship duties are not without their dilemmas.

Although it has been argued that in his later works Marshall exhibited a "growing ambivalence about the proliferation and assertion of rights" (Rees, 1995b, p 357), it is clear that the extension of rights rather than responsibilities is his primary concern in outlining a citizenship theory. Indeed many (Giddens, 1994; Selbourne, 1994; Roche, 1992) have since criticised his account for privileging largely unconditional rights to the neglect of the important duty/responsibility element. In his concluding paragraph Marshall (1992) states that his major aim was a

> ... wish to throw a little light on one element which I believe to be of fundamental importance ... a rapidly developing concept of the rights of citizenship and their impact upon the structure of social inequality. (Marshall, 1992, p 49)

A general concern with social rights rather than responsibilities characterises his approach to citizenship.

Membership

As the quotation that opened this discussion indicates, enjoyment of citizenship status in Marshall's theory is tied closely to membership of a community. The community he refers to here and elsewhere is the nation state. Although aware of the problems inherent in linking citizenship status and the rights and duties that it entails to such a remote form of community, Marshall seems unaware of the exclusive tendencies that the coupling may engender. Much feminist criticism of Marshall has concentrated on highlighting the extent to which women as a group inside the boundaries of the nation state were and continue to be denied substantive citizenship status. Many writers (Lister, 1998a, 1997a-b, 1990b; Walby, 1994; Pateman, 1992; Vogel, 1991; Allen, 1989) have been critical of the male assumptions that underpin Marshall's citizenship. They argue that his approach is male gender specific and, in recognising a false public/private dichotomy, is a factor in the continuing oppression of women. It assumes a standardised sexual division of labour reflecting Parsonian ideals of instrumental and expressive roles within a defined family unit. Furthermore, they point out that the full employment embodied in Marshall's duty to work ideal refers only to the full employment of males in the paid labour market. A consideration of many women's continued support of both the welfare system and the functioning of the market economy, via unpaid domestic labour and care provision, is completely overlooked. The vulnerability of many women to poverty because state provisions often assume a financial dependence on men continues to be a problem that impacts on their citizenship rights (Lister, 1997a, 1990b).

In many ways the labour market remains segregated; large numbers of women continue to earn less than their male counterparts in spite of legislation to end disparities. They face disadvantaged treatment and access to social benefits because the system of provision is largely biased towards traditionally male work patterns. In reality the basic right to sell one's labour freely on the open market does not exist for women with childcare responsibilities. The lack of any generally available, publicly supported childcare provision means that entry into the labour market is often blocked or only possible by negotiation with a partner. Allen (1989, p 7) notes, "Marshall maintains that rights properly constituted are not open for negotiation". For many women the private domestic sphere constantly interacts with and limits any public role. Although today there are fewer formal distinctions between the civil, political and social rights of men and women, the lived reality is often different. The shortcomings of a legal system, designed and usually applied by men, often impacts on the legal rights of women (Kennedy, 1992). Patriarchal structures and ideologies can continue to adversely effect women's citizenship status.

Citizenship has, however, had a profound effect on gender relations throughout the last century. The public/private dichotomy which Marshall fails to question facilitates a differential access to citizenship rights for women in comparison to men. The development of a female political citizenship bought about by the active struggle of women, and the consequent emergence of social rights and benefits, provided women with an alternative to dependence on the individual patriarch within a relationship. Walby (1994) notes,

> ... the development of social citizenship is constituted by changing gender relations as it is by changing class relations. Citizenship is about a transition from private to public patriarchy, not only about the civilising of capitalism. (Walby, 1994, p 392)

Dahrendorf sees the treatment of minorities as "the true test of the strength of citizenship rights" (1994, p 17). Measured against such a proposition, many would argue that Marshall's citizenship is found to be lacking. Its explicit link with the British nation state has proved to be particularly problematic for many ethnic groups. An analysis of British postwar immigration legislation illustrates that the British state has implemented a series of Acts that have negatively impacted on the citizenship status of the resident black community, and simultaneously sought literally to exclude black people beyond the geographical boundaries of Britain from attaining formal legally defined citizenship[2] (see Lewis, 1998; Spencer, 1997; Mason, 1995). As such, much immigration legislation has helped to define the presence of black people in Britain as problematic and racialised the notion of 'Britishness' (Gordon, 1989; Mullard, 1979). Brubaker (1989) distinguished between 'formal' and 'substantive' citizenship status and concluded that in reality many rights are denied black citizens. Similarly, Gordon (1989) argued that being black can imply a second-class citizenship status with racial violence, discrimination and prejudice constantly impinging on basic civil political and social rights. As Gilroy (1992) points out, the lived reality for many is that British and black remain mutually exclusive categories. For Modood (1992) this exclusion is directly related to the degree of difference exhibited by an individual or group from the norms that were inherent in Marshall's thinking. "The more distant an individual or group is from a white upper middle class British, Christian/agnostic norm, the greater the marginality or exclusion" (Modood, 1992, p 54).

The omission of a discussion of disability, Marshall's emphasis on the rights and responsibilities of able-bodied males within his account, and the fact that the vast majority of disabled people do not enjoy basic rights in any substantive sense (Oliver and Barnes, 1991; Barton, 1993) (eg the right to work, unrestricted access to public buildings) suggest that it would be premature to consider many disabled people as full members of the community of citizens that Marshall envisaged. In recent years disabled people and their organisations have articulated demands for a recognition of their rights as equal citizens (Oliver, 1996)[3]. Angered by a dominant, professionally constructed and administered 'medical model' of disability (intrinsically linked to ideas of dependency), they have challenged the status quo by developing, alongside like-minded intellectuals, a 'social model' of disability which focuses on the disabling attitudes, environments, practices and policies that are prevalent in contemporary society (Barnes and Mercer, 1997a; Oliver, 1990, 1996). As Williams states,

> An impairment affects the way our bodies and our minds work, but it is society's reaction to impairment which determines whether we may have a good quality of life. (Williams, 1995, p 215)

Barnes (1992, 1991) outlines how disabled people face institutionalised discrimination in most areas of their lives. Pointing to a combination of enforced segregation within the education system, the labour market, various welfare services and a hostile physical environment, Barnes argues that disabled people are effectively denied the civil, political and social rights that are central to Marshall's notion of citizenship (see also Oliver, 1996)[4]. He is also clear about the central role that the state has played in this denial.

> A great deal of the responsibility for the persistence of institutional discrimination against disabled people rests with the succession of

British governments since 1945. While there is a growing consensus throughout the democratic world that disabled people have the same basic human rights as non disabled people, and that it is the responsibility of governments to ensure that they are able to secure a standard of living comparable to that of their fellow citizens, this has not occurred in the United Kingdom. (Barnes, 1992, p 13)

In spite of repeated calls (Bynoe et al, 1991; Barnes, 1992, 1991) for the enactment of anti-discrimination legislation for disabled people, it appears that in Britain substantive citizenship rights for disabled people remain firmly anchored in rhetoric rather than reality (Barnes and Oliver, 1995). It also remains to be seen what impact the newly established Disability Rights Commission (due to start work in April 2000) will have on the lives of disabled people (see Wilkinson, 1999).

The extension of full citizenship rights to disabled people would offer new possibilities to many for higher levels of participation and increase both their individual and collective autonomy within society. This would to some extent challenge the traditionally dominant image of disabled people as passive recipients of welfare who lack both the competence to make decisions about their own needs and the ability to act as citizens in their own right (Oliver and Barnes, 1998). Increasingly disabled people and their organisations have called for the right to define their own needs and for the autonomous definition and control of any services that they may require to facilitate independent living (Oliver, 1996).

The general point to grasp is that Marshall's theory of citizenship with its (implied and explicit) terms of membership has problematic implications in terms of inclusion and exclusion for certain groups both inside and outside the community of the nation state. The developing notion of European citizenship (Lister, 1997a), an increasingly global economy and the movement of peoples across national borders (Ackers, 1998; Vogel and Moran, 1991) are additional complications. In outlining a theory of citizenship one of Marshall's stated concerns was, "an increase in the number of those on whom the status [of full citizenship] is bestowed" (Marshall, 1992, p 18); however, this brief consideration of the citizenship status of women and minority ethnic groups and disabled people helps to illustrate the limit of his vision.

A contemporary relevance for Marshall's theory?

As some of the above discussions illustrate, Marshall's theory of citizenship has been much criticised in recent years. His account has also been shown to be Anglocentric and of little relevance in other settings (Mann, 1987), his theory on the sequential development of citizenship rights shown to be flawed when considering the case of British women (Walby, 1994)[5], and the universality of the welfare rights central to his account to be limited (Williams, 1992; Alcock, 1989). In the light of these extensive deficiencies it is necessary to remember that much of Marshall's theory continues to have a relevance when discussing welfare and citizenship. Marshall's account and its emphasis on the "fundamental importance" (1992, p 49) of social rights forced welfare firmly on to the citizenship agenda. As Williams (1996) notes, Marshall's citizenship continues to be of use when asserting welfare rights as part of a combined package of civil and political and social rights. It remains a potential benchmark against which exclusion from full citizenship status can be measured and the dynamics of social divisions constructed around the several dimensions explored. Marshall's misplaced belief that his account of citizenship, with its additional extensive set of (largely unconditional) state-guaranteed social rights, would be widely accepted as an essentially apolitical concept of uncontested universal worth (Roche, 1987) is probably his greatest error. The values that underpinned Marshall's citizenship have been challenged, not least by the New Right; it is to their perspective on citizenship and welfare that we now turn.

The challenge of the New Right

The New Right's[6] approach to citizenship and welfare reflects the contradictions on which their general political philosophy is built. In drawing on the traditions of both libertarian liberalism (with its emphasis on individual freedom, a 'free' market, limited government and the basic right to property) and social conservatism which stresses government's central role in establishing and maintaining a particular moral order (that emphasises individual and familial duties), it seeks to combine liberal economic assumptions with political arguments that favour reducing the state's welfare role while simultaneously increasing an individual's responsibility to meet their own needs (Furbey et al, 1996; Roche, 1992; King, 1987). Broadly speaking the New Right can be seen as hostile to the idea of a welfare state and the closely allied notion of social rights. It is important, however, that the diversity of positions within the New Right camp should not be overlooked. As Faulks (1998) notes,

> The term New Right has tended to be used as a convenient shorthand
> for a diverse group of thinkers from the political right, embracing not

only neo-liberalism, but also neo-conservative thinkers such as Lawrence Mead (1986), monetarist economists such as Milton Friedman (1962) and public choice theorists such as James Buchanan (1962). The term New Right is, then, a very imprecise one because the range of opinions contained under such an umbrella term are often opposed and contradictory. (Faulks, 1998, p 53)

For example, the discussion of the 'underclass' that follows below illustrates the differing approaches of two such commentators; indeed, Teles (1996) sees Murray's economic concerns and the behavioural preoccupation of Mead as indicative of a deeper division within New Right thinking[7].

Given their philosophical predisposition towards libertarian liberalism (see Chapter Two), the New Right refute Marshall's claim that social rights are a legitimate part of the citizenship package. The idea that individuals possess a universal entitlement to make extensive welfare claims on the state is rejected, with only civil and (begrudgingly) political rights being regarded as essential to citizenship status (Pratt, 1997; Bellamy and Greenaway, 1995; Plant, 1992). Given such a predisposition a reasonable, if simple, assumption to make would be that governments which were sympathetic to the New Right approach (eg the Thatcher and Major administrations) would set about implementing policies that eliminated all state provision of welfare. Pragmatic politics and the diversity of positions covered by the New Right umbrella have dictated that this is not the case, but a strong antagonism towards state provision of welfare in particular, and unconditional social rights can be detected. The New Right have certainly mounted a systematic challenge to the collectivist assumptions that underpinned both the postwar welfare settlement and Marshall's conceptualisation of citizenship with its emphasis on state-guaranteed universal social rights. The old assumption that welfare and the state were somehow intrinsically and exclusively linked has been fractured (Clarke, 1996). The New Right regard the welfare state to be: inefficient and ineffective (in that it serves the interests of bureaucrats and professionals rather than meeting the needs of its clients); economically damaging (because it reduces the ability of the free market to deliver wealth and demands high levels of taxation); socially damaging (in creating and encouraging an 'underclass' characterised by feckless behaviour and long-term passive dependency on the state); and also politically damaging (in that a government's role is reduced to the management of the self-interested rights claims of competing interest groups, rather than the pursuit of its primary purpose of promoting the common good) (George and Wilding, 1994). The belief that a reduction of the state's welfare role is both positive and progressive, coupled to the idea that the future welfare of citizens will be best served by a system that encourages greater individual responsibility in meeting welfare needs, with only limited, often highly conditional, state provision, have became central tenets of the British Conservative Party's welfare policies. It may be useful to consider at this point the ideas of two American New Right theorists, Murray and Mead, whose influence appears to have been of particular significance in making the reduction of state-provided welfare and the principle of conditionality priorities in contemporary British social policy.

Murray, Mead and the 'underclass'

In outlining the development of an 'underclass' in Western societies, the accounts of Murray (1999, 1996, 1984) and Mead (1997a-c, 1986, 1982) are built on similar assumptions (Deacon, 1997a, 1994; Hill, 1994, 1992). First, that the right to extensive, state-funded welfare entitlements creates and reproduces an 'underclass' of welfare dependants; and second, that it is dysfunctional behaviour rather than economic inequality that distinguishes the 'underclass' from the mainstream society. Both commentators take an explicitly moral stance by highlighting and condemning aspects of that behaviour, and likewise both Murray and Mead see its solution in the fundamental reform of social welfare (Hill, 1992). Although their assumptions about the causes and effects of the 'underclass' phenomenon are similar, a more detailed analysis of their work illustrates, however, that they offer differing answers.

In defining his notion of the 'underclass' Murray is keen to state from the outset that "the underclass does not refer to a degree of poverty, but to a type of poverty" (Murray, 1996, p 23). He is keen to distinguish between two types of 'poor' people: those who simply live on a low income, but who nonetheless lead respectable lives; and those whose lack of money is combined with an irresponsible disregard for both themselves and wider society. The 'underclass' is not, therefore, defined by reference to a disadvantaged financial condition but in terms of common patterns of behaviour that violate respectable norms. Paralleling Victorian distinctions between the deserving and undeserving poor, Murray outlines the emergence of a British 'underclass' (with certain similar characteristics to its American counterpart), a distinct population characterised by three important dimensions: a disproportionate number of illegitimate children, a high incidence of (violent) criminal activity, and a lack of employment among able-bodied males. This group is vividly portrayed as a real threat to civilised society whose standards it refuses to accept.

> Britain has a growing population of working-aged, healthy people
> who live in a different world from other Britons, who are raising their
> children to live in it, and whose values are now contaminating the life
> of entire neighbourhoods, which is one of the most insidious aspects
> of the phenomenon, for neighbours who don't share those values
> cannot isolate themselves. (Murray, 1996, p 25)

Murray is clear that it is collective state welfare and not a lack of money or inequality that is the cause of this destructive phenomenon. Rather than alleviating poverty, the right to welfare is seen as actively encouraging dependence among the poor by making it easier for some to ignore their responsibilities and choose state-supported lone motherhood and/or unemployment instead of relying on their own efforts through engagement in the paid labour market (Deacon, 1997a). Arguing that the right to benefit on the simple demonstration of need has led to welfare dependency and, therefore, is in itself constitutive of much ensuing poverty, Murray's (1984) solution is simple: end all cash benefits except for short-term unemployment insurance payments. State welfare could then be replaced with locally administered relief subject to the terms and conditions of the local community. The lack of an adequate state-guaranteed minimum to fall back on would force individuals to be self-reliant once again and simultaneously "reinforce the work norms, family authority and individual responsibility", (Hill, 1992, p 117) necessary to counter the sub-culture of the 'underclass'.

Whereas Murray would do away with state welfare in an attempt to remove dependency, Mead attempts to use it to reform the character of the poor by establishing a principle of conditionality. In contrast with some of the New Right, Mead (1997a-c, 1982) consistently expresses the view that his primary concern is not with the economic cost of state welfare but with the behaviour that it engenders in the separate 'underclass' who are either unwilling or unable to work. He accepts that a lack of money and low pay may be issues that affect levels of non work within the ranks of the poor but believes that "their problem is now more a *moral* one than an economic one, and so is the challenge facing the welfare state" (Mead, 1982, p 19; original emphasis). In going on to state that a body of individuals 'out of the mainstream of society' exists who will not readily accept available jobs and that "the troubling behaviour and condition of the disadvantaged is due to social programs on which so many are dependent" (Mead, 1982, p 22), he echoes Murray's belief that state welfare exacerbates dependency. For Mead, however, it is not simply the existence of social rights in the form of state benefits that is the problem, but the fact that they are unconditional; that is, that the state offers support but expects little in return. Mead's solution is to enforce responsible behaviour.

> Government must now *obligate* [welfare] program recipients to work rather than just entice them. What is obligatory cannot simply be offered as choice – it has to be enforced by sanctions, in this case the loss of welfare grant. (Mead, 1982, p 28; author's emphasis)

In short, state welfare rights should be dependent on recipients accepting attendant state-defined work responsibilities.

Mead (1997b) revisits many of his previous assertions, and in relating his discussions directly to Marshall's perspective contends that linking limited social rights to compulsory responsibilities brings the poor back into the citizenship fold. His paper considers four possibilities for social policy to tackle the problem of poverty: entitlement, investment, privatisation and enforcement (compulsion). Arguments in favour of a universal unconditional entitlement to social welfare are dismissed, because such schemes, with their focus on social rights available to individuals who meet agreed criteria of need, fail to adequately consider the duties of welfare recipients. Within Mead's version of citizenship, state aid is not given on the basis of need or entitlement but is dependent on lifestyle and an acceptance of the principle of conditionality. The investment approach (ie state sponsored intervention programmes that target assistance at specific disadvantaged families/groups) is dismissed by Mead in a similar vein.

> The main drawback of family programs appears to be their limited authority. While they may be informally directive they do not overtly require that beneficiaries do anything to help themselves. (Mead, 1986, p 217)

Privatisation of state welfare along similar lines to Murray is rejected for practical reasons. Evidence[8] suggests, however, that Mead is not opposed in principle to the abolition of state social provision. He appears to regard it as an unlikely and perhaps counterproductive option, but then goes on to imply that it may be the only solution to welfare dependency if the preferred enforcement option fails; and for Mead enforcement provides all the answers.

> The final option for antipoverty policy represents a return to a citizenship rationale, but this time with the emphasis on obligations rather than rights. The argument is that, if nonwork and other incivilities have weakened the welfare state, then work and other duties should be enforced. If the dependent poor become better citizens, especially by working, then the Marshallian case for aiding them is restored. To do this is also instrumentally the best way to solve the poverty problem. (Mead, 1997b, p 220)

Mead argues here that not only is conditionality both generally popular and functional but also that the imposition of compulsory work conditions for the recipients of state benefit effectively re-establishes their right to be regarded as citizens. He believes that previously permissive welfare regimes and the unconditional nature of their benefits marked out the poor as recipients of state charity, rather than as citizens entitled to state support in return for their acceptance of specified responsibilities. Their right to equal citizenship status is thus restored because, as Mead has previously stated, "only those who bear obligations can truly appropriate their rights" (Mead, 1986, p 257, quoted in Hill, 1992, p 119). A case for recipients of social welfare to voluntarily accept their obligations could of course be made, but Mead has rejected this as unlikely to succeed. Those most in need of employment are, as Deacon (1997b) reminds us, regarded by Mead as "dutiful but defeated" (Mead, 1992, p 133); in such circumstances Mead sees it as necessary for the state to use its authority to compel individuals to return to the labour market. Mead's approach may be considered both 'utilitarian', in that the imposition of conditional benefits may prove harsh for some, but a greater common good will be served (Deacon, 1994) and 'authoritarian' (Deacon, 1997b) because it demands specifically that individuals take what are assumed to be readily available jobs and consequently places few demands on the state to ensure the quality or conditions of work.

It has previously been noted that Murray and Mead share some important views about the negative impact of extensive social rights on both the character of benefit recipients and also the contemporary values within wider society. Their differing solutions to the problem of welfare dependency have also been discussed. The importance of their common emphasis on the value of individuals largely assuming responsibility for their own welfare via paid employment should not be overlooked. The reaffirmation of the desirability of self-help and the view that the state should have a greatly reduced welfare role have been influential in challenging, both in principle and in practice, the existence of an extensive social rights element within citizenship. In Britain, to a certain extent, such views have found a political expression in the legislative programmes of the Thatcher[9] and Major governments.

Citizenship, welfare and the Conservative governments

The Commission on Social Justice[10] notes,

> The argument from the right [was] that the state had to be rolled back and the market extended, the public sector had to be disciplined and the private sector set free, collectivism reined in and individualism rewarded. Lower direct taxation, less trade union power, and a new emphasis on personal initiative and enterprise would, the Conservatives claimed, build both economic strength and a more responsible society. (CSJ, quoted in Franklin, 1998, p 110)

Successive Conservative administrations of the 1980s and the 1990s sought to redefine citizenship, particularly the welfare element, by drawing on aspects of the New Right agenda. If the addition of a set of universally available, state-provided social rights can be seen as being of pivotal importance to both Marshall's conceptualisation of citizenship and the postwar welfare settlement, then correspondingly attempts to reduce the state's role in funding and providing for the welfare of its citizens have been central to the challenge of Conservative welfare policy. This was combined with a general acceptance of the existence of a welfare dependent 'underclass' and the endorsement of a highly conditional approach to some aspects of public welfare. A brief appraisal of recent Conservative social policies shows the New Right vision of citizenship to be very different from the one advocated by Marshall.

Provision

Policies which sought to diminish the state's welfare role, reduce or at least contain public welfare expenditure, challenge the power of the welfare state professions, promote a residual welfare state and introduce quasi-markets (Le Grand, 1997; Wilding, 1997; Clarke, 1996; George and Miller, 1996; Le Grand and Bartlett, 1993; King, 1987) can be seen as consistent with Conservative hostility to extensive state welfare. The reduction of state funding in many areas moved some services largely into the hands of the private sector (eg residential care of senior citizens, childcare and so on, while some providers, notably local authorities, were forced to charge money for services that previously were viewed as citizenship rights freely available to those who met accepted criteria of need. In some instances what were once regarded as universal citizenship rights have become services available only to individuals who can afford to purchase them (Dwyer, 1998).

Increasingly, obligations that were previously met by the state have been transferred to private, charitable or voluntary services[11]. In terms of recent Conservative administrations, this has been apparent with the endorsement of the 'active citizen' who, through involvement in charitable and voluntary work, is defined as individually and socially responsible, while also meeting the welfare needs of the less fortunate (see Bellamy and Greenaway, 1995; Meikle, 1994; Oliver and Heater, 1994; Kearns, 1992; Oliver, 1991; Hurd, 1988; Thatcher, 1988). This citizen is one who recognises that they must accept, first and foremost, responsibility for their own (and their family's) welfare. Beyond this any philanthropic actions within the wider community are seen as enhancing that individual's right to claim their 'citizen' status. Recourse to increasingly limited state provision is viewed as a last resort. The effects of this ideal of citizenship may be positive for those who are able to volunteer in this way, but it also has negative implications for the citizenship status of those who are unable to engage in such activity. An inability to meet the important defining feature of the 'active citizen' (ie being someone who is actively engaged in the public giving of private time and resources to others on a charitable basis) marks certain individuals out as second order citizens. A further exclusionary tendency of this ideal of citizenship should not be overlooked. When urging us as individuals to take responsibility for our own welfare, self-interest may sometimes prevail; however, we can and do choose who we wish to direct our charitable endeavours towards. If a system of welfare previously based on institutionally situated rights gives way to a system based around charitable giving, there is less of a possibility that everyone's needs will be adequately met (Dwyer, 1998).

A detailed analysis of the Conservative's citizen's charter initiatives lies outside the main concerns of this discussion. Daly (1997), however, reminds us that their instigator, the then Prime Minister, asserted that the main functions of the charters were to "raise quality, increase choice, secure better value and extend accountability" (Major, 1991, p 4). In spite of their name it should be noted that citizen's charters have little to do with either the extension of social rights or notions of citizenship that allude to a publicly provided welfare element (Hill, 1994).

> The charter refers solely to the protection of contractual rights as consumers of public services.... We have no social entitlements stemming from mere membership of a community. (Bellamy and Greenaway, 1995, p 478)

Such an approach fits with previously discussed New Right assertions of the primacy of the civil rights of individual market actors and the denial of social rights within theories of citizenship.

Conditionality

The Conservative Party clearly endorse a principle of conditionality. An attempt to link an individual's right to welfare to the acceptance of certain responsibilities became an increasingly important aspect of welfare policy in the 1980s and 1990s. For example, the Child Support Agency, set up in 1993, was principally established with the aim of ensuring that absent fathers recognised their financial responsibilities to their children. In an attempt to ensure that women would cooperate, a mother's right to benefit was made conditional on her first agreeing to name the father of her children so that he could be pursued. It is the area of unemployment benefit, however, that perhaps illustrates the extent to which the Conservatives were prepared to make rights conditional on individuals accepting certain patterns of behaviour or additional responsibilities. During the 1980s the payment of unemployment benefit became more and more dependent on claimants meeting new obligations in order to receive full benefits; attendance at regular 'restart' interviews became compulsory and more stringent eligibility tests were introduced (Cook, 1998; Dolowitz, 1997a; Deacon, 1994). Simultaneously, levels of benefit have been systematically reduced, as has the number of individuals eligible to claim (Novak, 1997). It has been widely argued (Dolowitz, 1997a-b; Novak, 1997; ERAS, 1996; CPAG, 1995) that the Jobseeker's Act (1995) took this process a step further with the imposition of the jobseeker's agreement, and the new powers available to the client advisor who can now require claimants to alter their appearance or behaviour if they feel either may prejudice the chance of employment. Failure to accept such conditions may mean a disqualification from benefit. The establishment of the pilot 'Project Work' scheme and a (1997) manifesto commitment to expand it made plain the Conservative's endorsement of a 'workfare'-based system of unemployment benefits.

Within social housing, Part Five of the Housing Act (1996) also introduced some significant changes that linked the right to social housing to specific behavioural responsibilities. A new form of tenure was introduced (Sections 124-6) that enabled local authorities to grant introductory (probationary) tenancies to new tenants for a period of up to one year. On taking up a property the tenant is told that if they behave in an 'anti-social' manner within the trial period they are liable to eviction and any right to a future secure tenancy is revoked. Similarly sections 144-51 made it easier for social and private landlords to evict secure and assured tenants on the grounds of anti-social behaviour. Allied to this approach, sections 152-5 allow the power of arrest to be attached to court injunctions taken out by social landlords to deal with anti-social behaviour if violence has been threatened or occurred (Alder and Handy, 1997, p 104 and pp 120-2; Conservative Party, 1996, p 48; NHF, 1996, pp 51-63).

Membership

The acceptance of the notion of a separate 'underclass', defined by deviant behaviour and norms that run counter to 'civilised' society, has obvious implications for citizenship in which common membership is seen as being built on shared experience and values. That 'they' (members of the 'underclass') are not like 'us' (citizens) is an implicit assumption in the entire 'underclass' thesis (Hill, 1994). The New Right's protestations that the enforcement of work conditions ensures the restoration of citizen status is also problematic. The vision of a citizenship status built primarily around the idea that able-bodied individuals should be willing to work (and if not, forced to work) in order to secure their right to social welfare is not straightforward. Are individuals (including large numbers of women) with domestic care responsibilities to be excluded from membership of the citizenship club unless they agree to enter low paid, low status work in order to subsist? Are the 'idle rich' to be allowed to behave how they wish and continue to enjoy the fiscal and occupational benefits of state welfare, while the 'deviant' non-working poor are to have their social welfare rights tied to specified patterns of behaviour? Membership of a community of welfare organised according to the principles endorsed by the New Right may prove to be inherently exclusive.

Reducing public welfare: the New Right's twin strategies

Ideologically the New Right refute claims that citizenship status confers a general right to claim an extensive range of welfare benefits and services from the state. In Britain, a significant part of the New Right's political project is, therefore, directed at systematically undermining certain institutions of the welfare state, while simultaneously endorsing a central role for the state in promoting a particular brand of social order in the civil and political arenas (King, 1987). Although practical political considerations may ensure that an eradication of the state's welfare role is unlikely, an overt hostility towards the very idea of social rights, coupled with a belief that the state's role in the provision of welfare should at best be minimal, indicates the New Right's support for the state to be assigned a limited, residual role in welfare (George and Miller, 1996). If the state is to provide less in the future then it is likely that the fortunate will have to turn to privately purchased provision and the unfortunate to charity. Access to welfare in both cases is highly conditional, on the ability to pay in the former instance, and on the giver seeing a recipient as deserving in the latter; neither provide welfare on the basis of social right.

Within the field of social welfare, in order to reduce the state role the New Right in Britain have pursued two interlinked strategies, one focused on economics, the other on morals. They have attempted to dismantle public welfare provision by combining funding cuts with policies that either provide incentives or force individuals to make private arrangements to meet aspects of their own individual welfare needs. This has been coupled with an increasing use of the principle of conditionality (which holds that eligibility to certain basic, publicly provided, welfare entitlements should be dependant on an individual first agreeing to meet particular compulsory duties or patterns of behaviour) to ensure control over welfare recipients and enforce a particular moral order on the economically disadvantaged. Given that the New Right's philosophical foundations link economic liberalism and conservatism, we should not be surprised at this mix of money and morals in its social policies; however, we should be aware that many of the policies introduced have had a profoundly negative impact on the social rights of large numbers of Britons.

The new communitarian approach

The new communitarian approaches of Selbourne (1994, 1993) and Etzioni (1997, 1995)[12] share some common features that have certain implications for citizenship and especially the welfare element. Both commentators identify a crisis within Western society, a crisis caused primarily by the dominance of individualistic liberal philosophy and the expansion of unconditional rights. In turn each outlines a solution that places great emphasis on the role of ordered communities and on individuals recognising the importance of their obligations and duties to the communities in which they are situated. Importantly, both Selbourne and Etzioni appear to view extensive state welfare provision as undermining the establishment of a 'good' society, in that it removes duties of care from the realm of individuals, families and voluntary associations.

Selbourne's principle of duty

Faced with a proliferation of 'dutiless rights', which Selbourne (1994, 1993) concludes has led to a malaise that strikes at the heart of modern citizenship and threatens social cohesion, he makes a call for the reaffirmation of the 'principle of duty'.

> The principle of duty, the sovereign ethical principle of the civic order, demands both general and particular duties of the citizen – to himself [*sic*], to his fellows, and to the civic order as a whole – and, likewise, general and particular duties of the civic order and of its instrument, the state, to its members.... Such duties ... have ethical precedence over the rights, benefits, and privileges with which the citizen is vested as a member of such civic order; and, fulfilled, signify that the individual who fulfils them is playing his part. (Selbourne, 1994, p 147)

Rights here are seen as secondary to an individual accepting responsibilities and also subject to removal if the citizen fails to accept such duties as the community demands of them. Individual responsibility and duty are clearly identified as having primary importance over and above rights.

The distinction that Selbourne makes between civil and political rights on the one hand, and social rights on the other, has significant consequences for both social rights and for people who rely on publicly funded welfare for their day-to-day survival. Rights to public welfare are seen as 'generally lesser order entitlements' to privileges and benefits, "which do not possess and should not be given equivalent legal status" to civil and political rights (*The Independent,* 25 March 1993). Furthermore, he holds that "notions of egalitarian entitlement to such rights *which owe nothing to the individual's desert or merit*" (Selbourne, 1994, p 60; original emphasis) undermine the moral basis of the civic order. For these reasons Selbourne argues that publicly provided welfare benefits and services should not be seen as part of the package of rights that inform a universally held status of 'citizen', but that they should be seen as potential privileges that a society may bestow on dutiful members who behave in an approved manner.

Etzioni's new golden rule

Perhaps the most vocal contemporary representative of this approach is Etzioni (1997, 1995) who claims an emerging and wide ranging support that stretches across the entire spectrum of mainstream British and American politics. Etzioni's communitarianism is very much concerned with promoting a certain version of the 'good society', and is centred around the relationship between the individual and their wider community, and the expected roles each ought to play. The values essential to his approach soon emerge.

> Communitarians call to restore civic virtues, for people to live up to their responsibilities and not merely focus on their entitlements and to shore up the moral foundations of society. (Etzioni, 1995, p ix)

Central here is a call for the restoration of the 'correct' balance between rights and responsibilities. This balance is said to be dependent on specific historical and cultural factors, but Etzioni (1997, 1995) stresses the urgent need in the West for individual responsibility and obligation to be restored as a cornerstone of society. "The West is in the cold season of excessive individualism and yearns for the warmth of community to allow human relations to blossom" (Etzioni, 1995, p x). The right for local communities to develop a collective moral voice and 'chastise' those who violate communally defined norms is seen as a positive response to selfish individual behaviour.

A correctly functioning communitarian community is dependent on achieving the correct balance between the two key components of individual autonomy (ie rights) and the common good (an agreed order that recognises the importance of shared responsibilities). Etzioni's new golden rule, in stating "respect and uphold society's moral order as you would have society respect and uphold your autonomy" (Etzioni, 1997, p xviii), essentially asserts that neither should be privileged over the other. For Etzioni (1997) the establishment of a good society rests on a general acceptance of a shared core values that reflect this principle. It is seen as important that agreement about these values should be largely voluntary and not enforced. The formulation of a persuasive culture of "voluntary compliance" (Etzioni, 1997, p 13), that sets out a particular moral environment in which certain actions or behaviours are held to be both individually and communally acceptable or unacceptable, is, according to Etzioni, the best way for a community to reach agreement about the correct balance between rights and responsibilities. Communities should try to convince their members about the inherent worth of their moral commitments; so while it is important to realise that order and some structure are needed in any working society, such an order has largely to be based on the voluntary choices made by its members. While the individual autonomy of community members is recognised as important, any such autonomy is conditional on individuals first of all respecting the rules of the communities that they inhabit (Heron and Dwyer, 1999).

In outlining a thesis dedicated to the betterment of the moral, social and political environment, the new communitarians claim to be a radical new movement but it is one built on old 'truths'[13]. First, a belief that a recommitment to moral values can be achieved without puritanical excess; second, that the 'family' (in reality a particular traditional conception of what a family consists of) can be saved without women being forced into a domestic life; third, that schools can provide essential moral education without indoctrination; and finally, that powerful special interest groups can be curbed without stopping legitimate political lobbying. It is clearly an approach that attempts to address social relationships at a multitude of levels, but some important questions remain unanswered. Which values, which definition of the family and which special interests will be allowed to prevail? Where will these morals emerge from? The need for a set of basic virtues, some fundamental settled values, is seen as imperative and the backdrop from which this moral voice, the 'social glue' of society, is to emerge soon becomes apparent.

The institution of the family is to play a major role in this restoration. Etzioni is scathing of professional childcare provision, stressing that parents should have the dominant role in bringing up their children (Etzioni, 1995). In order to facilitate this, local communities are urged to push business and industry into adopting flexible working patterns which will then allow working parents to set up cooperative, largely self-financed, childcare schemes in which each parent serves approximately four hours a week. It is a scheme that appears to have negative implications for women and less affluent families. Etzioni acknowledges that his approach to childcare is problematic for single parents and low-income families, who often need to work long hours in order to survive financially; however, for such families he offers no alternatives. In spite of assurances to the opposite, a latent hostility to single parents surfaces. "There are several reasons why two parent families are the most suitable for children" (Etzioni, 1995, p 60). Whether or not agreement can be reached on this highly contentious statement is in some respects irrelevant. As the single parent family is a modern social reality, a more positive approach for communitarians may be the development of social policies that attempt to alleviate the stresses and hardships that such families often face, rather than seeking an implicit restoration of a traditional familial order. This hostility is evident in Etzioni's approach to divorce.

> The most reasonable conclusion based on a whole body of data, rather than dwelling on this or that study, is that divorce should not be banned or condemned but that it should be discouraged. Easy divorces for parents are not in the best interest of children, the community, or as we shall see the adults involved. (Etzioni, 1995, p 77)

It is unlikely that placing obstacles, legal or otherwise, in the way of couples whose relationships have broken down will lead to a reduction in the number of divorces granted.

Initially, crumbling moral foundations are identified: the mass exodus of 'both parents' (perhaps it would be more accurate to say mothers) from the home to the workplace and the consequent youngsters left with no one to teach them right from wrong; the greed of the 1980s and 1990s coupled with an attendant reduction in citizens' belief in political institutions. For example, Etzioni pays lip-service to the increasingly competitive world of the global market place but then emphasises the problems that will ensue if "workers will not stay sober all of the time they are on the job and give a day's work for a decent day's pay" (Etzioni, 1995, p 25), thus implying a problem and solution located at the level of individual responsibility rather than global economics. "It follows that we must shore up our moral foundations to allow markets, governments and society to work properly again" (Etzioni, 1995, p 25). The priority of listing in the last sentence is interesting: look after the morals and all else will follow. This outline of a free market approach combined with a strong government working for the good of a society that has become lax and irresponsible has a familiar ring to it.

Provision

An overt hostility to extensive state welfare provision in the case of Selbourne (1994, 1993) has already been noted. Similar concerns about substantial state provision undermining the important ethic of individual responsibility, and so weakening the social fabric, can be identified in Etzioni's approach. In his 1995 account national, unemployment insurance appeared to be the limit of any social rights that Etzioni envisaged[14]. In his later work, it is clear that he approves of the state agreeing to provide only a minimal safety net of welfare via the provision of 'social basics'.

Society has some responsibility to provide, but only at a basic level. This is appropriate because

> ... psychological security does not rely so much on the specific level of support available ... as on the firm conviction that they and their children will receive some basic help; that they will not be cast into the street, without medical assistance or basic provisions. (Etzioni, 1997, p 83)

Limiting the right to publicly provided social welfare, he argues, lowers financial costs, helps to reduce welfare dependency, and simultaneously helps to restore the balance within welfare away from rights back towards responsibility.

Further investigation illustrates that cutting the tax burden of the affluent citizen is not far from Etzioni's mind. He laments that people today "have to pay the hired hand for what used to be done by the community" (Etzioni, 1995, p 125). To illustrate this point he takes a superficial look at the condition of older people, who, he maintains, are increasingly institutionalised, where once they were cared for by the family. To point to a simple increase in the number of senior citizens in institutional care may be flawed. Today in affluent Western societies increasing numbers of people live longer lives and, consequently, some have to enter care homes but the majority do not. Again, the communitarian vision appeals to an illusory past without grasping the complexities of the present. The burden of past family care fell largely on female shoulders; are women to supply such care for kin both old and young in the future? The acceptance of progressive taxation as a means of funding social provisions seems to be deemed an inappropriate moral stance for the new communitarians to embrace. Given their emphasis on 'moral responsibility' this is somewhat surprising. In reality Etzioni's new movement may be little more than a hierarchy of self-help.

> First, people have a moral responsibility to help themselves the best they can. The second line of responsibility lies with those closest to the person including kin, friends, neighbours and other community members. (Etzioni, 1995, p 144)

The ordering of priorities is constant self-help, family help, local help. "Last but not least societies (which are nothing but communities of communities) must help those communities whose ability to help their members is severely limited" (Etzioni, 1995, p 146). Lip-service is paid to the ethic of helping those less fortunate than yourself, but at a national level any form of social right to state-funded welfare or entitlement is extremely restricted.

Conditionality

It should already be apparent that according to the new communitarian perspective rights are conditional on individuals accepting attendant responsibilities. Within the accounts of Selbourne and Etzioni, welfare rights as well as being limited are bound by this rule. Although both are clear that they prefer to persuade citizens of the importance of their communal duties, neither is beyond the use of compulsion or sanction (generally and in relation to welfare) so that the moral order is not corrupted by unacceptable behaviour. Selbourne notes that,

> Compulsion and deprivation in defence of the civic order may take many forms, including ordering the citizen to do certain things ... and the taking away of certain thing from the citizen, including his [*sic*] liberty, but also his privileges, benefits, licences, and rights, and even citizenship itself. (Selbourne, 1994, p 256)

Etzioni's endorsement of 'community jobs' and his acceptance that these may be organised along workfare principles "to replace part of welfare, for example" (Etzioni, 1997, p 82) shows a similar comfortableness with conditionality.

Membership

The terms of membership that communitarians outline may be problematic. First, in outlining a membership based on individuals accepting a socially defined moral order, the communitarian approach assumes that the individual is willing to subjugate their individual preferences in return for membership of a particular community. Second, in spite of assurances that a democratically agreed constitution will ensure that majority interests do not prevail above and beyond those of minorities, the major problem of all communitarian approaches, the right to be different, appears unresolved. Third, the tone throughout Selbourne and Etzioni's appeals is backward looking, with the authors seeking to restore a particular vision of community that, either intentionally or accidentally, embraces inherently conservative values which have proved highly exclusive for many individuals in the past. Etzioni's direct appeal to Tonnies' vision, in calling for the development of a 'new *Gemeinschaft*' society where strong community ties have an increasing relevance, is not as simple as it may first seem. Although the development of 'work communities' made increasingly possible by modern technology and the rise of urban village or suburban lifestyles are offered as two positive examples of this, little thought is given to those excluded from these closed worlds. Those beyond the paid labour market cannot reap the benefits of work communities and many inner city areas have suffered from increasing urban deprivation as more affluent suburbs have developed. Etzioni seems unaware that in his new *Gemeinschaft* communities will often be in direct rivalry with one another and appears to have little concern for the losers in any such competition.

New communitarians and the New Right: a common agenda?

The new communitarians may have much in common with the libertarians and conservatives that they claim to oppose. Essentially the whole 'new' communitarian agenda builds from an old liberal position whereby individual actors first and foremost take personal responsibility for their choices and actions. "We start with our responsibility to ourselves and to members of our community; we expand the reach of our moral claims and duties from there" (Etzioni, 1995, p 147). These individuals and the communities that they then choose to build are reaffirmed at a national level by a democratically agreed bill of rights and a written constitution; in short, a package of civil and political rights.

In spite of the community packaging which surrounds its ideas, new communitarianism shares several common features with the New Right in its approach to citizenship in general and welfare in particular. In each case rights are to be largely limited to the civil and political spheres, and intervention into the workings of the market and the promotion of social rights and entitlements is to be extremely limited. Any acceptance of wider communal welfare responsibilities (to individuals beyond family and other restricted communities) other than charitable giving appears to be lacking. There is certainly little room for a redistribution of social and financial wealth across smaller community or group borders. Their mutual endorsement of conditionality as a principle by which to arrange limited public welfare provision and a predilection for moral agendas and particular patterns of behaviour are also commonalties. Again like the New Right, against a backdrop of perceived social crisis (blamed largely on a sense of moral decay) the new communitarian appeal appears to rest on the assumptions that the restoration of strong community at all levels (family, neighbourhood and nation state) will restore a crumbling social fabric. This is the world of the moral panic, where complex changes in social relationships and their solution are reduced to a certain moral view of the world. Egalitarian considerations do not appear to be a central concern of the citizenship being mapped out by the new communitarians.

New Labour and welfare: a new approach?

As early as 1993 Tony Blair was using the language of citizenship to help map out the tasks for a future Labour government.

> A modern notion of citizenship gives rights but demands obligations, shows respect but wants it back, grants opportunity but insists on responsibility. So the purpose of economic and social policy should be to extend opportunity, to remove the underlying causes of social alienation. But it should also take tough measures to ensure that the chances are taken up. (quoted in Blair, 1996a, p 218)

While Blair's tacit acknowledgement that the welfare element and 'social conditions' are legitimate concerns of citizenship highlights a significant philosophical difference between New Labour and its Right Wing opponents, a closer consideration of the party's rhetoric and emerging welfare policies seems to suggest that it is keen to endorse a notion of citizenship that shares similar concerns to both the New Right and new communitarian perspectives that have previously been discussed. Certainly New Labour makes no apologies for making a reduction in costs a reason for its welfare reforms (Hills, 1998; Brown, 1997). In spite of a dislike for the New Right's "market dogma and crude individualism" (Blair, 1995a), the New Labour government is also willing to accept a pragmatic role for markets in the provision of public welfare, and it certainly expects those citizens with adequate means to assume a greater level of responsibility for their own welfare, particularly with regards to pensions and care in old age. Labour's 'new politics' suggests that in relation to welfare the promotion of a particular type of moral community in which citizens earn access to their social rights through a combination of hard work, responsible behaviour and personal contributions has become the primary concern. Consequently the New Labour government is concerned to use social policy to reward worthy citizens and discipline irresponsible ones. This can be seen as a central concern in Field's vision of stakeholder welfare, an approach that informed the green paper on welfare reform (DSS, 1998b).

Stakeholder welfare

More recently, direct appeals by government ministers to the concept of stakeholding have diminished; however, it is an idea that New Labour is able to accommodate comfortably (Jones Finer, 1997). Indeed the Prime Minister has added his own approval to its underlying principles (Blair, 1996b). Such support is hardly surprising as stakeholding clearly matches many of the important criteria on which New Labour is now building its approach.

> What underpins the fundamental idea of stakeholding is that social and economic inclusion, rather than equality, should be the overriding objective of the contemporary left. Inclusion implies membership; you cannot be included if you are not a member. But membership entails obligations as well as rights. So a stakeholder economy exists where there is a mutuality of rights and obligations constructed around the notion of economic, social and political inclusion. What stakeholder capitalism does is to apply those principles to the operation of free market capitalism and by doing so it places limits on the operation of unfettered markets. (Hutton, 1996, p 3)

This is to be an 'inclusive' politics in which 'rights' demand attendant 'responsibilities' from all levels of society. Importantly for New Labour, stakeholding has also been packaged as a new approach which challenges the inequality that was central to the economic neo–liberalism of Thatcherism, while simultaneously distancing itself from many of the redistributive ideals that (nominally at least) are seen as synonymous to 'old' Labour thinking (Burkitt and Ashton, 1996).

Stakeholder welfare shares similar concerns to communitarianism, in that it is keen to ensure that public welfare provisions encourage individuals to take control of their own welfare and ultimately to be responsible for meeting their own needs whenever possible. Significant contributions in mapping out the content and extent of stakeholder welfare have been made by both Hutton (1996, 1997-b) and Field (1996). Field's departure from government in July 1999 appears to be indicative of the fickle nature of power politics rather than a significant rejection of his ideas. There may well be a shift in emphasis; indeed, in his resignation speech, Field makes it clear that he believes economic considerations are marginalising important moral issues: "although the level of expenditure is an issue, the main concern is the cancerous impact that much of welfare has on people's motivations" (Field, 1998, p 2). Nonetheless, New Labour's welfare reforms continue to a large extent to share Field's concerns about individual behaviour and the wider moral order that welfare regimes may help to promote. A consideration of his views therefore remains valid.

Hutton's active welfare state

In terms of welfare provision, or more accurately social security benefits, Hutton (1996) envisages an inclusive role for the welfare state in the stakeholder society. However, inclusion is essentially limited to the condition that all must contribute, and in return contributors have access to potential benefits. In stating that in future public welfare must become more 'pro-active' (ie, move beyond merely offering benefit payment to individuals during periods of unemployment), Hutton is explicit in defining the role for a revised welfare state. In stakeholder societies, responsible governments will primarily concentrate on creating opportunities for the unemployed to re-enter the labour market. The relief of poverty via benefits assumes secondary importance. This may be seen as synonymous with New Labour's approach (Darling, 1998). Inclusion for stakeholding, then, largely implies inclusion into the paid labour market. Consequently, the desired role of the state in tackling the attendant problem of social exclusion is largely limited to offering opportunities that will enable unemployed individuals to return to paid work as soon as possible. As Levitas has commented, the use of the term 'social exclusion' in this way is highly problematic.

> The concept of social exclusion as it is currently deployed places people either inside or outside of the mainstream society, synonymous with outside the labour market. The concept works to both devalue unpaid work and to obscure the inequalities between paid workers. (Levitas, 1996, p 18)

New Labour (see, for example, Mandelson, 1997), however, seems to have few objections about continuing with this approach.

Field's remoralising of welfare

The essential elements of Field's proposed 'stakeholder welfare' are set out in Deacon (1996). Compulsory contributions based on an insurance principle are at the centre of Field's proposals. Crucially, unlike previous state insurance systems, each person will retain ownership of their own welfare capital, consisting of personal and employer contributions. An individual's welfare account will therefore directly serve to meet their own needs in periods of economic inactivity such as unemployment or retirement. Linking an individual's welfare entitlement to their personal contributions in this way will, Field maintains, ensure popular support at a time when people are exhibiting both a reluctance to pay high levels of direct taxation and also a tendency towards greater 'social autonomy'[15]. A strong redistributive element is ruled out within the envisaged scheme, but some degree of help from government could occur: namely, the payment of basic contributions for those who are excluded from paid work and therefore unable to contribute themselves. This, Field believes, would guarantee that the proposed scheme is both inclusive in its approach and universal in its coverage. It is made clear that basic welfare requirements (compare Etzioni's social basics) could be paid for by income raised through general taxation rather than the money paid in by wealthier contributors to the scheme. Furthermore, in spite of Field's demise, it appears that the language of stakeholding still informs government thinking on the reform of pension provision (DSS, 1998d).

Central to Field's approach is his attack on the Conservatives' expansion of means-tested benefits; not only because means testing dramatically increased the cost of social security provision (Field, 1996; DSS, 1998a) (this he believes to be unsustainable); but second, and more importantly, because:

> ... means tested welfare is the enemy within. Its rules actively undermine the whole fabric of our character. In doing so it is a cancer within the public domain helping to erode the wider moral order of society. (Field, 1996, p 20)

Criteria by which means tests are applied, Field believes, go against all the values that a 'decent society' should be promoting. If a person who is receiving means-tested benefits seeks to improve their position via paid work, the automatic application of a new means test cuts their eligibility for benefit. It is often more worthwhile for an individual to remain on benefits rather than take up low paid work. Those thrifty enough in the past to save for future contingencies such as unemployment find they do not qualify for assistance. In effect, their 'good housekeeping' is penalised by the state. Similarly, other claimants may be actively encouraged to lie about their assets in order to maintain eligibility for means-tested benefits. In short, means testing actively promotes a benefit trap and encourages deceit on the part of claimants. Both of these factors are seen by Field as instrumental to increasing costs and promoting a dependency culture.

> Means tests ensure that claimants' energy is channelled into working the system rather than working themselves off welfare. It is in the

way they have an impact on effort, savings and honesty that means tests are the most potent recruiting sergeant there is for the dependency culture. (Field, 1996, p 17)

It appears that New Labour is now less concerned than Field about the negative effects of means testing. Recent legislation (ie the 1999 Welfare Reform and Pensions Act) indicates that certain incapacity benefits will be subject to a means test in the future (DSS, 1999c; Thomas and Wintour, 1998).

One of New Labour's underlying beliefs is that welfare is a powerful force in shaping our individual and collective characters, and that its influence can be both positive and negative. Any actions of government which attempt to foster 'responsible behaviour' in benefit recipients are viewed as wholly legitimate (Darling, 1998). Self-help and an independent striving for self-improvement are two examples of the responsible behaviour that New Labour wishes public welfare to promote, and consequently both have a major part to play in their vision of the future welfare state.

The system as it stands promotes fraud and deception, not honesty and hard work. It has led to growing poverty and dependence, not independence. It has fuelled social division and exclusion, not helped the creation of a decent society.... *The new welfare state should help and encourage people of working age to work where they are capable of doing so.* Work offers the best escape route from poverty and dependence, a platform on which to save and a sense of individual purpose. (DSS, 1998c, pp 1-2; original emphasis)

By basing their Green Paper on a contributory principle, New Labour hopes to maximise each individual's potential for self-improvement and reward rather than penalise paid work, effort and saving.

New Labour continues to tacitly support many of Field's assumptions about human behaviour and the effect that collective welfare may have on individual actions. This approach could be seen to imply a separate 'underclass' whose behaviour needs to be remoralised, in part by welfare reform, an approach clearly rejected by many on the left (Bagguley and Mann, 1992; Roseneil and Mann, 1994). New Labour's fixation on what they consider to be the dysfunctional behaviour of some recipients of social welfare and their emphasis on individual strategies of self-help under the guiding hand of a moral community shares common concerns with communitarians such as Etzioni and Selbourne.

Beyond Left and Right: Giddens' blueprint for New Labour?

The recent work of the sociologist Anthony Giddens (1998, 1994) reads almost like a blueprint for New Labour's approach to welfare reform. This should not be too surprising as his ideas were deemed important enough to warrant an invitation for informal discussions with the present Prime Minister. *In beyond left and right*, Giddens (1994) takes a similar view to the government and urges a fundamental rethink of the state's long-term leading role in the provision of welfare. He argues that we must ditch the state-led, top-down approach to welfare, believing that this will facilitate greater levels of individual autonomy and encourage a new 'positive welfare' in which individuals recognise their personal responsibilities both to themselves and wider society. Within Giddens' work there is stress on the importance of both individual and group agency as a counterbalance to the dependency that he associates with some state-led programmes of welfare. In looking for an expansion of political participation at all levels, he encourages a recognition of the importance of our responsibility to fellow citizens, but this stress on political participation, of citizenship in its most active sense, coupled as it is with a rejection of a fundamental role for the state in the provision of welfare, is not without its problems.

Although aware of the problem of solidarity within his theorising, Giddens (1994) maintains that the possibility of social renewal rests on individual agents recognising the importance of obligations to others that are binding and authoritative. A centrally important question, however, remains unanswered. In a world of disparate views and needs, and the inevitable disagreement that ensues, we must ask which voices will endure and come to dominate. His entire approach in this particular work appears to rest on the highly contentious view "that for the first time in history we can speak of the emergence of universal values" (Giddens, 1994, p 20). The twin problems of differential power and conflicting values remain unresolved and seriously weaken his approach.

More recently Giddens (1998) has revisited some of the above themes and once again his ideas and concerns for welfare reform appear to mirror those of New Labour. He outlines a new role for the envisaged 'social investment state'. This is a state that will in future meet its commitments to social justice and equality via the redistribution of 'possibilities'(opportunities) rather than wealth. "Government has an essential role to play in investing in the human resources and infrastructure needed to develop an entrepreneurial culture" (Giddens, 1998, p 99) [compare Page, 1997 below]). Giddens is also unequivocal in making a reciprocal relationship between rights and responsibilities central to his approach.

> One might suggest as a prime motto for the new politics, *no rights without responsibilities*.... As an ethical principle 'no rights without responsibilities' must apply not only to welfare recipients, but to everyone ... because otherwise the precept can be held to apply only to the poor and needy as tends to be the case with the political right. (Giddens, 1998, p 65-6; original emphasis)

Although the above declaration that the new rights/responsibilities rule must be evenly and universally applied is commendable, it fails to reflect reality. In relation to the social element of citizenship it is almost exclusively the rights of the poor and needy that are being reduced, while simultaneously the attendant responsibilities required to access those rights are being increased. A further, and perhaps more worrying, aspect of Giddens' theorising is the general lack of vision when considering 'welfare' and the 'problem' of dependency. Titmuss (1958) reminded us long ago that we are all welfare dependants to a certain extent. Giddens' analysis would perhaps have greater authority if he also considered the fiscal and occupational benefits available to the better-off rather than (taking his cue from the New Right) concentrating solely on the more visible 'social welfare' element discussed by Titmuss.

New Labour and social citizenship

Provision

It appears that New Labour sees the welfare role of the state predominately in terms of what Page (1997) has called endowment egalitarianism[16]. The state provision of benefits, although seen as important for a minority who are unable to work, seems to have become an issue of secondary consideration, behind attempts to ensure the highest possible level of labour market participation. In terms of provision, therefore, New Labour accepts that the state has to assume a leading role in the provision of training and work opportunities, but in return it expects citizens to take up those opportunities (see below) and contribute to both their own and society's well-being or alternatively accept that they have no right to expect support from the national community in the form of welfare (Darling, 1999; Powell et al 1999; Stepney et al, 1999). In this way New Labour is moving towards the endorsement of a principle of mutual responsibility rather than agreed definitions of need as the basis for social rights. Furthermore, the New Labour government's policies of keeping a cap on welfare expenditure, refusing to raise income tax rates, and cutting the benefit of lone parents suggest that in certain areas they think about the reform of public welfare provision along similar lines to their Conservative predecessors (compare Hills, 1998).

Conditionality

The individual responsibility/duty theme central to both the New Right and new communitarian critiques of Marshall has also become a central tenet of the New Labour government's thinking on citizenship and much of the social welfare provision that they envisage. Reforming the welfare state is now a stated priority of the new administration but access to certain social and economic rights, and the opportunity and security they can bring, looks increasingly likely to be conditional on some citizens accepting "that rights offered go with responsibilities owed" (Labour Party, 1997, p 11). The recent rhetoric of ministers and the various policies emerging from government departments support this view. The reality of the Prime Minister's call for a "fundamental reform of our welfare state, of the deal between citizen and society", based on "compassion with a hard edge" (Blair, 1997, p 10) is apparent in Labour's New Deal Welfare to Work proposals for the young unemployed, lone parents and disabled people (see Blunkett, 1998; Blair, 1997; Harman, 1997). While currently it is stressed that both lone parents and disabled people will only be encouraged back to paid work, it is clear that ultimately the government feels that such individuals have a responsibility to return to employment if it is at all possible. The recently announced plans (DSS, 1999b) to extend the New Deal initiative to all new benefit claimants reiterates this stance. In the case of the young and long-term unemployed the link between rights and responsibilities is already more clearly defined: a failure to take up one of the work/training options offered by government will lead to the application of benefit sanctions. Beyond the world of paid work the government's emphasis is still very much a mixture of persuading and compelling individual citizens to recognise their responsibilities.

> This is why our reform agenda is dominated by a new emphasis on responsibilities as well as rights: the responsibility of parents, absent and present, to care emotionally and materially for their children; the responsibility of adults of working age to work; the responsibility of

welfare recipients to take opportunities to escape from dependency. (Field, 1997, p 6)

Such an approach should not be surprising; as early as 1995, Tony Blair was emphasising the importance of responsibility and duty within New Labour's politics.

> Duty is the cornerstone of a decent society. It recognises more than self. It defines the context in which rights are given. It is personal but it is also owed to society.... It draws on a broader and therefore more accurate notion of human nature than one formulated on insular self-interest. The rights we receive should reflect the duties we owe. With the power should come responsibility. (Blair, 1995b, p 5)

Generally the application of the principle of conditionality within many aspects of social welfare is presented as an unproblematic and a common-sense part of the citizenship advocated by the present government. Labour's unemployment policy has undergone a significant shift so that it now endorses what it previously referred to as "the blunt Tory strategy of compulsion" (Labour Party, 1994, p 28). As previously noted, state regulation of the behaviour of unemployed people has become a greater feature of policy with the launch of Labour's New Deal. This is particularly the case when considering young people. All 18 to 24 year olds who have been unemployed for over six months now have a choice of a job with the private sector, a job in the voluntary sector, a place on an environmental task force, or full-time education and training; "staying on benefit will no longer be an option" (Blunkett, 1998, p 1). It is already clear that harsh benefit sanctions for refusal to work or train are at the heart of New Labour's strategy for the young and long-term unemployed (Powell, 1999; Tonge, 1999; Finn, 1998; Milne and Thomas, 1997).

Similarly, within the social housing sector the Labour Party (1996) clearly endorses the last government's attempt to deal with tenants who misbehave, and now endorses a stricter regime in the Crime and Disorder Act (1998). The Act includes a new type of injunction, the 'community safety order', to cover cases of serious violent harassment or anti-social conduct, and also creates for the first time a new category of 'racially aggravated' offences which will deal specifically with incidents involving racial violence or harassment (Home Office, 1997). It has been argued that such measures would not lead to "a general reduction in tenants' rights" (Blair, 1995b, p 10), but one outcome must surely be a reduction in the welfare rights of particular tenants. In future only those tenants deemed to behave in a responsible manner will be tolerated in public housing. If individuals who have been evicted because of anti-social behaviour are regarded as having made themselves intentionally homeless by other councils or housing associations to whom they apply for shelter, then effectively they will have no right to be housed.

Membership

The Green Paper *New ambitions for our country* (DSS, 1998b) has further confirmed that membership of the citizenship club and the welfare rights that it entails will only be available for those (able-bodied) individuals who agree to contribute positively and in an approved manner to the community that they inhabit. The centrality of paid work within New Labour's welfare reform agenda has been widely noted (Lund, 1999; Oppenheim, 1999; Powell, 1999; Stepney et al, 1999; Deacon, 1998; Plant, 1998; Levitas, 1998, 1996; Page, 1997) and certainly a willingness to engage in paid work is central to New Labour's perspective. The acceptance in principle of a 'citizenship pension' (DSS, 1998b, p 37) payable to carers, however, indicates that the government recognises the performance of unpaid domestic care work as a valid enough contribution for an individual to claim their social rights. It should also be noted that while the government believes that all those capable of work have a responsibility to enter into employment if at all possible, at present it is at pains to stress that lone parents will only be encouraged back to work and that sanctions will not be applied to those who remain on benefit. This may be a tacit recognition of the social value of parenting. What should not be overlooked is that those individuals who refuse to accept the rules of membership as laid down by the government will be deemed 'undeserving' and excluded from certain communally provided benefits and services.

A new and inclusive approach?

Deacon (1998) views New Labour's Green Paper (DSS, 1998b) as an attempt by the government to promote a particular notion of the common good ('social well-being') by using the state's power in three interlinked ways. In making work central to its welfare policies and offering incentives[17] to individuals who choose work above welfare, the government is attempting to use social policy as a way of harnessing self-interest for the good of both individuals and the wider society. Field's stakeholder welfare vision can be seen as an example of this approach. The Green Paper also sees the government exercising its authoritative power by imposing punitive benefit sanctions on the young unemployed who do not act as the government wishes and refuse to take up one of the work opportunities being offered. Finally, Deacon argues that the state is also using "welfare as a mechanism for moral regeneration" (1998, p 2) by setting out within its proposals an appeal for a society in which the 'proper' balance between rights and responsibilities is achieved. As such, New Labour is using its welfare reform agenda in an instrumental way, as a tool to persuade citizens of the superiority of its citizenship perspective which emphasises notions of individual and mutual responsibilities rather than individual rights.

The suggestion that New Labour is mapping out a new and inclusive approach to welfare, a 'Third Way' (Blair, 1998a; Giddens, 1998) somewhere between the residual welfare state of the New Right and Marshall's vision of citizenship with its extensive package of social rights to benefits and services is, however, more contentious. Hay (1998, 1997), for example, strongly argues that a new bipartisan consensus has emerged and that New Labour now pursues policies that were until recently closely associated with the New Right. It has also been stated that New Labour's welfare reform is based closely on issues and policies that had previously been central to the Conservative approach (Lister, 1997c). New Labour's concern to use welfare as an agent for moral regeneration and its endorsement of conditionality are clear indications that the present government also draws heavily on New Right and new communitarian approaches in relation to the social element of citizenship (Heron and Dwyer, 1999; Driver and Martell, 1997). In borrowing heavily from both New Right and new communitarian perspectives, New Labour's approach to welfare may be novel in terms of party policy but it cannot be seen as a distinctly new 'Third way.' We should also be sceptical about claims about its inherent inclusiveness; clearly those who do not accept their responsibilities, as defined by New Labour, will be excluded from certain communal welfare provisions.

A Muslim perspective

As Bin Hamzah and Harrison (2000) note, an understanding of Islamic perspectives on welfare is a relatively new but developing area of interest within British social policy. This section attempts in a modest way to provide an understanding of how Islamic principles may relate to Western notions of citizenship and its welfare component. Issues relating to an individual's right to welfare provision, the obligations of a community's members to meet the needs of the poor and the redistributive mechanisms necessary are common concerns of both Western and Islamic perspectives.

Ahmad (1982) notes four characteristics which define an Islamic economy: first, that "an Islamic economy is an integral part of an Islamic society and state and cannot be studied in isolation" (1982, p 5); second, that material (economic) and moral (behavioural) issues are intertwined and, therefore, rightly both are the concern of policy makers; third, that an Islamic economy is neither free market nor command economy[18] but that it stands somewhere in between; and finally, that the primary objective of an Islamic economy is to establish a just social order, one in which the *Shari'a* (the Islamic Law) sets out the rights and duties of community members in terms of meeting their own needs and the needs of the less fortunate. The institution *Al-Hisba* as laid out by al-Shaykh al-Iman Ibn Taymiya (1263-1328) is an important influence in determining the extent to which the ethic of the market place or the ethic of social justice prevails within a community.

> *Al-Hisba* is a moral as well as a socio-economic institution in Islam through which public life is regulated in such a way that a high degree of public morality is attained and the society is protected from bad workmanship, fraud, extortion and exploitation. (Ahmad, 1982, cover note)

Islam suggests, therefore, that the justice of the market alone cannot prevail and adequately meet the needs of all citizens. A regulatory role for the community is considered appropriate so that the welfare interests (both economic and moral) of all the community members can be met.

Provision

Maintaining the provision of essential supplies, at a reasonable price, to those in need is seen as a legitimate practice for the state to engage in (Taymiya, 1982). Indeed the state is seen as having a dual role in ensuring that the wealthy producers meet any shortfalls in the essential needs of citizens. Initially it would encourage those who were in a position to help to do so but ultimately it is deemed reasonable to use force to ensure that the collective requirements of an entire community prevail over the wishes of affluent individuals to make profits. This can be seen to be consistent with Ahmad's (1982) view that Islam represents, to employ a well-used contemporary phrase, 'a third way', and what Dean and Khan (1997) have called Islam's 'ambiguity to capitalism' in supporting private wealth and enterprise but challenging the excessive hoarding of capital in the face of unmet need because it may damage the moral foundations of a community (*Ummah:* see overleaf).

One of the main mechanisms for financing welfare provision within a Muslim system is by the giving of *zakat*. *Zakat* is a religious duty imposed upon all who are Muslim to give a fixed percentage of their disposable wealth (usually 2.5%) to members of the community who are in need. Interestingly, the giving of *zakat* has benefits both for those who provide as well as those who receive. A respondent in the fieldwork that informed this book was at pains to explain that "the giving of money first and foremost benefits the giver; it secures your own position and cleanses any remaining personal wealth" (Dwyer, 2000, pp 35-6). In this way *zakat* upholds both the economic and moral principles of a good society as set out in Muslim terms. The individual citizen who provides for less fortunate kin reaffirms their own righteousness by recognising and acting upon their duty to the community, the right of the needy to welfare is validated, and a moral order in which mutual duties are seen as fundamental is established.

Conditionality

Although it has been contended that *zakat* is unconditional in that it is given out of duty to meet the needs of other, anonymous, community members (Dean and Khan, 1997), limited research (Dwyer, 2000) suggests that the removal of certain rights to welfare may be justified if an individual continued to ignore the *naseha* (sincere advice) of his fellow Muslims by not recognising his responsibilities to the community and continuing to behave in an immoral way. A parallel may be drawn here with Khan's (1982) discussion of the treatment of what he describes as 'voluntary parasitic beggars' in early Islamic society.

> Invalids and the economically infirm were provided the basic necessities of life from the *zakat*.... The Muhtasib[19] would compel healthy able-to-work individuals to engage themselves in some gainful pursuit. (Khan, 1982, p 146)

Although Khan goes on to recognise that unemployment at contemporary levels was unknown in ancient times, it would appear that Islamic welfare provision tacitly endorses the principle of conditionality and that rights to welfare can be, in certain circumstances, reduced or withheld from irresponsible individuals.

Membership

Each individual Muslim is held to be a member of the *Ummah*,

... a community of the faithful, possessing similar beliefs and goals and sharing material benefits, intellectual responsibility and a vision of the worldly life and the hereafter. (Bin Hamzah and Harrison, 2000, p 7)

It should be noted that this community of faith is not limited by ethnicity, national borders or kinship but that its general well-being is held to prevail over the specific interests of individual members. The extent to which certain individuals and groups, most notably women, may lay claim to rights other than those specified in *Sharia* and accepted by the community is a point of much discussion with Islamic scholars (Dean and Khan, 1997), but principally it appears that the *Ummah* is a community whose citizens are bound together according to principles of duty, and acceptance of those principles is instrumental in allowing members access to their rights.

'British Muslims'[20] and welfare

Dean and Shah (1999) suggest that there may be two different traditions that Muslims draw on when negotiating their position as citizens in non Muslim Western states. Those who adopt the 'modernist or pragmatic' tradition appear to be more open to active engagement with the Western societies in which they are located.

To the extent that this is a tradition that defines a Muslim identity, it is the identity of an outward-looking ambassador for Islam who engages with and exploits the opportunities that a liberal democratic Western constitution offers. (Dean and Shah, 1999, p 7)

In contrast, the above authors also draw attention to a more 'conservative or neo-revivalist' tradition within Islam that condemns the secularism and materialism which it sees as fundamental to Western values and lifestyles. Central to this approach is a belief that Muslims should keep themselves separate from the prevailing concerns of the society that surrounds them and that they should instead work to promote Islam so that in time that society may itself become Islamic.

To the extent that this tradition defines a Muslim identity, it is the identity of an introspective stranger who, though strongly committed to solidaristic principles, can only protect the integrity of his/her life project by placing strict limits upon engagement with the non Muslim world. (Dean and Shah, 1999, p 8)

While these traditions are rarely explicit in the dialogues that British Muslims use, it is argued that they do, however, provide one way of making sense of the popular discourses on social citizenship and the part that Islam plays in the relationship between individual British Muslim citizens and the state.

Dean and Khan (1997) draw attention to the pragmatic way in which British Muslims have adapted their faith to set up systems of welfare that run parallel to those of the British state. Such moves should not be surprising, given the state's role in limiting the welfare rights of Muslim minorities in the past (Ahmad and Husbands, 1993) and the continuing socio-economic disadvantage and cultural discrimination that many Muslims face (Modood, 1998). The Muslim approach to welfare is not wholly capitalist or socialist/egalitarian. It sees entrepreneurship and the accumulation of capital as acceptable as long as individuals recognise their duties as members of a community and provide adequately for those in need. In terms of the 'good society', differences in income and status are seen as acceptable as long as no one is abandoned to poverty or hopelessness.

> The Qu'ran assumed an economic system based on individual enterprise and reward, but set within a moral framework that ensures support for the weak through the compassion and self-discipline of the strong. (Dean and Khan, 1997, p 198)

What is particularly interesting in the context of this discussion is the extent to which the sentiments expressed in the above quotation resemble those of certain other Western perspectives on citizenship that have been discussed earlier. In outlining a welfare system based on a state endorsement of a particular, ordered moral community, in which individual contribution and mutual responsibility are regarded as badges of membership, the Islamic perspective on welfare may be closer to New Labour's vision than many people realise.

Conclusions: a new orthodoxy?

Plant (1998) highlights two contrasting notions of citizenship.

The first sees citizenship as a status that is not fundamentally altered by the virtue (or lack of it) of the individual: it does not ask whether the citizen is making a recognised contribution to society.... You should thus be able, as a citizen, to claim benefits even if you are not discharging what others may regard as your proper obligations to society.... The second and alternative view, places much less emphasis on rights, and focuses instead on obligation, virtue and contribution. On this view citizenship is not a kind of pre-existing status, but rather something that is achieved by contributing to the life of a society. The ideas of reciprocity and contribution are at the heart of this concept of citizenship: individuals do not and cannot have a right to the resources of society unless they contribute to the development of that society through work or other socially valued activities, if they are in a position to do so. (Plant, 1998, p 30)

Marshall's rights–based approach sees citizenship very much in the terms of the first position outlined above; however, it is the second view of citizenship that is now predominant (Dwyer, 1998). The New Right, the new communitarians and New Labour may all call upon differing philosophical traditions in the attempt to secure what they would see as differing objectives. However, by endorsing a concept of citizenship with 'obligation, virtue and contribution' at its heart, they all promote similar outcomes, particularly in relation to social rights. A new welfare orthodoxy that stresses reduced access to public welfare provision, a stronger link between rights and responsibilities, and an increasingly moral agenda is now dominant. Discussion of the state's responsibility to meet the needs of its citizens is limited; certainly any expansion of the state's welfare role through the promotion and provision of an extensive package of social rights appears a secondary concern. The social component is essentially undergoing a redefinition, in which certain welfare rights are increasingly conditional upon citizens first agreeing to conform to appropriate patterns of behaviour as defined by the state or other provider of welfare. This newly dominant approach to citizenship which is built around the pivotal notions of individual and mutual responsibility serves two purposes. First, the exclusion of certain individuals from public welfare arrangements becomes less problematic for the provider of welfare. The welfare rights of those deemed 'irresponsible' because they cannot, or will not, meet certain state-endorsed standards or regulations may be withdrawn or reduced. Second, the state can then place the blame for the predicament of those whose right to publicly funded welfare is reduced or removed firmly at the door of the individuals concerned, while simultaneously justifying the withdrawal of an individual's welfare rights and a reduction in its own role (or the role of its appointed agents) in guaranteeing or financing provision.

Notes

[1] Refer to Dean (1996, ch 2) for a good account of the differing principles underpinning rights to social security in Britain. See also Lister (III.10) in Alcock et al (1998).

[2] The 1962 Commonwealth Immigration Act for the first time limited entry into Britain to those citizens who held UK-issued (or UK government representative overseas issued) passports and work vouchers. The 1968 Commonwealth Immigration Act, from a Labour administration, further tightened controls in the face of the so called 'Ugandan Crisis'. The 1981 British Nationality Act removed the ancient right of *jus soli* and created three levels of British citizenship, with British Overseas Citizens having no real rights of abode anywhere. In 1986 new visa requirements were introduced for visitors from five named Commonwealth countries; all five have predominately black populations. 1995 saw new moves to tighten the right to asylum in Britain.

[3] Oliver (1996, p 148) discusses the important role played by coordinating organisations such as Disabled People's International (DPI) and the British Council of Organisations of Disabled People (BCODP). See also Part Two of Oliver and Barnes (1998) for a selection of policy statements from disabled people's organisations such as the DPI and the Union of the Physically Impaired Against Segregation (UPIAS), an organisation set up in the 1970s.

[4] Beresford and Wallcraft (1997) raise an important related point in their discussion of psychiatric system survivors, noting that the restriction of survivors' rights is enshrined in the legal system and seen as both necessary and legitimate.

[5] Walby (1994, p 385) notes, "In the case of British women, political citizenship was as least as often the powerbase from which women were able to win civil citizenship as vice versa. Many civil rights have only recently been acquired". For example, married women were granted independent tax status as late as 1990.

[6] See, for example, the following authors for a more detailed examination of this term and its diverse approaches to social policy: George and Wilding (1994); Andrews (1991); Levitas (1986).

[7] Refer to Teles (1996, pp 60-75) for a more detailed account of various American New Right theorists' views on the causes of, and solutions to, 'welfare dependency'.

[8] Refer to Mead (1982, pp 25-9 and 1997b, p 220) where he sees the abolition of state welfare as 'impolitic' because of continued popular support for helping those in need.

[9] The Conservative governments of the 1980s and 1990s are often referred to as 'Thatcherite' administrations. For those readers who wish to specifically explore 'Thatcherism' and its link to the ideas of the New Right in more detail, a good place to start is chapter 5 of Faulks (1998). The influence of what I have referred to previously as 'libertarian liberal' or 'libertarian New Right' thinkers (and which Faulks refers to as neo-liberal) is clearly stated. He notes, for example, that, "The Thatcherite governments rejected the kind of citizenship advocated by social liberals such as Marshall and instead sought their inspiration from the neo-liberalism of Hayek" (Faulks, 1998, p 96).

[10] The Commission for Social Justice was an independent body set up by the late John Smith in partnership with the IPPR. It presents, in its own words, "a forward thinking programme for social and economic reform" that attempts to radically confront the "bankrupt dogmas of the free market economy" (1994).

[11] Certain New Right thinkers may have been influential here. Opposed to the 'paternalistic collectivism' of an overbearing state, Marsland (1996, 1995, 1992) has argued that state welfare provisions should be greatly reduced. Both Marsland (1996) and Green (1996) outline strategies to replace state welfare with a system that combines the 'individual freedoms' of market purchasing with a restored role for voluntary/charitable organisations in meeting the needs of poorer citizens.

[12] It is not intended to give the impression that these two authors represent the full extent of new communitarian thinking; however, they do outline the main concerns of many of their colleagues. For two similar and more recent accounts refer to Tam (1998) and Sacks (1997).

[13] Deacon and Mann (1999) have drawn attention to Etzioni's (1997, p 177) assertion that he is not attempting to 'rerun history'. Given the tone of his historical analysis of American morality and values (1997, ch 3), in which he appears to be lamenting the way in which many of the ordered certainties of the 1950s gave way to the permissive 1960s and subsequently increasing

anarchism, and his (1995) call for a 'new Gemeinschaft', it is reasonable to argue that Etzioni's communitarian vision is inherently backward looking. Compare also Stacey (1998) and her paper on the combining of new communitarian and conservative thinking in the Clinton administration's endorsement of 'traditional' family values.

[14] A position that Etzioni shares with New Right theorists such as Murray (1984).

[15] That is to say people assuming a more active role in defining their relationships to each other and to welfare institutions.

[16] Page (1997, p 10) defines endowment egalitarianism as "providing fair opportunities for all citizens to acquire the necessary education, skills and training that will allow them to compete in a changing and uncertain labour market".

[17] In the summary version of the Green Paper (DSS, 1998c, p 2) the government promises, "We will ensure that work pays by introducing the Working Families Tax Credit, reforming the tax and benefits system, introducing the minimum wage and modernising the National Insurance scheme".

[18] An Islamic economy "affirms the right of the individual to own property and engage in private enterprise but transforms the concept of ownership into that of trusteeship and subjects individual freedom to ownership and control" (Ahmad, 1982, p 6).

[19] A free Muslim scholar of high integrity and social status, well versed in the community's traditions and norms who administered the Al-Hisba according to the rights of God, and the rights of people.

[20] Although this section discusses generally a Muslim perspective on welfare, it is important to state that terms such as 'British Muslims' and 'Muslim welfare' do not adequately reflect the diverse reality of Muslim populations in Britain or disputes within Muslim thought worldwide.

Part 2
Three dimensions of citizenship: welfare service users' accounts and debates

General introduction

Having considered relevant theoretical discussions in Part 1, the purpose of this second part of the book is to allow the perceptions, experiences and expectations of some welfare service users[1] to become a part of ongoing debates about citizenship and, more particularly, its welfare element. In order to achieve this aim the next three chapters draw extensively on the voices and opinions of users as expressed in a series of focus group discussions that took place in 1997 within the metropolitan district of Bradford, England. It was intended that these focus group sessions would provide the book with a series of group interviews to act as located case studies that were relevant to an analysis of both citizenship and welfare.

Given previously stated concerns about contemporary citizenship and welfare debates being dominated by powerful 'expert' voices (compare Beresford and Turner, 1997) a decision was taken to set up group interviews with as wide a range of users as possible. In an attempt to ensure that the research did not exacerbate the social exclusion experienced by certain sections of British society, it was resolved to make use of a broadly inclusive sampling framework so that the accounts of men and women, young and old, white, African Caribbean and Asian citizens and so on could be drawn upon. Some further purposively driven sampling decisions were also taken. First, given the extent of the exclusion of 'welfare state service users' from welfare debates in the past, and the aim of documenting and interpreting service user experiences and opinions, it was decided to largely (though not exclusively) sample a number of groups whose members, for one reason or another, were reliant on various state social welfare benefits for their day-to-day survival. Second, because of Bradford's relatively large Muslim community and a noted absence of research into their views on the central themes of the book (Dean and Khan, 1997), it was resolved to include several groups of British Muslims within the sample. It is hoped that this book builds on the earlier insights offered by Law et al (1994) and Cohen et al (1992) into the perceptions and experiences of the Muslim minority population in relation to welfare issues and the notion of citizenship.

Some basic information about the focus groups is available in Table 1 of the Appendix that appears at the end of the book; however, as a way of introducing the chapters that follow it may be useful to further briefly outline the focus groups. In all, 10 groups were convened: two were exclusively female in composition, two exclusively male, while in the other six groups both men and women were members. In three of the groups all the participants were of the Muslim faith.

Overall a total of 69 respondents took part in the research; of these 36 were men and 33 women, with ages ranging between 19 and 80 years. Forty-three of the respondents could best be described as white, 23 as Asian and a further three as African Caribbean. Ten respondents were in work (five full-time and five part-time) and a further eight respondents were largely dependant on various retirement pensions for their upkeep. In total 59 of those involved were outside the paid labour market at the time of the study and 17 people (16 of whom were female) identified themselves as having caring responsibilities within a family. These respondents without paid work (except the retired pensioners noted above) were reliant on a range of state benefits which included JSA, various disability benefits, a war pension and Income Support. Forty-one out of these 59 respondents specified which state benefits they claimed, with the remainder preferring to offer no further comment.

For various reasons[2] many voices and groups may be missing or poorly represented (most notably African Caribbean), but this book still offers many insights into a range of 'grassroots' service user views that are of relevance to ongoing contemporary citizenship and welfare debates. It is important that such voices are heard, especially in the present period of welfare resettlement. As New Labour's reform of welfare continues, it seems reasonable to allow a platform for the opinions of some of those citizens whose welfare rights and responsibilities are effectively being redefined; Chapters Four to Six present such opinions.

Notes

[1] As previously stated, the term welfare service user is utilised as a shorthand to denote ordinary citizens who are not normally involved in the formulation or implementation of welfare policies.

[2] The research that informs this book was originally undertaken for a PhD. The practical, that is financial, constraints that this imposed limited a more wide ranging study.

FOUR

Provision

Introduction

A specific purpose of this chapter is to address the central question of who should provide welfare from a service user perspective. Throughout, the qualitative data presented will relate to the three areas of welfare chosen as the basis of the study, that is, healthcare, housing and social security. Initially, the users'[1] views on the appropriate role(s) of the state, the individual, the market and so on in terms of welfare provision are explored. This is followed by a consideration of several allied issues that were often raised in the group discussions. Opinions and experiences concerning the adequacy or inadequacy of current provisions are then investigated, and a discussion of the extent to which welfare service users feel stigmatised because they are in receipt of public welfare follows. The subject of how benefits and services are to be financed, a topic with obvious and important implications for public welfare, is then considered, prior to some concluding comments.

The role of the state, the market and other agencies in providing welfare

The state: a leading role in provision

Healthcare

The initial point to make is that the majority of users clearly located the ultimate responsibility for the provision of welfare firmly with the state. This was particularly the case when healthcare was discussed; indeed only two users deviated from this view. Many indicated a strong attachment to the NHS and its principle of universal 'free' care, provided as and when people required treatment, and financed from general taxation. Two justifications were prominent. First, people believed they had an individual right to healthcare through past contributions; in effect that they had previously paid contributions on the tacit understanding that publicly provided healthcare would be available as and when they required it.

"I have worked all my life, so I have paid in all my life." (Linda, Women Benefit Claimants Group)

"If you are giving taxes to the government then it becomes the government's responsibility to provide healthcare. Whoever is earning a sufficient amount for his own private care, then yes, he can take private care, but for the individual who is not working or who pays taxes, then it is the state's responsibility to provide healthcare. Care should be provided on the basis of taxes given." (Ahmed, Informal Mosque Group)

Recent and continuing changes in the range and type of free public health services guaranteed by the state as free led to at least one group (Disabled Claimants Group) being pessimistic about enjoying access to free healthcare in the future. As Jane makes clear, she and her colleagues believed that in certain areas they had been 'robbed' by the state of provisions that people had expected to be available in return for their contributions.

Interviewer: "Do I get the impression from what you are saying that you think that the state should take a leading role?"

Jane: "Well, we have paid for that, my grandparents and everybody before us have paid for that and it is not there any more, is it?"

Harold: "No, the state is relinquishing its responsibility for even basic care with teeth and glasses."

Second, there was also a strongly expressed and recurrent opinion, whereby the users endorsed a more universalistic approach which emphasised a collective right to healthcare, based on need, in which the issue of past contributions was no longer centrally important.

"I was brought up to believe that the Health Service should be a universal service. It should be available to those who require those services, not dependant on their income; it should be dependant upon need." (David, Benefit Claimants Group)

"When you pay your contributions it is for the rest of society not just yourself; it is for everybody else as well. I don't think that you should make exceptions because you could then say, well, children are not entitled to it or whatever, or old people once they have got over a certain age and stopped paying contributions." (Linda, Women Benefit Claimants Group)

The following comment from Ahmed, who earlier had outlined a justification for free healthcare linked to past contributions, perhaps illustrates best of all how the users also viewed access to free healthcare as a basic human rights issue.

"Some of us have no income and have a large family, say, then it is a humanitarian issue if someone is ill; then the state has to provide more from compassion for the people who live in the country. Mankind should help one another and that aspect should be present in regards to the state and the individual." (Ahmed, Informal Mosque Group)

The other notable opinion expressed by a user was that healthcare should be offered on the basis of "a tripartite relationship of responsibility between government, individuals and also the communities." (Mary). This opinion was endorsed by Mary's co-users in the Middle Class Charity Group, but all saw a continuation of the state's role in funding services as centrally important, and they also believed that the state should continue to be the dominant providing partner in any future welfare coalition.

Housing

Questions concerning the provision of housing for those in need of shelter elicited a more complex response, but once again the most commonly held opinion was a strongly expressed belief that it is the duty of state to provide low-cost housing to meet needs where necessary.

"Well, the only people who can give a lead on that are the people who have got the money and that is the government, isn't it? Government has got to fund local councils so that they can afford to do it. They have been doing it in the past but with all the bloody cutbacks consequently stopping all the local councils from funding not just houses but police forces etc there is only one sector that can do it, the people who have got the money and that is the government of the day." (Harold, Disabled Claimants Group)

The Middle Class Charity Group, while endorsing the need for state support of social housing, were, however, openly hostile to local authorities providing houses. This group maintained that a switch in policy which endorsed a greater provisory role for independent housing associations would be positive as they make a better job of managing and maintaining properties.

"You have a situation in some parts of Bradford where some housing that was originally owned by the local council needed quite a lot of repairs doing to it and they sold it to a housing association and even in the short time that I have lived here you have seen the transformation. The housing association seems to look after the property better than the council." (Mary, Middle Class Charity Group)

A number of users expressed the opinion that it did not matter who provided a house as long as a person had shelter at a reasonable price. This appears to reflect desperation rather than a strong conviction that individuals should be left to fend for themselves. Two users who held this view were, by their own admission, technically homeless: one was sleeping at various friends, while the other admitted only to "a roof over my head". Their sentiments were echoed by the group of unemployed Asian men interviewed, whose spokesman, when asked if there was any preference towards council accommodation over that of private landlords, stated,

"There is but like they say, beggars can't be choosers, now, can they? If you are looking for a house and say you have got your family with you, you don't get the option every day of what house you want; you have got to go for something where you can at least keep a roof over your head. Once you've got it, once you've got a roof over your head then you can actually start to look around, you can actually choose." (Mohammed, Asian JSA Claimants Group)

Social security

When considering the issue of social security provision the overwhelming majority of users were adamant that ultimately only the state had the ability to deliver benefits to the people who needed them most. Moves to encourage individuals to take out private insurance type schemes were dismissed as being of little relevance by most of the users as the low paid, the unemployed and many disabled people couldn't afford them anyway because of their disadvantaged position in the labour market. Most were openly hostile to such ideas. For example, two women reacted angrily to the question.

Linda: "That's bollocks!"

Paula: "It is, yes, what if you can't work because you are sick? You can't provide your own.... Yes, it is bollocks, yes!" (Women Benefit Claimants Group)

Similarly,

Harold: "To start off with, a lot of people are not in a position to pay into a private pension scheme. A lot of people on social security and welfare benefits are not there because they want to be; it is because they are forced to be, not through their own fault."

Jane: "The first thing that they will do if we get this is exclude people.... They will never see a payout."

Paul: "How does a 16 to 18 year old get it – they don't. Doesn't have a job, can't get dole." (Disabled Claimants Group)

A couple of the users from the Middle Class Charity Group did express the view that in future individuals should be encouraged to purchase their own pensions and requirements such as mortgage protection privately, rather than rely on collectively financed state provisions. William especially had few misgivings about such a switch in policy, but he did imply that the expectations of those individuals who had been told in the past that the state would provide adequately for the majority of their welfare needs had to be met in any difficult period of change.

"I think that the last government was moving along those lines towards private healthcare, wasn't it, but certainly it was moving along that road with pensions, for instance. It is part and parcel of what we are talking about, I suppose. I think in some ways it would be a good thing if the responsibility was shifted from government to the individual but it is the transitional period which concerns me somewhat, as to how it might be bought about." (William, Middle Class Charity Group)

Mary agreed with this notion, that those who were able should privately purchase some provisions, but she added the important proviso that if such a change was encouraged by the state then the state itself would have to increase its regulatory function with regards to private providers. This would be necessary to avoid a repetition of past instances when private insurance policies had proved to be in effect worthless, due to insurers invoking conditional clauses that were not pointed out to purchasers when the policies were initiated.

Individually purchased provision: a welfare role for the market?

Raising the profile of the private sector as an alternative to state welfare provision has been an important aspect of government policy in recent years. Attempts to reduce the amount of public revenue spent on the various aspects of welfare provision have often been accompanied by tax incentives for those who sought to make greater use of privately provided services (tax relief on private pensions, healthcare schemes and so on). Similarly, the introduction of quasi-markets (see Le Grand and Bartlett, 1993) was partially justified as a means of introducing an element of fiscal responsibility to publicly provided welfare, while simultaneously enforcing some competition between providers in order to force down costs. In spite of the state assuming a major role in providing welfare for the past 50 years, the private sector has continued to flourish. In Britain, welfare has never been a simple question of exclusively either state or privately purchased provision; the relationship between the two is much more complicated. Users' opinions on privately purchased welfare seem to reflect this element of entanglement between public and private provision.

Healthcare

When considering healthcare, the most extensively held view (80% of users) was that any attempt to encourage a major expansion of a private healthcare system would be to the detriment of the NHS. It was widely believed that this would reduce public provision to little more than a second rate, residual service reserved for poor people. People clearly valued their right to free treatment and viewed privatisation as a threat to that right. Maxine's comments are illustrative of similar concerns voiced in four of the focus group sessions.

> "This is a European country; it is not a third world country. It isn't somewhere at the back of beyond; it has got an NHS. This country will go down the pan, there will be people dead all over the streets if everybody has to start paying and they privatise the NHS as they have done in America. If you don't get yourself private insurance you don't get treated. I mean, even in the depths of depravity you still get treated.... When it comes to something like that and healthcare is going to be privatised and you have to have private insurance to get treated, there is going to be a definite line between poor and rich."
> (Maxine, Residents Group)

The members of the Disabled Benefit Claimants Group were likewise convinced that if the moves under "the Conservatives to encourage people to take out private medical insurance" were continued, a two-tier system of healthcare would inevitably develop. The group feared that access to the best (ie private) care would then be reserved exclusively for those people who could afford the required premiums or fees. If an individual had a medical condition, then often they would be denied private insurance cover.

> "That [private medical insurance] sounds okay, but I have tried for the last two years to get into a private medical fund and because I have had ##### within the last five years no one will touch me."
> (Elaine, Disabled Claimants Group)

As Harold ironically commented, "Yes, you can only take medical insurance out when you are fully fit": bad health or a limited income would deny access to care. However, as Roger later pointed out in another discussion ("If they paid privately they would be operated on, wouldn't they? There's an irony"), once a certain level of wealth is reached and people are able to directly purchase private treatments then the ability to pay, rather than the extent or type of illness, becomes the dominant decisive factor in deciding access to care. The possibility that the group with perhaps some of the greatest healthcare needs relative to others in British society (that is, those people who were both poor and in ill health) would be doubly disadvantaged by an expansion of private healthcare, particularly if accompanied by a corresponding reduction in public provision, was a clear concern.

Several of the focus groups identified the NHS reforms under the Conservatives and the imposition of internal markets as being responsible for a reduction in the standard of care that they had received. A recurrent concern was the increased wait that many patients faced before receiving treatment on the NHS.

> "Three years after my accident I was diagnosed with kidney stones and by the time they had finished it were like a rock. They took it out and it was that big ... but the thing was I had to wait two years to have it removed. For those two years I was in pain." (Chris, Disabled Claimants Group)

> "I had a minor operation on a trapped nerve. I waited and then went to St #####. They couldn't do it within the twelve months and the reason given was the sheer volume of operations and the lack of resources to do those operations. It was actually fourteen months after I was told I should have the operation. I had to have the operation at ##### General, 20 miles away. The job was done as a package of over 200 that were transferred to ########; of course ##### had to pay for them. To me there is something drastically wrong when you get to a stage that there are not enough staff, are not enough funds or the funds have been used in the wrong places." (Joe, Residents Group)

Joe's last point was also echoed by a large number of those who took part in the survey. Rather than reducing bureaucracy, it was a commonly held belief that internal markets had added another expensive administrative dimension to public healthcare which diverted funds away from clinical services. Stephen's comments were typical.

> "I worked in hospitals many times and they are allotted a lot of money each year for buildings, but the biggest lump always goes on administration, new carpets, furniture, curtains, all this before it gets to the patients on the ward." (Stephen, Disabled Claimants Group)

When considering areas such as dentistry, opticians and prescriptions, some 38% of users held the view that the state should provide some assistance to those without adequate private purchasing power; however, these users also believed that due to budget limitations people in employment should be encouraged to contribute either fully or partially to the costs of their treatment. On two separate occasions different groups proposed a means test type system with a sliding scale of remissions of charges linked to individual income. This was thought to be fairer than the present system of flat rate charges which favoured the better off and penalised those on low pay. The Muslim/Pakistani Women's Group went further, stating that everybody (adults) should pay half the cost of their treatments as this would encourage responsible behaviour and it was unfair to expect the state to take on the full financial burden. The justification for this stance was a belief that many people on benefits were squandering their money on non-essential items.

> "People on benefits, they have got cars but when they go to the chemist they just sign, and people who are working, they have got to pay full. It is not fair so everybody should have to pay half. People are going in pubs and drinking, they spend money. That money they have to save for the dentist." (Raharna, Muslim/Pakistani Women's Group)

A further influence on this stance of everybody contributing a certain flat rate amount may have been the women's Islamic faith. When later discussing taxation levels and the financing of public welfare, the group were unanimously in favour of a *zakat* type system (where each individual, rich or poor, gives the same flat rate percentage in tax) rather than more 'progressive' methods.

A small number of users (22%) spoke against additional payments for health provisions such as dentistry, prescriptions and so on. They saw a future universal system of free treatments as the best way to ensure that cases of borderline hardship were avoided. They maintained that contributions were paid to meet public provisions and if the public purse could not stretch to the full amount then taxation should be increased accordingly.

Barry: "The point is that the cost of the service should be worked out and then taxation should be related to that. They are doing it the other way about and saying we have got so much in taxes so you can have that bit for health."

Len: "It should be the responsibility of the state exclusively. They [the state] should look after the health of the population, It shouldn't be left to private individuals or commercial institutions or anybody else. It should be

> down to the Health Service and that was the idea of the
> Health Service when it was introduced, to look after
> people for the whole of their lives, and that is how it
> should be and it should be financed out of taxation."
> (Senior Citizens Group)

The application of more stringent means tests and the reduction in the
number of criteria for exemption from additional dentistry and so on
charges has been a part of the drive to curtail public spending, but as one
respondent made clear, the switch from public to private provision may
not be entirely painless.

> "Privatisation, that is the truth, on the dental side and your glasses. I
> would be the first to admit that I don't get my eyes tested like I used
> to because I can't afford it. As it happens I don't need dental care any
> more, but like my husband and that, you just think to yourself it is
> £31 for this and £40 odd for that. Well it isn't hurting me yet so I
> will wait and while you are waiting you are in increasing pain." (Gail,
> Residents Group)

Housing

Very few people offered positive support for the private rented sector,
although two of the Muslim/Pakistani Women's Group did say that they
had past positive experiences with private landlords. The rest of the users
were quick to condemn private landlords for several reasons: rents were
often high, properties poorly maintained and two women spoke of
landlords appearing uninvited in their homes. Significantly, several people
also talked of the problem of securing a private tenancy when drawing
benefits. Even if the state is willing to finance certain individuals,
conditions stipulated by many landlords exclude large numbers from
looking to the private housing market to meet their needs.

> "It is like that with benefits. You cannot get, it is practically impossible
> to get, a private tenancy when you are on the DSS, because [they
> assume] you are scruffy, you are on a lower income, you are not going
> to have a nice house. My house is beautiful. It took me a long while
> because I had to save up but when I was looking and was on the
> waiting list and going round and whatever, it was 'no DSS no DSS!'

You are lucky if three out of one hundred will accept you. There is stigma attached to it." (Elaine, Disabled Claimants Group)

Perhaps the final word in condemning private landlords as providers of social housing should go to one respondent with personal experience.

"They are the worst kind of landlord of all, and I can say this with my hand on my heart because unfortunately I used to be one. I had two flats. The people who have got one, two, maybe three places, it may well be that the rent is their income that they have got to live on and when faced with major repairs they have not got the money, and so they can't do the repairs." (John, Benefit Claimants Group)

Social security

Previous comments in support of the state retaining the major role in the provision of social security benefits have already indicated that the overwhelming majority of users believed that the potential for privately purchased schemes to form the basis of future benefit provision was limited. The New Right's competitive market road to freedom was rejected because of its inherently exclusive tendencies for those with limited finances. Generally, it was recognised that individual private provisions had a part to play in certain limited contexts, but users held that they could never replace the proper role of the state in funding collective provision that currently is available in one form or another as a welfare right.

"Say I was fully employed and I wanted to insure myself against being unemployed, what would be the premiums, I mean, who is going to pay out £100 plus per week once I am out of work?" (Harold, Disabled Claimants Group)

When discussing privately purchased pensions, healthcare plans, meeting the costs of long-term care in old age and so on, only two users voiced a preference for a shift in responsibility from the state to the individual (one was in secure employment and the other was a retired company director), but both were also very keen to stress that the state would have to establish a strong regulatory role over private providers. Apart from this minority view, the most prevalent opinion was that, in principle, there was little wrong with purchasing private healthcare, housing, or various social welfare insurance schemes if and when you could afford them. For example, within the Muslim/Pakistani Women's Group there was a general agreement that their preferred option was to purchase their own homes as soon as they could; other users looked forward to returning to work and being able to contribute to private or occupational pension schemes. Several of the interviewees also spoke of having purchased private healthcare in the past in order to ensure quick treatment for their families, particularly children.

> "I am not ashamed to say that in the past with my loved ones I have gone private and paid in order that they get immediate attention.... I found the money, I didn't particularly have the money but I found it to get immediate attention for my children." (Harold, Disabled Claimants Group)

> "It is going to be 12 weeks before she can see the specialist with a nine month old baby. She is having to pay to go private and to see the specialist will cost between £50 and £100 and I think that is wrong when it is a baby." (Gail, Residents Group)

Users often had pragmatic reasons for sometimes choosing privately purchased options, not least the deficiencies that they identify in present public provisions, but importantly the majority of them strongly supported the continuation (and in many cases the expansion) of collectively financed state social welfare provisions. For many, their present disadvantaged situations had re-emphasised the need for the state to maintain its central role in the provision of welfare. People were not against the purchasing of private provision (if and when they had the ability to afford it) *per se*, but saw the imposition of privatisation and the market mentality on publicly provided welfare services as inappropriate.

> "I don't really go along fully with the idea of privatisation of the things that were controlled by the state, things like we have got going in the Health Service which is kind of like pseudo privatisation, where they have set up quangos and internal markets. I think that the idea of privatisation works in things like British Telecom but in other areas it is just complete nonsense. It has been used as an overriding ideology of the past government, who just wanted to privatise everything. I can see why they had to privatise some things. On some things the state did need to improve its act." (Peter, Lone Parents Group)

Family and charitable provision

The brevity of this section reflects the fact that the users had little to say on these two themes. Although much informal welfare activity takes place within family settings, the most noticeable feature throughout the empirical work was a lack of discussion on the appropriate role of the family in terms of welfare. Only on very few occasions was the role of the family in providing welfare explicitly commented on by a user. The most obvious comment came in response to a discussion question about the appropriate agencies for meeting housing needs.

> "It depends on your circumstances. Sometimes you might not be able to help because you are only on a low income and your own house might be overcrowded so then you can't give anyone accommodation. So then maybe you need to go to your council and get accommodation. It depends if you've got kiddies or what. Some might have to end up staying in hostels due to different circumstances."
> (Sabrina, Women's Benefit Claimants Group)

In this instance, the respondent's comments seem to imply that even if a family is willing to offer accommodation to another family member with housing needs, circumstances will often dictate that it is impossible to do so. Sabrina quickly moved discussion on to the duty of the local authority to meet housing needs and it was this aspect of her reply which the rest of the women present chose to develop in their discussions, rather than returning to the family theme.

In a similar vein, the role of charitable organisations in welfare provision was only mentioned on two occasions throughout the discussions. First, the Middle Class Charity Group, not surprisingly perhaps, believed that charities such as their own did have a minor role to play in attending to some of the needs which public provision left unfilled. Second, Molly, a single parent, noted,

> "It is debatable that, isn't it? I wouldn't like to see charities take over the welfare state. I think they would be even worse than the government. I think there would be people who would come in your homes and say, well, what are you doing with that and with that? I prefer to see it as it is, still in the government's hands." (Molly, Single Parents Group)

While noting the drawbacks of current state provision, this respondent clearly thinks that to be dependant on charitable provision would be even more problematic. This appears to echo criticisms of the charitable provision that existed before the state became extensively involved in providing welfare (see, for example, Fido [1977] on the Charitable Organisation Society). Further comments from other users on either family or charitable provision were scarce; on the few occasions when the subject did arise, discussions were centred on the duty of the state to recognise the value of such work, rather than users endorsing family or charitable work as the central basis for provision.

Adequacy/inadequacy of present state welfare

Although there were never any direct questions put to the focus groups which looked to specifically explore the subject of the adequacy or inadequacy of state provision, the issue was a recurrent theme raised spontaneously by most of the focus groups. The inadequacy of state-provided welfare in one or more of the three areas investigated frequently dominated group discussions and was raised by eight out of the 10 groups.

Healthcare

In the area of healthcare, the length of waiting lists has already been mentioned as a major reason why people with limited incomes had used private medicine in the past. The other major concerns of the users have also been dealt with previously. Joe's comment neatly encapsulates many shared anxieties.

> "To me there is something drastically wrong when you get to a stage that there are not enough staff, are not enough funds, or the funds have been used in the wrong places." (Joe, Residents Group)

The belief that the NHS is seriously underfunded, and that its capacity to treat patients promptly has been undermined by recent reforms which wasted money on expensive additional levels of bureaucracy, was a common perception among users. This is hardly surprising, as several were able to draw on their own personal experiences of long painful waits for treatment.

Housing

Recurrent themes when housing was being discussed were the inadequacy of much council provision and the lack of any provision, particularly for young men.

> "I find that they are not very sympathetic towards single people, young males. They tend to say to them, oh, you can go to hostels, you don't need accommodation.... The young woman is much more likely to get accommodation than the man, but they need a roof as much as we do." (Doreen, Women's Benefit Claimants Group)

> "There should be more provision made by the council and the local authorities really. When you think about the number of empty properties that are around and the number of homeless people.... I don't know all the facts but I think that perhaps they should do more to buy properties to provide accommodation." (Linda, Women's Benefit Claimants Group)

Many were sure where to attribute the blame for this rise in homelessness and the poor condition of a large amount of the public housing stock.

> "The municipality has been stopped from building houses, stopped from repairing houses. We have had a situation where houses are actually falling to pieces because there is no money available to repair them, so we have people crammed into individual properties in the centre of the city and it is partly due to the policies of the Conservative governments that advocated the private ownership of housing and the complete abrogation of public, that is municipal, housing. What I hope is going to happen is that the £6 billion that is in the bank accounts of the local authorities will be used to build houses, and doing a lot of repairs to accommodate the growing population that we have." (Len, Senior Citizens Group)

The need for immediate improvement in the quality and quantity of public sector housing was seen as an issue that required the urgent attention of both national and local government. These users were aware that the social housing initiatives that they envisaged required substantial financial outlay, but believed this to be a cost worth paying in return for a reduction in homelessness and an improvement in the living conditions of those currently resident in unfit housing.

Social security

Some of the most telling comments about the inadequacy of state provision were made by those who were either partially or fully dependent on social security benefits for their day-to-day existence. The actual benefit being drawn seemed to make little difference; again the opinions were regularly of unmet need.

> "I am a widow and I've got a widow's pension. I'm penalised in not being able to get other things and it just leaves me over the – well, I'm on the breadline, I'm scraping by. Well I don't have entertainment. It is just a basic living." (Ivy, Women's Benefit Claimants Group)

> "There is one thing, the law states at the moment that the minimum income is supposed to be £97 per week. I get benefits of £47 a week. Will somebody explain to me why there is that difference?" (David, Benefit Claimants Group)

> "I mean I live on my own with two kids and the money that the social security give me supposedly to live on is just laughable, when you think of Christmas, birthdays, if you wanted to go on holiday or owt like that. I mean I work and I never want to give up work but they make it very hard for people who give up work to actually go back, because they take an awful lot off them straight away. I mean, like now if I didn't go to work I would be £15 a week worse off and I am getting out of bed and going to work every day. So a lot of people think, £15, what's £15 to me? They don't give people the incentive to actually want to go back." (Lorraine, Residents Group)

Lorraine's comment is interesting because it illustrates a double dimension to her perception of the present social security system's inadequacy. Initially she strongly asserts that benefit levels do not allow some recipients of social security to enjoy what might be regarded in contemporary British society as a 'normal' family life; subsequently, by drawing on her personal experiences, she makes clear her belief that the benefits system offers inadequate support for those people who are in part-time or low paid work. Although this issue of what is often referred to as the 'benefits trap'[2] was not a subject that was regularly referred to across the range of focus groups, its consistent appearance in philosophical and political debates and, perhaps more importantly in the context of this chapter, the lengthy debate that ensued in the Residents Group make it worthy of further note. Lorraine and several of her female co-users argued that complex regulations often combined to deny them access to certain benefits even though they were attempting to support themselves through paid work as much as possible.

> "Can I just say that I was originally on family credit and as you know I work in the school kitchen anyway, and because my claim for family credit came up in the six weeks holiday they refused it, and they said I could not have family credit because I did not work for 52 weeks per year; I only work 36. So then they changed it and I had a fellow from the DSS in my house for an hour and he said, 'well, you can't claim income support' because then I worked 17 and a half hours per week so I was over the level for income support of 16. Then he turned round and said, 'well, you cannot have family credit because you work 17 and a half hours but for less than 52 weeks per year; you only work 36'." (Lorraine, Residents Group)

Rules about the minimum amount of payments required in order to gain access to contributory benefits (which tend to favour those in full-time employment and so disproportionately effect women[3]) had a similar negative effect.

> "In the school holidays I am not allowed to sign on. I have paid NI and income tax all year for 36 weeks and that is a quarter of my wage taken in deductions, and I am not entitled to sign on and I am not entitled to any benefits during the school's holidays. Also because I am not allowed to sign on there will be no National Insurance credit going in. So when I come to retire the credits that are going in are not going to be enough. I have to pay for a private pension as well as for the National Insurance and I cannot get enough credits to get my stuff in the holidays, my bit of money that I need to live on." (Maxine, Residents Group)

Although she was employed as a school teaching assistant, Maxine's remarks serve to illustrate that the growing numbers of individuals whose work is in one way or another part-time have inferior benefit rights to full-time workers, often despite paying a substantial percentage of their income in contributions to the state. The extent to which this may force people on a low income to purchase private forms of social security (provided they can afford the premiums) is also illustrated.

The view that present social security benefits were adequate was very much in the minority, with only 4% of users throughout the discussions voicing such an opinion. Two members of the Middle Class Charity Group did believe that social security provision was adequate to get by on, significantly neither was heavily reliant on the state for their income, and one was firmly of the opinion that many of those on benefit squandered money on pastimes such as drinking, drugs and gambling.

> "The tragedy, of course, is that today, under the social security system, the majority of people except for old age pensioners like us. The majority of people do get sufficient from the state to live, anyway I won't say they live well but they get sufficient to live. The tragedy is, of course, that lots of these people on the estates, is that they drink, they smoke, they gamble, they don't work and they probably take drugs and the money that they get is being directed into those things instead of being used to provide food and warmth and what have you, and clothes for the kids. It is a tragedy but that is the situation. What the answer is, who knows?" (William, Middle Class Charity Group)

It is apparent that William and his ally believe that the behaviour of claimants, rather than the level of benefit, is the primary cause of any hardship suffered by those who rely on social security. The most vocal supporter of the notion that the state provided adequately to meet the needs of those on social security was, however, a member of the Informal Mosque Group. As the following quotation illustrates, Ali firmly believed that the state should take a leading role in the provision of welfare.

> "Britain is privileged. Britain is a place where to be perfectly honest and truthful they have been around the world and mugged the whole world. It is not necessarily the case that people have to come here from mother countries and loot back what they have lost. Britain is a pinnacle of Western society, even though I don't agree with it, it is the pinnacle of Western society. You can come here, you can get healthcare, welfare, you can get everything and it should never change. It should never change or Britain will no longer be Britain." (Ali, Informal Mosque Group)

His strongly stated view that the British state should retain a fundamental welfare role was qualified, however, by a strong belief that individuals had a duty to both themselves and their communities to first and foremost be self-supporting. In some ways Ali shared common ground with William.

Later remarks such as "There would not be layabouts in the same way. They would not be wasting time in the same way ... people hanging round bars" (if Islamic welfare principle were to be applied) indicate a similar preoccupation with the imprudent behaviour of welfare recipients, rather than a belief that current social security benefits are insufficient. To this end he outlined a personal view of limited state support in which it was generally up to the individual to strive to make their own living, even to the point of not taking (and presumably the state not providing) unemployment benefit.

> "As long as you are going to pay my rent, help me with my rent, then it doesn't matter if you give me unemployment benefit. You help me make sure I've got a roof over my head, help me with my electricity bill and my gas, leave the rest to me. Help me with my rent and such things, but all this unemployment benefit, I've never had it anyway.... Yes, housing, and if we can't afford the rent then our rent but everything else you should be able to do yourself." (Ali, Informal Mosque Group)

As far as Ali was concerned, at times the British social security system was in certain instances overgenerous and this he believed could have potentially damaging effects on society by encouraging indolence.

The problem of stigma

The more specific problem of the stigmatisation of individuals in receipt of social security benefits was seen as being of enough significance for half of the groups to raise the subject without any prompting from the interviewer. Users in half of the focus groups strongly believed that negative assumptions on the part of DSS staff and others were part of the everyday experience of those claiming benefits. Many, as the following dialogue illustrates, complained that they were perceived to be 'scroungers' or 'layabouts' by staff who were often unsympathetic to their needs and the reasons why a person had found it necessary to claim benefit in the first place.

Rita: "I think that when you go down to the DSS it's very degrading, you are classed the same as everybody else. It is like you're...."

Maxine: "Like a scrounger."

Rita: "Yeah, like a scrounger, you are all the same. We are not.
            Some of us have worked. I mean, I am not saying that
            these who haven't worked are the scum of the earth or
            whatever, but that is the way you are classed. You are
            stood there saying thank you, and you are begging that
            women to help you fill this form in so you can get some
            money. It is so degrading and there is junkies, there are
            all sorts of people, and you've got to take your kids in
            there half the time and there is nothing for them there."
            [angry] (Residents Group)

This negative stereotyping of claimants was not limited to government
workers and agencies, but was seen as a widespread phenomenon that
had serious implications when individuals attempted to find
accommodation or seek employment.

"People on benefits are categorised as well. I mean, whether you are
on benefits because you have been made redundant or whether it's
the employers because you just can't be bothered to go out and get a
job, you are thrown into the same pot. If you go to a landlord and say,
'I'm on benefits', they turn round and say, 'I don't want anyone on
benefits, I've had so and so happen'. You are categorised. You are
penalised for what one person might have done just because you are
on benefits. They seem to think everybody is the same and they are
not." (Doreen, Women's Benefit Claimants Group)

"There is also stigma at places. I've worked at places, I got friends
jobs at places where I have worked. They have been out of work on
the dole for a couple of years, then they get a job and after a couple of
months all they [the employers] start saying is, 'it is the unemployed,
they don't want to learn.'" (Paul, Disabled Claimants Group)

Implicit within some of the above dialogue is a belief, held by a number
of the users themselves, that certain individuals have a more deserving
claim to benefits; for example, according to Maxine and Rita past workers
deserve better treatment than junkies. This distinction between deserving
and undeserving, or perhaps more accurately in the context of the
discussions generated by the focus groups, individuals that users identify
as having a more or less deserving claim to welfare, is a theme that will be
discussed in detail in Chapter Seven. The essential point here is that
while the users accept that there is a small number who may be actively

avoiding work, they resent being categorised as indolent because they are temporarily claiming benefits.

> "There is always going to be a hard core, a certain number of people who don't want a job and who are never going to get one in a million years. You are always going to have that. The rest of the people, I find most of them do want to work." (Linda, Women's Benefit Claimants Group)

Linda's remarks are particularly apposite here, as prior to a debilitating illness that forced her to rely on incapacity benefit and Income Support she worked for the Employment Service interviewing clients, and having experienced the reality of claiming "from both sides" felt well qualified to comment. It is important to note that when discussions about shirking the responsibility to work occurred, users expressed opinions that went beyond a mere willingness to work; indeed, many apparently longed for a return to employment and its potential attendant financial and personal reward. Work wasn't something they would put up with, but had become a central desire in their lives.

> "I would love to be earning now and subscribing to a private pension and organising my own future. I would love to be able to do it. I need a job, I need to be in work.... I think there is something like two and a half million of us unemployed at the moment and a tremendous amount of them do want to work, do want to get up at seven o'clock on a Monday morning and then go to work and become an active member of society." (Harold, Disabled Claimants Group)

Importantly, sentiments such as those presented above and similar comments like that of Elaine (Disabled Claimants Group), "As far as I'm concerned state benefit is not there to keep a person for the rest of their life. They are there as stop gap" appear to refute the powerful popular notion that a benefit-dependent underclass, with different norms and aspirations from the mainstream, has somehow become a threat to 'civilised' society. Users consistently expressed opinions that stressed a fundamental wish to end their own reliance on state-provided social security as soon as possible.

Financing public welfare

Previous discussions have illustrated that many see current public welfare provisions as often inadequate. Correspondingly, this may suggest that many of those interviewed would like to see an improvement in state-provided services and benefits; an outlook that has obvious financial implications. While aware of the fact that improved or increased public welfare would cost extra money, the majority of users still went on to outline a position in defence of higher income tax in order to pay for an improvement in benefits and services.

> "Yes, more, more tax depending on your income. I am not saying that the better off should be penalised because of their qualifications but yes, it should be related to what you earn." (David, Benefit Claimants Group)

> "Back to my point: the whole system needs overhauling. It is alright a government saying that there are all these scroungers tossing it off, drawing benefit and contributing nothing. What the government never says is 'will you willingly pay more income tax?' If you cut income tax who is going to pay for all these bloody services? [mmmm, yes in agreement in background] You have got to have money coming in to pay for them. I would willingly pay £5 a week I would, being a working person, if that money was going to provide extra services all round, not just social security, and I'm sure a lot of people in this country feel the same." [general agreement] (Joe, Residents Group)

> "I don't mind when I am working my taxes going up. I don't mind at all because it doesn't just benefit everybody else, it benefits myself anyway, because of the taxes that are paid." (Chris, Disabled Claimants Group)

As the following comment indicates, this approach is consistent with the opinion offered on numerous occasions by users, that if every individual is to enjoy a decent minimum measure of welfare, provisions have to be adequately financed and that ultimately only the state has the ability to guarantee universal access to such provisions as a right.

> "That at the end of the day the benefits can increase overall, not just for people like Lorraine but for all people who need social security at some time during their lives and there must be very, very few people

down here who won't need it at some time during their life. On the other hand this business of asking people to provide extra pension, extra money for themselves through private pension schemes, I think that can only really apply to people who are in full-time employment and have got the spare cash to put into it. And I think that the spare cash would be better employed either as NI contributions or in tax to the state and the state doing the providing." [general agreement] (Joe, Residents Group)

Only the Middle Class Charity Group saw an expansion of services as unlikely because of budgetary constraints. As one of their number put it when talking about the limitations on the NHS, "the state would fund everything in a perfect world; as I said earlier on the NHS would provide the lot, but unfortunately it is not." They clearly felt that present levels of taxation were adequate and that they were meeting their responsibilities to society by currently "paying tax at a very heavy rate", and being involved with charitable work. The point to stress is that more generally people were willing to endorse a return to a more 'progressive' tax regime, an obvious exception to this being the Muslim/Pakistani Women's Group and their previously noted *zakat* approach.

Conclusions

A specific purpose of this chapter has been to identify welfare service users' opinions and views on the appropriate role of various agencies in providing for the welfare needs of citizens; several conclusions can now be drawn in relation to this question. First, all the users see the social element of citizenship, social rights, as a valid and valued part of their citizenship status. They articulate a defence of their rights to publicly provided healthcare, housing and social security provisions by drawing on two distinct discourses: an individual right to welfare because of the payment of past contributions combined with the understanding that the state would provide; and a more collective approach that emphasises a universalistic right to welfare for individuals who are considered to be living in state of basic human need. Second, the majority also believe that the state should continue to have a centrally important role in providing to meet those needs in the future. This is based on a large majority view that a welfare system largely built around an ability to individually purchase provisions has inherently exclusive tendencies for those who cannot afford the necessary premiums and fees. Recent attempts to impose a market mentality on the welfare state are therefore regarded as short sighted and detrimental to the welfare rights of many vulnerable citizens. A third point to stress here is the widespread approval of a continuing welfare role for the market above and beyond that of the state. There was an acceptance of the right for people to privately purchase welfare provisions as long as the state continued to guarantee universal access to an adequate minimum of welfare rights as part of a citizenship package. This pragmatic approach towards private welfare should not be viewed as incompatible with the solid support for publicly provided welfare previously outlined. The endorsement of a strong role for the public sector does not necessarily indicate a hostility towards private agencies providing additional welfare services. The notion of social citizenship promises no more than a universally available guaranteed minimum of welfare, a minimum that is subject to constant redefinition and one which appears to be increasingly subject to reduction; the users appear to be aware of this and so are keen to reserve the right to make future use of private welfare as and when they can afford it.

It is important to reflect on certain other important issues concerning welfare provision which have been raised in this discussion. In spite of strong support for publicly provided welfare, all but three of the users share a belief that much present state-led provision is inadequate and they wish to see an improvement in this state of affairs in the near future. Similarly, they recognise that this will cost money but there is a general willingness from many to accept increased progressive taxation in order to fund this improvement. The urgent need for such improvement and the hidden costs, both financial and social, if present inadequacies are not addressed, were noted by certain users.

"It is absolutely outrageous, you can go to the courts every day and you find what young people are subjected to. They have cut out the unemployment benefit and there is no subsistence, so what do they do? It is a question of either you starve, you beg or you steal." (Len, Senior Citizens Group)

"Yes, if I could get to the specialist I would be back at work now but because there isn't one in ###### and they keep cancelling appointments, well, I could be leading a worthwhile life now, back at work and not reliant on state benefits." (Jane, Disabled Claimants Group)

Users in half of the focus groups also spoke of feeling stigmatised because they were reliant on public welfare. Interestingly, this stigma appears to be restricted almost exclusively to those individuals who are in receipt of social security; few feel guilty about living in a council house, and to try to brand someone as undeserving because they use the NHS would widely be regarded as a nonsense. The important point to make here is the powerful resentment among benefit claimants about being stereotyped as 'scroungers'. The strong desire to work, to be self-sufficient rather than to be reliant on state benefits, was clearly voiced on every occasion that the users instigated discussions about their stigmatisation.

If the state is to provide less in the future, and given current political trends this seems likely, then it appears that increasingly the fortunate will have to turn to privately purchased provision and the unfortunate to charity. Access to welfare in both cases is highly conditional, on the ability to pay in the former instance, and on the giver seeing a recipient as deserving in the latter. As neither provide welfare on the basis of right, both approaches were rejected by the users as suitable foundations on which to build any new welfare settlement.

The concluding comment by Ali draws heavily on his Islamic beliefs but it also has a resonance with the dominant view on welfare provision outlined by the users. With several noted exceptions, those who took part in the research aspire to a welfare state which is built on collectively financed, universal rights–based provision. For many of those interviewed, their own past personal experiences had emphasised the need for the state to continue to take the lead role in providing adequately financed welfare in the future.

> "The state should take the lead in everything. That is what the state is there for. The state is the living embodiment of what we are. If we are a just nation then the state is supposed to be just as well and administer justly all of these provisions. The provisions for mankind are vast, they are enormous, there is no such thing as there isn't enough, there is more than enough. It is just that people have and they don't share and this is basically the problem." (Ali, Informal Mosque Group)

Notes

[1] This term is used as a shorthand for the term welfare service users and in these three chapters that draw on the empirical study it refers specifically to those respondents who took part in the fieldwork that informs this book. For a fuller consideration of the sample and methods involved, please consult the Appendix.

[2] That is, that in some cases people may choose to remain on social security because a return to work, and the consequent loss of benefits, leaves them financially either worse off or in a very similar position.

[3] *ONS Social Trends* 28 (1998, Table 4.11) reports that in 1997, 5,367,000 women worked part-time as opposed to 1,328,000 men.

FIVE

Conditionality

Introduction

The relationship between rights and responsibilities is an issue of central importance to any notion of citizenship. It has already been made clear that this relationship is a dynamic one that is open to challenge and renegotiation over time. Indeed it has been argued in Chapter Three that in Britain the welfare component of citizenship is increasingly under the influence of a new political orthodoxy which is keen to stress that individuals have to accept certain responsibilities or duties in return for the right to specified benefits and services. The central focus of this chapter is, therefore, a study of some users' views on what Deacon (1994) has called a 'principle of conditionality', that is, that eligibility to certain basic, publicly provided, welfare entitlements should be dependant on an individual first agreeing to meet particular compulsory duties or patterns of behaviour. Initially the extent to which the users endorse this principle in the three areas of welfare under consideration is discussed. A brief exploration of three related areas then follows. First, the issue of financial conditionality and access to social security benefits is considered. Second, users' opinions on the desirability of an unconditional benefit in the form of a universally available citizen's income are explored. Third, the users' reflections on the plausibility of applying a principle of conditionality to fiscal and occupational welfare is briefly discussed. Finally some concluding comments are offered.

Welfare rights and the 'principle of conditionality'

Recent changes in legislation (eg the Jobseeker's Act, 1995 and the Housing Act, 1996) and many policy statements of the present New Labour government indicate that the issue of conditionality is very much part of contemporary political welfare debates. Although understandably there were on occasions a number of differing views on a particular issue within each group, in more general terms the extent to which users as a whole approved, or disapproved, of the imposition of a more conditional link between rights and responsibilities varies according to the specific area of welfare under consideration.

Healthcare

When discussing health provision one respondent, who was a former health service worker, pointed out that the issue of NHS doctors taking into account an individual's habits or lifestyle when making a decision about treatment was nothing new:

> "... there has always been discrimination in the Health Service since it began. There has always been judgements made. Is this one worth the time and the effort? ... [but] it is becoming more public now." (Jane, Senior Citizens Group)

However, an overwhelming majority of users stated clearly that they believed that an individual should not lose their right to treatment because they choose to engage in a form of behaviour that may have a negative effect on personal health. Healthcare was the area of public welfare provision in which many users argued most strongly for unconditional rights; the issue of personal responsibility, although not ignored, was clearly seen as being of secondary importance to a universal right to healthcare as required.

> "Well yes, we all either drink, smoke or are doing things which are bad for our health. We all know that and we do them. I mean, I smoke and I have been told umpteen times how bad it is for me. I drink, but I don't drink in excess. I don't take drugs but that is my own decision. I could do if I so wanted to but I have no desire to because I feel that it is irresponsible to. Now, people can say, 'well, it's irresponsible smoking, because at the end of the day you are shortening your life', and what have you, but we all take risks and you analyse those risks yourself, and I sincerely hope that I do not get a cancer related disease through smoking. My grandfather was 96 when he died and he smoked all of his life, so I am hoping that the few genes left in me will keep me going like. But everybody takes risks, a lot of people eat the wrong kind of things for various reasons and then they put on a lot of weight, or they don't eat enough, they don't have a proper diet. So we all take these risks but at the end of the day if we become poorly because of that, initially, I would expect treatment. If

the doctor turned round to me and said that 'you know what has caused this, it is smoking cigarettes. Now we can do an operation and we will probably extend your life X amount but to accelerate that extension, change your lifestyle: give up smoking.' Then we come to individual choices as to what we do. And I think that most responsible people would accept that and would do it." (Joe, Residents Group)

Users recognised that many of the activities that they chose to engage in may have negative effects on their well-being but saw any attempt by the government to specify a list of criteria (drug abuse, smoking, obesity and so on) on which to base denial of care as arbitrary; one respondent noted mockingly, "They wouldn't be treating a right lot of people then would they"?:

"I feel there are just too many different criteria on which to apply a value judgement: it would be impractical to apply it. You can't just take an isolated thing whether it be smoking, weight or age or nice person/bad person. There is just no limit to it, so the universal thing is the only real way out of it." (Darren, Benefit Claimants Group)

"You could say that people who do dangerous sports or whatever are endangering their health, so there is nowhere to draw the line really. I don't really think that you can say that you have got an unhealthy lifestyle. It is so subjective, so subjective." (Linda, Women Benefit Claimants Group)

The clear feeling was that the state was in no position to set down rules that would penalise individuals with certain habits by denying them care, particularly when it was actively engaged in raising large amounts of revenue from the alcohol and tobacco industries (see discussion below). Given that the British government accepts and sometimes even promotes certain types of behaviour with known or potential health risks as reasonable, the clear majority of users believed it to be equally reasonable to expect the state to provide healthcare to individuals who took risks such as smoking, drinking, playing dangerous sports and so on on the same terms as other citizens who chose not to do any of those things. As Joe's comment above illustrates "... initially I would expect treatment", the users are willing to recognise that they ultimately have a responsibility to themselves to try and change their lifestyle if a doctor advises it is necessary for their treatment or recovery. Resentment arises when doctors or other health service professionals base their decisions to provide care on personal moral judgements rather than clinical considerations.

> "I think first and foremost it should be a clinical judgement. Any kind of treatment should be a clinical judgement, but I think that we are seeing some doctors with bias creeping into their judgements and I think that should be resisted. I certainly am opposed to refusing to treat someone because they happen to be a smoker. Smokers should fall into the same category as alcoholics and drug abusers." (Barry, Benefit Claimants Group)

Although the users clearly valued both their right to publicly provided healthcare and the right to choose their own lifestyle, several groups resented the simplistic assumption (implicit in calls to deny public healthcare to people who behave in certain ways) that behaviour is always exclusively the outcome of an individual making some kind of socially isolated rational choice. For example, three women in the Pakistani/ Muslim Women's Group stated that everybody should have the same right of to access to care whatever their habit or vice, because they believed fallibility to be an inherent part of the human condition and that most people were liable at some time to do things that are not in their best interest. In particular, one drew attention to peer pressure and/or a disadvantaged social location as reasons why people may start to take drugs or drink excessively. Echoing her sentiments, another woman said that individuals often turn to drink or drugs or abuse themselves in other ways in an attempt to forget personal problems. It became clear from such comments that these three women would not be party to attempts to deny access to healthcare to people with health problems brought about by certain habits. They argued that such individual behaviour was often grounded in a particular social, cultural or environmental context; educating people about the potential harm that certain habits may cause was seen as a better way for the state to proceed, rather than punishing irresponsible individuals by denial of care. As the following quotations illustrate, a recurrent theme within the interviews was that to condemn the behaviour of certain individuals and to deprive them of the right to care without consideration of the wider circumstances in which people live would be shortsighted and unjust.

> "It would be very simplistic to say that it is a person's fault for being unhealthy. But say you have a scenario of somebody who smokes who lives in a tower block of flats, the resources are low in that family

etc, their parents smoke. Okay, everybody knows that in theory people say that you shouldn't smoke for the health of your children, but if you are looking at why somebody in that situation may be smoking, it may be helping to control stress and therefore it may be preventing those children from being abused or mistreated or whatever. Therefore if you are looking and saying just because these parents are smoking then they should not have the same equal access to healthcare it is oversimplifying the issue and it is making some moral judgements without actually considering some of the wider implications of what is actually going on in that environment. Really, if somebody is drinking then we should be saying, what are the wider social and welfare issues involved in this situation? It is not just about health, it is about the holistic approach to it, what are the environmental issues, what are the social issues, and therefore we have got to start to understand those and perhaps do something to see why people are drinking or smoking or whatever, rather than just victim blaming. To deny somebody who smokes healthcare without looking at the wider implications is really to victim blame." (Mary, Middle Class Charity Group)

Another respondent was more explicit and believed that the issue of class was central to a better understanding of the causes of ill health.

"When it is about individual provision we cannot ignore the Black[1] argument about the class gradient thesis, where if you are born into a poor family you are more often than not, in British culture, retaining the characteristics of poverty, or deprivation throughout the whole of your life, judging by the mortality statistics. So what really needs doing is a raising of the class system and hopefully that will produce a better situation. The class gradient factor is essential and it seems valid, as Townsend has pointed out." (Don, Senior Citizens Group)

This discussion of conditionality as it relates to healthcare would not be complete without reference to the small minority of users who believed that access to public healthcare should be conditional on a 'healthy' lifestyle. In contrast to the other members of their group whose views have already been outlined, three of the Pakistani/Muslim Women's Group felt that if individuals were drinking excessively or taking drugs then the provider of healthcare was right to deny them care. The view was expressed that if a person was not going to show a level of responsibility for themselves then it was reasonable for the provider of healthcare to deny access to treatment. Three users from other groups also expressed similar views, but in addition they were keen to stress that rights should be removed only in particular situations. Two were of the opinion that if a person's lifestyle was causing obvious harm to their health, then it was reasonable for the provider of care to operate a system of reduced rights, where prior access is given to those who conform to medical advice to alter their behaviour.

> "I think that people like Joe has just mentioned, with heart disease and things like that, who are smoking and things, if they are not prepared to give up smoking. I am not saying don't give them the treatment but what I am saying is put them on the list, and they have to wait on that list until they come up to the top, and if in between times that somebody comes in who doesn't smoke they can have the operation, then fair enough. I mean, I do think that everybody is entitled to care whether they smoke or not, but the ones that are prepared to stop smoking, then yes, they could have the operation done a lot quicker than the ones who are not prepared to stop smoking." (Gail, Residents Group)

Similarly, Rita was adamant that drug users should only be given one chance of treatment and if they went back to drugs afterwards they should be left to fend for themselves. The harshness of Rita's attitude in this case was directly connected to her past experience of 'losing' her long-term partner to heroin. She was particularly scathing of the practice of prescribing methadone to addicts, which she believed to be little more than a publicly financed system of drug abuse which failed to help either the drug abuser or their families.

> "But they dish methadone out 'there you go, – there is your methadone, ta ta' [mocking].... Yes, they are taking water samples in off their mates. There is an illegal trade in that, methadone and all the sleeping tablets that they can get. What they will do is they will go and get their heroin and then they will think, 'well, I have got five milligrams of methadone, I'll sell you it if you want', and the person who has the methadone is saying, 'well, I am not a smack head any more', but by rights he still is.... I think that such as drug abusers, they should be given one chance and one chance only, because they do and I know, I really do, that they take the mick they do, they really do." (Rita, Residents Group)

The users above clearly believe that it is fair to allow an element of moral judgement about the behaviour of certain individuals to become part of the process when deciding who should get treatment. The other respondent who shared this opinion was much more explicit in expressing his views.

> "We are looking at national healthcare here basically, aren't we, and I think that we are agreed that everyone, irrespective of their lifestyle, within reason, should receive healthcare on an equal basis. To follow on from that, what you have just said about a doctor choosing who he treats, then I would agree that a doctor should have a right if he has to choose between two people – one who has lived a fairly clean life and somebody who has drunk and smoked and taken drugs and all the rest of it – for the same operation, then I feel that the doctor is justified in choosing the one who has lived a clean life. On the basis of someone who has lived a fairly clean life you can probably rightly say that that person has made a greater contribution to society and probably to the income of the National Health Service than some one who drinks and smokes and takes drugs, because they probably don't work anyway, a lot of them." (William, Middle Class Charity Group)

It is apparent that the six users in favour of conditionality all share a common belief that those individuals with 'irresponsible' lifestyles do not deserve the same rights to healthcare as citizens whom they deem to be more responsible; where they differ is in identifying the circumstances in which sanctions should be imposed. This theme of individuals being seen by their fellow citizens as deserving or undeserving of rights to welfare and the implications that this has for the notion of citizenship will be discussed more fully in Chapter Six.

While acknowledging the small number of users with opinions to the contrary, it appears that the unconditional right to healthcare is seen by a large number of users as a foundational principle on which the notion of citizenship should be built. It is clear that the majority of users are opposed to the idea of the right to healthcare becoming more conditional in the future. The imposition of such policies is seen as unrealistic in principal and serving neither individual nor wider social needs in practice. Although they draw on a personal Islamic perspective, Salim and Ahmed reiterate the prevalent view held by the users, specifically that it is reasonable to encourage citizens to adopt a responsible attitude to their own health, but individuals who fall short of the ideal should continue to enjoy the same rights.

Salim: "There is a principle in Islam that goes like this: if you do bad by someone, or if you do revile someone, then you sink them further into the mire. So you have to advise an individual and you have to provide what they call in Islam *naseha*. That means that you have to provide them with good conduct, sincere advice and you have to put them in a situation where they can improve. So in Islamic society you help the person to improve and you do not revile them or undermine them and again that is a principle that should be followed."

Ahmed: "You have to look at everyone as an individual and everyone has deficiencies of some sort, humans have faults, but you can't remove from them the basic things that are required to live because of this. Society won't function if we are to target everyone's deficiencies and then revile them because of their deficiencies. Wherever that individual may be, whatever land he is in, he has been created with the disposition to make mistakes; we all make mistakes. Whatever the norms of the society in which the individual is living, they will accept that person. So individuals in this state are free to drink and whatever and there is no restriction on them. A Muslim obviously can't drink or eat excessively, so therefore there are restrictions upon us, but in terms of the question, do we withdraw the services from a Muslim who is an excessive smoker? etc etc, hopefully in a Muslim community you won't find these excesses. If you do find a Muslim who does these things, then there is no difference between him and a non Muslim from compassion to the individual, then you should provide healthcare." (Informal Mosque Group)

Housing

The discussions concerning conditionality and housing were designed to assess the extent to which the users felt that it was reasonable for a housing agency to tie the right to a home to both the individual behaviour of tenants and their willingness to accept further welfare responsibilities for the communities that they inhabit. In order to assess this debates were focused on three specific areas: anti-social behaviour, Probationary Tenancy Periods (PTPs) and Mutual Aid Clauses (MACs). In contrast to their views on health provision, in the cases of both anti-social behaviour and PTPs the most prevalent view shared by the majority of users was that the right to a house should be contingent on tenants behaving themselves. When debating the idea of MACs, this position was reversed, but it is important to note that a substantial minority (a little more than a quarter) of the users were in favour of their inclusion into tenancy agreements.

Anti-social behaviour was strongly condemned by all interviewees. Across all the groups there was strong unanimous agreement that individuals should be expected to "behave reasonably and considerately towards other people". This was widely seen as a matter of "common sense, or common courtesy". Irresponsible behaviour that infringed a neighbour's "basic right to peace and quiet" was clearly frowned upon.

> "It is important, I think, that everybody is entitled to their own space and everybody is entitled to their own privacy and it shouldn't be a case of, well, somebody making a noise, playing loud music, playing with motors, or people shouting and screaming in the garden. They should consider what other people think." [general agreement] (Joe, Residents Group)

> "Neighbours have rights upon each other and you can't infringe upon those rights. Those rights have been clearly defined, as Salim will probably state better than I can. These rights have been clearly defined by the lifestyle of the prophet and what he has told us. This is a big thing in Islam, your neighbour's rights." (Ali, Informal Mosque Group)

When asked what they thought of probationary tenancy periods (PTPs) and whether or not it was reasonable for an agency to ultimately evict someone who persisted in anti-social behaviour, again there was strong support from a clear majority of users. Most saw PTPs as a logical extension to the views on responsible behaviour that they had previously given. Strong feelings were again expressed that people had a right to reside in their home undisturbed, and that one of the consequences for people who were always "causing bother" should be eviction. Users in several of the groups outlined past experiences of bad neighbours that served to reaffirm the view that those with a persistent disregard for their neighbours should be evicted. A respondent recounted how in the past she had been forced to move to get away from nuisance because the council's measures to control the anti-social behaviour of her neighbours had proved to be ineffective.

> "Where I lived, I lived in a block of flats and I had a drug dealer working on one side and druggies used to come to my house, thinking it was me. The other side was a drummer who thought nothing of playing his drums until three or four in the morning. Downstairs I had a psychopathic alcoholic who used to run out at three in the morning with a bread knife in her hands, shouting 'come and get me'. So I went down to the council who sent letters to them all and it would be OK, but then it would start up again and they had six or seven letters written but it did no good, so in the end I packed my bags and said, 'right, I am going'. I went to a house that is totally unsuitable for my medical needs. I was already on the waiting list to be moved but I couldn't hack it any more so I just went." (Elaine, Disabled Claimants Group)

Support for a more conditional housing regime was, however, often dependent on a number of important qualifications. The manner in which the policy was implemented was a major concern; similarly it was widely believed that a warning should first be issued to enable tenants to alter their behaviour and so avoid eviction.

> "If they have been notified of the rule and they are a nuisance, yes, I think that the council or housing association has got a right to evict them because they can become a damn nuisance. It depends what they call anti-social. I don't mean for petty things but for anti-social behaviour, people who are always causing bother, always burgularing [sic] people's houses, you know. I think they should get a warning first, not just throw them out. There should be a procedure like." (Molly, Lone Parents Group)

> Doreen: "It would have to be a process though, as well, wouldn't it? It would have to have like a verbal warning then a written warning."

> Linda: "Yes, a contract so that you have got something to measure behaviour against." [general agreement] (Women's Benefit Claimants Group)

A small number of users (including the entire Residents Group) showed little enthusiasm for PTPs, with concerns about the interpretation and practical application of the rules causing most disquiet. These users believed that PTPs would be difficult to enforce and that once the probationary period was completed, irresponsible tenants would be inclined to do "whatever they want to do". The problem of malicious complaint was also discussed, with a woman relating how she had become ill after receiving a warning letter from the council following a complaint from a next door neighbour. This tenant was obviously scared that she could have lost her right to a council house in spite of having a good past record. One respondent was adamant that housing was "an absolute right" and that attempts to enforce a stricter regime on tenants were misplaced.

> "I think that housing is an absolute right and no local authority should have the right to push people about, and if there is any behaviour which is criminal, and it is really criminal behaviour I am referring to, the decision should be a court decision and not made by a local authority or a local official. But housing is an absolute right and people should be housed. We shouldn't have people on the street and this is a problem. We have already got plenty of people who are homeless." (Len, Senior Citizens Group)

Interestingly, although Len appears to condemn PTPs and believes that they could cause an increase in homelessness, ultimately he approves of a court exercising its power to order the eviction of tenants if necessary. This tacit acknowledgement of the principle that, in the final analysis, an individual's right to housing should be dependent on them accepting responsibility for their own (and in some cases their children's) behaviour appears to be a common perception with those who objected to PTPs. Within the Residents Group, in spite of their previously stated reservations, no one objected when Gail clearly implied that past behaviour should be taken into account before rehousing tenants.

> "I do think that it is important that you get on with your neighbours and that they get on with you, but I also think that when they are housing that particular person, I also think that it should be looked

into their background to see how they have been previously to where they have lived. For the simple reason, say for instance that you have got an elderly couple either side, and there is a middle house empty and you put a group of people in there who are young parents with six screaming kids who just don't care, obviously there is no consideration for the neighbours on either side." (Gail, Residents Group)

It would appear that the majority of users (possibly even those who voiced objections to PTPs) believe that the right to a tenancy should be dependent on individuals recognising that they have a responsibility to behave in a manner deemed reasonable by the housing agency and the immediate community; for many the simple equation of irresponsible behaviour equals diminished rights seemed appropriate.

Mutual Aid Clauses, whereby people who wish to live on a particular estate are under obligation to give up some time to help meet the welfare needs of other local residents, proved to be a highly contentious subject. Under such schemes the link between the right to a house and communal responsibilities becomes unambiguous; anybody who refuses to sign the 'Mutual Aid Clause' is refused housing. Initially, it is important to stress that all the users in the various groups were in favour of enhancing "community spirit" where "neighbour helps neighbour"; the major differences of opinion centred on the issue of whether or not it was reasonable and/or necessary to formalise local community relationships in a way that directly impacted "upon the basic right to live somewhere". A majority of the users (67%) had serious apprehensions about imposing this level of responsibility on tenants; for many it was "enforced paternalism" and a step too far. Typical comments were,

"You should have responsibilities attached to a right to housing, like just not being bad to neighbours, not being a nuisance, that sort of thing. Those things are expected of you but if you go further I think, to go further is a form of paternalism. It is social engineering. You are trying to make people into a certain type of person which perhaps they wouldn't be if they were left to themselves. There are other ways of building community." (Frank, Benefit Claimants Group)

Similarly,

"I actually think that it is a good idea. I would like to live on an estate where I knew everybody on that estate would be willing to help me, but I think that it is absolutely ridiculous that you would be refused a house on the grounds that you would be unwilling to do certain things. Most people would be willing to look out for their elderly neighbours, and watch over children when their parents might not be about, but to put it into a agreement, it is like a dictatorship. If every housing association did that in this country then where would everybody be, you know. It is ludicrous, it is silly and I'm afraid I would not sign on principle although I would want to help people. I mean, many a time in meetings I have said that we should go round and do gardens for people. It is only what you would expect yourself. As for throwing it down your throat, that you have to do it I do not agree with that. I certainly don't think it should be linked with whether you are eligible for accommodation." (Millie, Residents Group)

"I do think it does create community responsibility when neighbour helps neighbour, people get to know each other and you don't feel isolated, but not to be compulsory. That's stupid." (Molly, Lone Parents Group)

Several other strong objections were also raised. It was pointed out by the Pakistani/Muslim Women's Group that many people may already have family care responsibilities, and that these could clash with the requirements laid down in a MAC. When the question was posed as to who would be likely to shoulder the extra burdens (of childcare, care of elders and neighbours) as proposed in the scheme, it was generally agreed that the women in the community, rather than the men, would be the ones most likely to actually have to do the work. Mutual Aid Clauses were seen as having a gender bias and were not well received. Further strong objections by users included the opinions that the compulsion element in such schemes amounted to little more than 'blackmail' and a way for agencies such as the state or local authority to save money on care services. Some users also resented the possibility of "interference by busybodies" and expressed a desire to be left alone. In addition, a common view was that mutual help and support were already a part of their everyday lives and attempts to enforce 'community' through formal contracts were both unnecessary and unworkable. Problems of implementation and non-compliance were also raised.

"The theory is to get a more closely knit community, but how can you enforce it? By throwing them out of their homes – that seems a

big stick to wave for the sake of getting the community involved."
(Joe, Residents Group)

Interestingly, the possibility of discrimination against people deemed 'abnormal' or unwanted by a local housing community was as much a part of the dialogue of the substantial minority of users (30%) who were in favour MACs as of those who were its critics. The problem of difference and having to fit in was raised in several contexts (Asians, gay and disabled people), but in contrast to the users who opposed the clauses on the grounds that they could infringe an individual's right to housing, supporters identified a distinct lack of community spirit in contemporary society and emphasised the positive role that carefully administered MACs could have in restoring mutual responsibility.

> "I think that it is an indictment of society that you need to have things like this. Unfortunately we do need to have these things, and we need to start encouraging people to care again and to look around them and not wrap themselves up in their own problems. I am a practising Christian and this is an area where perhaps the Church has fallen down for the whole of this century, but it is starting to look and turn it round again which is absolutely brilliant. It is about time that people did start caring for the people around them in the area they are living, and generally be more thoughtful. If the only way forward is to have that kind of compulsory attachment to where you live, then I'm all for it, yes. I would want to see it extended." (Barry, Benefit Claimants Group)

It is obvious that Barry believes that 'community' is sadly lacking in many parts of British society and that making housing rights conditional to the extent envisaged in MACs is a price worth paying in an attempt to foster closer relationships between neighbours. A commitment to the Christian faith influences his view, and similarly religious belief was clearly an influential factor in the Informal Mosque Group's support for MACs.

> "Get it [the MAC] signed. That's Islam. Everybody should be doing that." (Ali, Informal Mosque Group)

> "This is a form of engineering to create community but community isn't just created like that. If the basis of the community is that they will give you a house, that is not enough of a basis. Community is something that the individual embraces because they have a desire to

help people, altruism, and to enable us to be caring and compassionate. That would be created as far as I'm concerned through religion and generally by cultivating a sharing society, so in a way this is a form of engineering. If it succeeds it would be good to see, but it is just half the way." (Salim, Informal Mosque Group)

Mutual Aid Clauses were also positively received by those who had felt isolated in the past. Ahmed spoke of his isolation when housed on a predominately white estate where he was subject to racism and had a series of regular burglaries of his home. Several of the Disabled Benefit Claimants Group also saw the potential that MACs could have for integrating marginalised individuals into local communal networks and so help to reduce their isolation.

"You are thankful for owt, we have all been there at three o'clock in the morning where we have been shut in behind four walls, in agony, depressed or whatever, and all of us have been on us own. This is maybe where we have got the other side of where we wanted company at three o'clock in the morning. You would have loved a neighbour to come round and knock and say, 'are you all right Harold, are you all right, Paul, can I make you a cup of tea.' I know I would at three in the morning, when I have been crawling around on my hands and knees in agony, so maybe again you are talking to the wrong people." (Paul, Disabled Claimants Group)

What is obvious from consideration of the users' opinions about MACs is that there is a basic difference of opinion over the relative importance of rights and responsibilities. The majority are reluctant to see a basic right attached to additional communal conditions, believing that moves to enforce mutual aid responsibilities could have a detrimental effect on the rights of some individuals to a house: rights take precedence over responsibilities. The minority remain similarly convinced that rights should be conditional on individuals first recognising responsibilities to their local community.

Social security

Attaching additional conditions to the right to unemployment benefit has been an element of political debate and policy initiatives in recent years (see Chapter Three). It was primarily around this area of social security that the discussions on benefits and conditionality were focused.

Another concern of the research was to investigate the extent to which the users would endorse a future social security system centred around an unconditional basic citizen's income. Initially the focus falls on two developments in unemployment benefit policy that make the right to benefit increasingly conditional on recipients agreeing to new responsibilities: the implementation of the new conditions of the Jobseeker's Act (1995) and the more recent 'workfare' elements of Labour's Welfare to Work policies. This approach of making the right to unemployment benefit more conditional resulted in a significant two way split in the users' views, with a narrow majority in favour of conditional benefit (either in every case or in certain specified situations) being marginally the more popular opinion. There was always, as the following discussions illustrate, a very substantial minority (of around a third to a little less than a half of those interviewed, depending on the point under discussion), who were strongly opposed to the majority view.

The right to unemployment benefit has of course long been conditional, with 'signing on at the dole' a long-term standard requirement. The question of whether or not it was reasonable for the state to require additional responsibilities from the unemployed split the interviewees, with strong opinions on both sides. A majority of the users (53%) believed the imposition of the jobseeker's agreement with its actively seeking work clause was reasonable and justified. The following comments were typical.

"They don't have to get a job, they have to be seeking a job. They have to be active in seeking a job and I think that is the least that you can do, to go out looking for a job." (Paul, Disabled Claimants Group)

"I think that it is up to everybody who is out of work to do everything they possibly can to find work. If they are not prepared to do that they do not deserve any benefit. That's my view." (William, Middle Class Charity Group)

"Do they want to work? If they are desperate enough to get a job they should get off their bum and make the effort. I mean, you are signing on so that you are available for work, so yes, it should be." (Amy, Women's Benefit Claimants Group)

"Yes, they all agree with it because there are so many, right, that are not looking for work. I mean, there are so many that are better off on benefit. At least then they can see that you are looking for a job and if you are not looking for a job and you have signed the agreement then that puts extra pressure on you to go out looking for a job." (Mohammed, Asian JSA Claimants Group)

"There is nothing wrong with having to do something to get your money. You have to stand up at some time in your life and if it means you have to have a kick up the behind from the state, then so be it. There are so many people sitting around doing nothing. It is a fact that they have got this complacency." (Jarvid, Informal Mosque Group)

The notion that the unemployed have a responsibility to be doing everything in their power to get a job is apparent in the above comments, as is the strongly expressed view that some people need compulsion to look for work. In fact, a small number (7%) argued that conditions and sanctions should only be applied to those individuals who were deemed lazy. They understood that the general premise underpinning the jobseeker's agreement was that all unemployed people needed cajoling into looking for work because some individuals were happy to get by on benefits. These users were keen to make it clearly understood that while they resented being looked upon in this way, they believed it was reasonable to withdraw benefits from other 'undeserving' claimants who were actively engaged in trying to avoid work.

Opposition to the Jobseeker's Act (1995) and its regulation of claimants' behaviour was also strongly expressed by a significant number (43%) of users, and many were scathing of an approach that attached more stringent conditions to benefit. Typically, a respondent believed such measures to be "absolutely bloody ludicrous". Another, referring back to a previous experience of drawing benefit, maintained that,

"They have semi-criminalised being unemployed now. Going back 20 years, being unemployed you signed on every week and they used to have the vacancies in the labour exchange and they would match you with vacancies. You never needed to see how many vacancies they had got. If they had got any they would send you after them. If not, then well, that was it. That was the system that they had; they had boxes of cards with jobs in. Now all the paraphernalia of the jobseeker's allowance, the restart interviews – this is just to manipulate the figures. We have got back to the undeserving poor again." (Frank, Benefit Claimants Group)

Another user (incidentally in full-time employment) drew general support from the other members of his group when airing his views.

> "The state should get themselves organised and sort out more jobs for a start. If there were more jobs, then there would be no need for a jobseeker's allowance. It is absolutely appalling that people are thrown out of work through no fault of their own, and they are treated like the lowest of the low. Absolutely diabolical. Then the whole attitude is wrong right from the top of the government to the bottom." (Joe, Residents Group)

It was extensively felt by the users who objected to the Jobseeker's Act that the jobseeker's agreement was largely unnecessary as most unemployed people who were capable of work were already seeking work, and that the state would be better occupied in trying to promote an environment in which there were sufficient numbers of suitable jobs available.

> "What the state seems to be doing is, rather than encouraging people to take jobs that are available, that people want, and doing something about the work market to create jobs for people that they actually want, they punish you if you don't take the crap jobs that they are offering. It is carrot and stick, isn't it? I think it is much better to encourage people through having a work environment that people want to go to." (Peter, Lone Parents Group)

> "Good jobs do not remain unfilled. We do not need all these incentives or punishing people." (Frank, Benefit Claimants Group)

The issues of poor pay and conditions were never far away when users critical of conditional unemployment benefit were expressing their opinions. The stricter regime was commonly seen as being in line with DSS attempts to force people off benefit and often into unsuitable and low paid jobs, or a cynical attempt to "just exclude more and more people from unemployment benefit".

> "They are also putting things like restrictions on your wages. When I put down, I think it was around £170, that would have been enough because I would have come out with about £130. Well, they say that is not really on, is it, and then you have to argue. and I say, well that is what I need to live, my rent is £44 per week and gas, electric, everything

else – I need that to live. They are kind of pressuring you to lower your limits each time." (Tom, Benefit Claimants Group)

A young graduate looking for her first job stated,

"They are living in a dream world at the benefits office.... They are not bothered as long as you are not on their books.... I mean, I am asked what are my qualifications, and then they say, have you looked downstairs. But I can't drive a forklift truck and that is the sort of thing going." (Kate, Benefit Claimants Group)

Consideration of the question of whether or not it was right for the state to demand that claimants alter their appearance or behaviour in order to make themselves more employable also split the users into two camps. Those users (29%) who were opposed to the client adviser having this power thought that such measures were at best misguided and unnecessary, and at worst potentially ethnically and individually discriminatory.

"What gives one person the right to say to someone else your appearance is not acceptable, your hair is too long, you can't have your toenails painted. It is taking away that person's individuality, isn't it?" (Shelly, Women Benefit Claimants Group)

"They are affecting your civil liberties, aren't they, if they are coming round saying, 'have you got your hair cut?' or whatever." (Harold, Disabled Claimants Group)

It was pointed out that the possibility of a decently paid job was seen as an adequate enough incentive for most people.

"If there were good wages about, then people would smarten themselves up and go keenly looking for a job, but if there is nothing about, well then." (Tom, Benefit Claimants Group)

The majority in favour of appearance/behaviour conditions (54%) believed that it was unreasonable for people to present themselves to a prospective employer in anything other than smart attire.

"Yes, you go to an interview clean and tidy because it is good manners." (Raharna, Pakistani/Muslim Women's Group)

Similarly, others saw it as reasonable that the DSS should be able to tell you to smarten up if necessary, as it was first, in the individual's best interest (because the number of unemployed people meant that employers could and would demand certain dress standards of potential employees); and second, that adopting appropriate dress for interviews had in effect been previously agreed to by the client as a reasonable condition of benefit when they signed the jobseeker's agreement.

> "I think in one sense it is good. If you are getting jobseeker's benefit and you have got shabby clothes on, there is no chance that anybody is going to employ you. I can see where they are coming from, if you signed it saying you are looking for employment and you are not going to get a job because of the way that you are dressed. I can see where they are coming from. I think it is right. I think they have got a point." (Susan, Lone Parents Group)

With both major political parties now committed to an element of 'workfare' within their unemployment policies, the users' views on the state requiring that certain groups of unemployed people attend compulsory work or training schemes make interesting reading. A definite split in opinion which closely mirrored previous disagreement concerning the introduction of the JSA was obvious; again overall, the most common opinion (by a majority of 51% to 45%) was that it was reasonable to link unemployed people's right to benefit to these additional work or training conditions. Those users in favour of the imposition of compulsory work/ training for unemployment benefit claimants highlighted two main justifications for their stance. First, they believed that such conditions were reasonable because they felt that compulsory schemes would provide the new skills and training to help unemployed individuals re-enter the labour market on a more permanent basis.

> "This is what I have thought for a long time, in every city, every town across the country there should be a big complex. I mean, old skills, there is no skilled workers now. They are all cowboys, aren't they, who have done a bit here, done a bit there. Years ago, they left school and they done an apprenticeship, five years, right, joiners, electricians, plumbers, the lot. I think when children leave school now, if they haven't got a job it should be made compulsory that they go to one of these big complexes and do a skill of some kind, an apprenticeship. If they haven't got the academic thing they could do something practical like an electrician, or joining, like I said, and I think it should be

compulsory that they should go there for two years and yeah, get a wage." (Molly, Lone Parents Group)

"Yes, they agree with that. I mean, if you are not studying then you should be looking for work…. If they have [just] been signing on, well I mean, there is going to be so few jobs in ten years time, there is going to be less and less, isn't there? It is just going downhill. I mean they will have no experience, so if they take this system up, at least they are getting some kind of experience." (Mohammed, Asian JSA Claimants Group)

Clearly, these two users could see the value of training in a shrinking job market and both believed (in common with other users who held workfare type schemes to be fair) that it was reasonable to apply benefit sanctions if people refused to attend.

"If they were to bring these big training centres in across the country, and they refuse to go on a training scheme for two years then yes, they shouldn't be just sat around at home, out of their heads on whatever. I mean you have got to think of all the people out there working and paying tax." (Molly, Lone Parents Group)

"Yes, they all agree with that because if a person disagrees with doing all this then he is not actually looking for a job, is he? He is not interested in that. All he wants to do is sit on his arse." (Mohammed, Asian JSA Claimants Group)

"If you sign on you are saying that you are available for work and so you should be looking, shouldn't you, and if you don't want to end up on a scheme then you should try harder to get a job…. Well, some people are content to just sit back and do nothing, aren't they, just live on benefits." (Amy, Women Benefit Claimants Group)

It was seen as unsatisfactory for some people to be content to take from the benefit system without giving something in return, in this case making themselves available for training or work schemes. These users seem to be endorsing the view that rights to certain types of social security should have attendant responsibilities. This leads us to the second justification voiced by the users in favour of workfare, namely that unemployed citizens should be charged with the responsibility to make some form of contribution to society in return for their right to benefit.

"There are jobs advertised and there are loads of jobs about that people could get but that they don't try to get. Sorry, but there are a lot of people who don't work and who don't want to work and I don't see why we who have worked all our lives and paid our dues, why these younger ones coming up should not put their bit into this community work. This countryside needs a damn good clean up and if they won't work then get them into the habit of working." (Jane, Senior Citizens Group)

"At least they should make some form of contribution. So many things that the local councils have fallen down on these days, like keeping streets clean. I know it is a menial job but at least it is something that people who don't have a job could use as a community contribution." [Mary and Colin are voicing agreement.] (William, Middle Class Charity Group)

Some important beliefs that are expressed here need to be considered. First, the underlying importance that these users attach to the duty of making a contribution to society. Second, the extent to which they equate this concern directly with paid employment. The implication of the stance taken above appears to be that once an individual is not able to meet both their formal responsibility to contribute to collective welfare through the payment of statutory taxes and dues, and their more informal duty to provide for themselves and their families, then that individual is seen as having broken the contract between citizen and state. Third, a consequence of disengagement from this ideal of the economically active citizen appears to be that it is now right for new rules to apply. The users seem to be saying that if an individual cannot or will not find available waged work, then it becomes reasonable for the state to then demand that the unemployed person contribute by working in reduced circumstances, in return for the right to benefit.

In contrast to the above, policies that compel claimants to go on training or work schemes were, however, unpopular with a large number (45%) of those interviewed, and many were highly sceptical of the motives behind the introduction of such policies. The following participant summed up criticisms that were raised on a regular basis throughout the interviews.

"To start imposing conditions like that, I don't think that it is any good, and they are having work done on the cheap as well. All these workfare schemes are having people doing things, tidying up and the like, which is work done on the cheap and it is another way of the state saying, 'oh well, we have slashed the unemployment figures by another 50,000. We have got these people back to work aren't we wonderful', but they have done naff all. They are saving money for the government but they are not enhancing anybody's pride or long-term object of keeping a job for ever. I mean, how long will these workfare jobs last." (Joe, Benefit Claimants Group)

The users who were critical of workfare also believed that in many cases it was employers rather than the unemployed who would benefit from the schemes due to the creation of a potentially cheap and expendable pool of labour.

"I went on one once at a printers and I was having to do overtime there. You were only supposed to do 30 hours a week but they said if you want a job after this, you will have to do overtime. Then you get to the end of the course and it is, 'oh, we don't have a job for you'. That's the way that they do it. They get as much work out of you as possible then dump you and get somebody else." (Paul, Disabled Claimants Group)

"The guy who is going to benefit is the owner of the business. He is going to get cheap, dirt cheap labour. He is going to be laughing his bloody socks off and making a fortune." (Harold, Disabled Claimants Group)

It was also pointed out that the widespread introduction of government-sponsored work schemes could lead to reduced wages for some and, ironically, an increase in redundancies in certain sectors.

"If you get a decent job, say you were cleaning the streets, you are taking jobs away from the people who are earning a reasonable wage cleaning the streets." (Tom, Benefit Claimants Group)

"It is putting pressure on those already employed, like they can just reduce the wages of anybody really, then. It is creating a bad situation for people who are unemployed and also for people who are in jobs as well." (Kate, Benefit Claimants Group)

Encouraging claimants by assisting them was seen as the best way to proceed, with compulsion regularly identified as a major problem and of little long-term value in ensuring that people will work in the future.

> "It is this element of compulsion – I mean if they are planning on bringing it in for so many groups and forcing them. If there was enough decent schemes that people wanted to do then there should be no need for compulsion. In a way, it is up to the government to provide things to make people want to go to work. If they are trying to create a new work ethic where people want to work, then you are not going to do it by forcing people into it." (Peter, Lone Parents Group)

Two concerns were also consistently raised whenever compulsory work schemes entered the discussions: low pay and poor quality training. Many users believed that in order for future compulsory work or training to be of any real value to them, the problem of low pay had to be addressed by considerably improving the money paid to trainees. The quality and range of the schemes offered was also seen as important, and a number of users stated that schemes needed to be of a better standard with higher financial rewards than the 'slave labour' of the YTS schemes that some had experienced in the past.

> "By making it compulsory you don't have to up the quality. If you came up with a really good quality scheme and paid a reasonable wage, not £10, something like doubling the benefit, that would give you quality training in a work environment. By making it compulsory all you need to do is say that we have this variation of £10 a week and you are now going to restore this dry stone wall." (Barry, Benefit Claimants Group)

A further insight into the twin problems of a lack of quality training and employers exploiting the schemes for their own ends was offered by a respondent who prior to falling ill had worked in the Employment Service for a number of years.

> "The schemes in my experience, and I worked at the ES, I don't think that they are of sufficient quality to be attractive to people. Either because I don't think the schemes should be compulsive [*sic*]. They should be marketed and be more attractive and actually mean something to people.... The wages are low and employers are not

necessarily fulfilling their side of the bargain.... We used to get people who came back of schemes and they hadn't done anything for eight weeks. They just swept the floor or God knows what else. That really is the reputation of the scheme for everyone." (Linda, Women's Benefit Claimants Group)

The users who were forthright in their condemnation of highly conditional workfare regimes showed little faith in compulsory schemes leading them to 'real' jobs in the future. They also clearly rejected the idea that rights to unemployment benefit should be contingent on individuals meeting state specified work or training criteria. In this way they indicate a position in which the benefit rights of the unemployed individual are seen as overriding the wider demands of society for them to accept additional 'work' responsibilities. Rights rather than responsibilities dominate; this clearly contrasts with their pro workfare co-users who emphasise that social rights do not have priority over social responsibilities. However, as the following quotations indicate, for those users opposed to conditional benefits rights are the primary concern.

"The next step in this argument is, 'if the blighters will not work then make them sweep the street'. Well, let them sweep the streets but pay them for it, employ a road sweeper." [general agreement] (Barry, Senior Citizens Group)

"If there are no jobs people should be paid unemployment benefit." (Len, Senior Citizens Group)

In spite of the difference in emphasis between certain users, some favouring rights above responsibilities and vice versa, it is important to note that while those who supported increasingly conditional unemployment benefit rights, support for such welfare regimes was regularly qualified. For example, two of the groups that were staunchest in backing both compulsory work schemes and benefit sanctions (the Informal Mosque Group and the Pakistani/Muslim Women's Group) were keen to stress that their support was dependent on how the schemes were implemented and administered. Although both these groups saw no problem with the wider community setting work responsibilities for the unemployed, the Women's Group was keen to stress that work offered had to match the individual's qualifications and requirements in order for the system to be just, a concern shared by others who had spoken in favour of conditionality.

> "People need to work but equally if I was out of work, say as a lecturer I got made redundant tomorrow, there are certain jobs that I would not do, that I don't want to do, but I will happily do other things." (Mary, Middle Class Charity Group)

The Informal Mosque Group was also adamant that it was proper for a society to demand withdrawal of benefit if individuals refused to join a work or training scheme; however, they were also keen to stress that sanctions must be applied in a manner that took account of wider social circumstances.

> "To a certain extent, yes. With regard to young people, yes certainly, they should be encouraged to work and if not then benefit should be withdrawn from them and this will then motivate them. There are conditions to that and the conditions are that you should look at what real opportunities does this person have to get a job. If a person is not able to get a job for genuine reasons then fair enough, you should make allowances for that, or likewise if a person's health is deficient, but you should encourage people to get a job. People who are of an older age, 30 plus, then again they may find it harder but as long as you are fair in terms of the people that you are dealing with, it is all right to put those conditions upon them." (Ahmed, Informal Mosque Group)

It is important to note that these are not isolated examples: support for conditional benefit was rarely unequivocal. For example, two female users in the Lone Parents Group could see a positive aspect in appearance conditions, agreeing that it would stop individuals who were workshy from "deliberately going scruffy ... so that they didn't get it (a job)"; one of them then went a step further and stated that there were some young people who "don't want work" and who should therefore be compelled to train. Later on in the interview, however, both agreed that a lack of jobs, lack of support for the young unemployed and poor pay in those few jobs on offer were the major reasons why many school leavers are unemployed; a realisation that situations beyond the control of individual claimants complicated matters. It appears that very few of those interviewed were in favour of the rigorous implementation and administration of a highly conditional benefit regime.

Although, as the above discussions illustrate, common concerns inform the views of both those opposed to, and those in favour of, conditional unemployment benefit, it is important to reiterate that the two bodies of opinion differ in several important ways. First, those in favour of conditionality believe that some jobs are available and therefore claimants must at the very least be actively looking for work. Second, they also believe that it is appropriate to use unemployment and benefit policy to regulate and control the behaviour of claimants through benefit sanctions, so that the workshy are discouraged and the work ethic promoted. This in turn may imply that some users in favour of conditionality believe unemployment in no small way is the fault of the individual claimant. Indeed, some would go as far as to argue that many individuals prefer to avoid work and draw benefit; hence support for comments such as,

> "I think at the end of the day some people do need a kick." (Chris, Disabled Claimants Group)

In contrast, those opposed to a conditional regime largely reject such thinking and see the underlying causes of unemployment as having little to do with individual behaviour. Policies built around such limited individualistic assumptions that simultaneously reduce people's social rights are therefore rejected as ineffective and unjust.

> "Yes, just that unemployment in this country is structural I think, and many experts would also say so. Without radical solutions you cannot solve structural unemployment. It is a vicious and difficult one to solve and some have said that the only solution will be to curtail certain freedoms and have a siege economy. So the unemployed cannot alter the problem of structural unemployment. It is not their fault. It is just a very difficult one to solve." (Don, Senior Citizens Group)

Social security and financial conditionality

The research also attempted to gain insight into the users' views on the issue of financial conditionality, that is, whether or not it was reasonable for the state to use means testing as a way of limiting the right to social benefits. Two specific aspects of means testing were explored in the study. First, the inclusion of the market value of an elderly person's privately owned residential property when applying a means test to decide if the state will meet the costs of any long-term residential care. Second, if it was reasonable for the state to take into account an individual's savings when assessing the right to certain benefits.

Long-term residential care

The present requirement that some senior citizens (who own private housing) should sell their property in order to finance long-term care in old age generated strong opinions, particularly among the 64% of users who were opposed to the policy.

Len: "I think it is an outrage, an absolute outrage, because you pay insurance all your working life. I've paid for 50 years, I've worked for 50 years and at the end my house might be taken away if I've got to go in a private nursing home. That is the situation and I think it is an outrage." [very angry]

Edna: "It is the same for all of us." [general agreement] (Senior Citizens Group)

"I think that it is wrong because they have worked all their lives, God, 60 or 70 years some of them, and have paid to be in that home, state run homes for the elderly. The state should pay for it. Those people have gone through wars and kept this country afloat through jobs, proper jobs not things like Macdonalds, something with a trade what are barely about any more, and I think that it is absolutely disgusting that they would ask a person or a family of a person who is too incompetent to make their own decision to sell that house, everything they own, to give them the money back. I think it is disgraceful, absolutely diabolical and that is why the Conservatives want to be out." (Millie, Residents Group)

Ivy: "I think it is absolutely appalling that."

Paula: "Disgraceful, that has happened to my auntie."

Ivy: "Disgraceful, when they have worked all their lives for what little bit they have got and it is all being taken off them really quickly at the last."

Dorreen: "What is happening there, is that they are making them sell their houses and when they have got over £8,000 in the bank they are making them use that for their accommodation."

Ivy: "I think it must be the most upsetting thing for any old person to actually lose their home."

Shelly: "As far as the government is concerned, elderly people are second class citizens." (Women Benefit Claimants Group)

As the above comments illustrate, many believed that as senior citizens had previously made valid contributions (financial and otherwise) to society throughout their lives, the state now had a reciprocal duty to fund long-term care. It was also believed that present policy was flawed as it penalised those individuals who had worked hard and had managed to purchase their own home. This policy was generally seen as running counter to the encouragement of 'responsible' actions such as saving and meeting one's own housing needs, while simultaneously sending out the message to individuals who spent all their money that such 'irresponsible' behaviour did not matter as ultimately the state would pick up the costs of their long-term care anyway. Jane succinctly expressed this view.

"What about those who have lived in council houses all their lives? They have got no money, they [the state] do it all for them anyway." (Jane, Disabled Claimants Group)

Another recurrent concern of those opposed to the enforced sale of homes was the extent to which it interfered with an individual's right to pass their assets on to their children as inheritance. The following comments were typical.

"That person has bought his house and he should be entitled to pass the proceeds on to his relatives. I don't see why not. He has worked to have his own house and I suppose he has worked damned hard and he is probably proud that he has got it and I am sure that the majority of elderly people would not want the government to snatch it off them but to pass it on to their nearest and dearest, either in the form of the house is yours in the will or sell the house and split the proceeds. It is wrong." (Joe, Residents Group)

"They think it is not fair, right, because in the Asian families we are very close as a family and once your parents go to live abroad, right, they actually leave you things. So say like there are three brothers, they will sell their house and divide the money and that shouldn't affect your benefit because you haven't actually earned it. You have been given it as a gift. It is not as if you are saving that money. You can't even live off benefit these days.... It is not exactly savings, is it? You have been given it by your parents and family." (Mohammed, Asian JSA Group Claimants)

Some users (28%), however, believed that it was reasonable for the state to demand that an elderly individual sell their home in order to help meet the costs of long-term residential care. All these users took the pragmatic view that this was an acceptable approach, as the elderly individuals concerned would have no further use for their former homes.

William: "Well, why? You don't want your house – because you can't live in it."

Darren: "You have got beyond living in it." (Middle Class Charity Group)

William' and Darren's views are particularly interesting in that they are both retired and in their early seventies, but as William makes clear they have no objection to funding their own long-term residential care if or when it becomes necessary.

"For example, in my own case, I own a house. If my wife or I had to go into care then I wouldn't object if the proceeds of my house were used to pay for our care as long as the funds were there. At the end of that time I would hope that there would be state funds or whatever if we were still living, to carry on us receiving care. I don't disagree. [With using assets in this way].... Maybe Darren and I would have reason to complain. I started work at 16 and I retired at 68 and fought in a war, and what I have got I have had to work for and I don't object if I have to use it to look after myself." (William, Middle Class Charity Group)

Although William is also keen to state the full extent of his past contributions to wider society, he is at odds with those users who view the funding of long-term residential care for elderly people as a duty for the state; clearly, those with sufficient assets, William in the first instance, view the meeting of such costs as a matter of individual rather than collective responsibility.

Personal savings

When discussing the question of means testing personal savings, those users who were opposed to the practice again highlighted the payment of previous contributions as sufficient grounds on which to stake a claim to benefit.

"If a person has paid their dues and demands while they have been working and they are all of a sudden unemployed, then they should be able to claim. If they have put money away for a rainy day then that's there for a rainy day. If they have paid their dues and demands, yes, they should pay them." (Molly, Lone Parents Group)

"If they have worked a lot of years, it is like my uncle Alf, when you went into a job years ago you were put into a trade. He became a sheet metal worker and luckily he stopped in that trade. You didn't swap and move about jobs like you do today. You just stuck to that one trade and worked your way up. Eventually he just couldn't work but he never signed on, he didn't know what sick money was, he didn't know what he had to do, what he didn't have to do. It finished. He had to go to Australia and spend a lump sum of his money which he didn't really want to do, just so that he could claim benefits, because he wasn't going to give them the pleasure of passing this money on to somebody who wasn't bothered about working when he had worked all his life for it, just to keep his head above water. I mean such as elderly people, like with my granddad every saving that he had was taken into account as to which benefit they were entitled to. We were comparing it the other day. There is a friend and her uncle and my granddad are the same age. The uncle has always worked but he has never paid a stamp. My grandfather has worked all his life and paid a stamp and the difference in pensions is £4. My granddad gets £4 more than the man who has never paid a stamp in his entire life, plus the man who has never paid a stamp is entitled to benefit because his money is made up by income support. My grandfather's isn't made up without income support, so he is not entitled to any benefits." (Gail, Residents Group)

As Gail's comment illustrates, means testing personal savings was again widely seen as running contrary to the work ethic and the idea that individuals via their contributions earn a right to benefit from the state when they are no longer active in the workforce.

In contrast to those users, 27% who supported the selective targeting of benefits via means testing believed that it made financial sense to restrict benefits to those people who had the most obvious need for them.

> "There should be some kind of means test. The perfect example there is family allowance, paid at birth. Now you get, I don't know what you get, let's say it's £10, if you are unemployed and you have one child you get £10 a week. If your husband is a circuit judge on £700,00 a year with one child you get £10 a week. That is the most ridiculous benefit going." (Jane, Disabled Claimants Group)

These users clearly felt that benefits should be reserved for those with pressing financial needs (established via means testing), rather than more universally available on the grounds of specified criteria or on the basis of past contributions.

> "When I got hurt I got vast amount of compensation and I didn't claim any benefits. The only ones I claimed were mobility allowance and my pension but I couldn't get rid of them. It was like throwing a bloody boomerang. They kept coming back. I couldn't understand it because I told them I had an excess income of £900 a week, so why should I worry? So I sent it back 'well you're in a wheelchair'. So what, 'It's yours, you've earned it'. I sent it back three or four times I said. 'You don't understand, I've got £X of compensation'". (Chris, Disabled Claimants Group)

In general terms, the users opposed to the use of means testing share common ground with those in favour of means testing, in that they all endorse the belief that individuals should be able to accumulate assets as best they can; however, they differ in the extent to which they believe that the ownership of private assets should determine a right to publicly provided provision. Those against the application of means tests are keen to stress that past contribution to society should be enough to give individuals the right to claim extensive, collectively financed support from the state once they are no longer economically active. In contrast, those users in favour of means testing appear to believe that the right to benefit or care should be more closely tied to need defined according to stringent financial criteria. They hold the view that state welfare should operate more as a safety net for those with insufficient means, and that beyond limited financial state support people should largely be expected to meet their own requirements.

Unconditional benefit: a case for Citizen's Income?

A specific question asked the users to air their views on the idea of reforming social security by replacing the current 'hybrid' system (Dean, 1996, pp 91-117) which combines means tested, contributory and contingency benefits with a single basic Citizen's Income (CI) payable to everyone regardless of their need. The initial lack of response from the focus groups to this question appears to suggest that it is not commonly part of user debates[2]. This should not be surprising, as although basic income has been part of academic debates for a number of years (see, for example, Clarke and Kavanagh, 1996; Purdy, 1994; Twine, 1994; Jordan, 1988; Alcock, 1985), it still appears to be of minor interest in political and media debates that often inform wider popular discussions.

The users' reactions to the idea of an unconditional CI were varied. The most prevalent opinion was that its introduction would prove to be a positive step. Those users who supported the idea (22%) felt that it would be a fairer system as a right to benefit would no longer be tied to past contributions or means testing. Similarly, it was thought that a CI would reduce significantly the need for benefit policing, which in turn would remove the threat of benefit sanctions being applied by the state.

> "But you would have less policing though, less benefit policing. At the moment you have got various people attending different organisations to prove that they are sick or prove that they are whatever, and you would get away from that." (Linda, Women Benefit Claimants Group)

What must be stressed is that on many occasions support for the introduction of CI was dependent on certain financial stipulations. As discussions ensued, it became clear that some users were happy to support everybody having the right to CI as long as the tax system was reformed so that individuals whose income exceeded a certain level had the amount they received in CI clawed back in taxation. In effect, the universal right to CI would remain but the application of an earnings limit would ensure that those whose income exceeded an agreed level would not be entitled to draw the benefit.

> "Well, I suppose that is another form of taxation but at least it would give everybody a fixed sum, and what you are saying is if you earned more than that sum the government would claw the difference back in tax." (Joe, Residents Group)

> "And we are absolutely in favour of this basic minimum living allowance which can be withdrawn, based on earnings, yes." (Ben, Senior Citizens Group)

This idea that actual payment of CI should be based on an agreed criterion of need also informed the views of the Informal Mosque Group where parallels were drawn between the right to *zakat* and the right to basic income. It became apparent that the group had no problem with using a means test to identify need; the problem which they believed had to be addressed was how to remove the stigma associated with drawing benefits from genuine claims for welfare. The key point about CI was that it had the ability to do this, but in line with their general view that welfare should be targeted at those in need, these Muslim users felt that a universal right to CI would be acceptable as long as it was linked to some form of means test to determine those in need. It was felt that CI would only work if either regulations limited the right to actually draw the benefit or if people chose not to 'abuse' the system by taking it when they did not really need it.

> "As a just person in a just state is the way that I'm looking at it. You take out what you need. If I don't need it I will leave it there in what is called the bait ul mal [national community fund] for the state to use for those people who are in need." (Ali, Informal Mosque Group)

Given that ideas about conditional welfare, being the best way to prevent unrestrained idleness in the working population, have long been a feature of public welfare in Britain, a number of the supporters of CI were also sceptical about it ever being introduced. It was seen as unlikely that moves to initiate an unconditional benefit system would receive popular support.

> "Yes, I am all in favour of that but I don't think that it will ever get introduced. Because people like others to have incentives, like the unemployed have incentives like threatening the loss of benefit and things like that." (Frank, Benefit Claimants Group)

This assumption would seem to be valid in light of the comments from those users 12% who were opposed to CI. The view that it would act as a disincentive to certain people who would then choose to rely on state benefits rather than their own efforts was commonplace.

> "It would [be a disincentive] because there would be people sat back doing nothing." (Amy, Women's Benefit Claimant Group)

> "But what do you do about people who just will not get a job, who refuse to work, blatantly refuse, who say 'I'm not working' or 'I'm not working for that pittance when I've got this nice little income here that I'm entitled to without anyone applying a means test'? I certainly agree with people who will go out to work, or may fall pregnant that can't go to work. It is something that is a good idea for them to fall back on, but for people who won't work I think that they should get the same as they get now, in fact less if you possibly can, because I work all year." (Millie, Residents Group)

A concern that a universally available CI would break the link between rights and responsibilities and encourage irresponsible behaviour was also central to the critique offered by those who believed that the right to CI should be reserved for certain deserving individuals. The view here was that CI should be available only to those people who were striving to better themselves and/or providing some kind of service to society. It was believed that such an approach would give recognition and reward to the valuable work carried out by many citizens outside the paid labour market (informal care work, voluntary work and so on) while simultaneously ensuring that freeloaders were discouraged.

> "If somebody is providing care for an elderly relative, then if they couldn't do it then social services would have to do it for someone, so there is a cost implication there. So if you are looking at providing people like that with some cash, some sort of income, or whether it is somebody who is partially disabled, and again providing them with an income so that they can actually do some voluntary work – I think that is fair enough." (Mary, Middle Class Charity Group)

> "I am a single woman and I have been claiming benefits for a few years but I am only doing that so that I can train to be a teacher. If it comes to a choice, between sitting at home or accepting some personal responsibility and training to get a job. I see people who have got

kids who sit on their backsides and spend their benefits money on a drink or whatever,. and I think that they shouldn't be getting it. There should be guidelines if you are getting this money. You should be trying to get a job." (Elaine, Disabled Claimants Group)

"A reasonable minimum wage, something where you can have a social life as well as pay your way in society – now I have always said that should be a right. But you should not get it free. You should have to work for it. Now again, if that means that you take a lesser paid job, let's just say for argument sake your basic minimum to give you a reasonable wage is £200 per week, you should now be allowed to go out and get a job for £120 per week, then collect the other £80 from somewhere, government or whatever, but at least you have contributed to the economy of this country." (Harold, Disabled Claimants Group)

Overall support for an unconditional CI was limited. Those who opposed it saw its introduction as an impractical and expensive burden on taxpayers that would encourage people to remain idle. Among those who in principle approved of the idea, there was widespread scepticism about its practical viability: who would decide the minimum requirement? How would the issue of individuals with differing needs be resolved? Would claimants end up financially worse off? Although the majority of users agreed that the social security system needs to be reformed as present provision is largely inadequate, the general opinion was that unconditional CI would not be part of that reform. To some this was a disappointment; to others a relief.

The irregular application of conditionality

At one point a respondent attempted to broaden the discussion on welfare by pointing out that the benefits which the state administers to those in need were only one aspect of welfare in Britain.

"We talk about the welfare state and social security but people getting social security is not the be all and end all of the welfare state. There is tax relief for people with money for various things, mortgage relief and things like that, that is all part of the welfare state, so when we talk about welfare it is no good just talking about people who signed on or sick people. We are talking about better off people who are also taking something out of the state. It is the same sort of thing. That is the welfare state." (Frank, Benefit Claimants Group)

Several of the users were aware that the recent changes in policy impacted largely on the rights of poorer citizens. There was a realisation that the principle of conditionality was being applied largely so that it affected the benefit rights of poorer citizens. In healthcare it has previously been noted that money buys the right to treatment without the need to change lifestyle or habit. The changes in social security legislation obviously impact on those with limited funds: it is the unemployed who are being asked to perform additional tasks for benefit. In housing it was clear to certain users that any introduction of PTPs and MACs would have no effect on those people who could afford to purchase their own home.

> "Again it is separating a class of people and saying that poor people have got different rights from people with a healthy income. Look what happens in the private market – people just move into their house and look after their own little bit. They don't necessarily put anything back into the community and certainly they aren't forced to. So why because you are poor should you have those stipulations made on you?" [Molly, Ross and Susan strongly agree.] (Peter, Lone Parents Group)

> "There is an anomaly here, where you get council estates where there are a lot of people who have bought their own houses. You can get one person who does something who can be thrown off the estate and the person next door who they can't do anything about. They have created a situation where only some people live in real fear of the results of their actions." (Frank, Benefit Claimants Group)

In response to these concerns, several groups were asked whether or not the fiscal and occupational welfare rights of the better off should be made conditional on them accepting wider communal responsibilities. The Disabled Claimants Group and two other users were in general agreement that this should be the case.

> "I am sure that they [the wealthy] should have [additional responsibilities]. You are going back now to what you were saying, we should all have a responsibility to each other. We have just been talking about housing and communities being responsible for other people. Yes, I am in full agreement with that, but I am also in agreement of wages, welfare for everybody." (Harold, Disabled Claimants Group)

Ivy: "If they are going to make council tenants sign an agreement that they have got to do something into the community, voluntary working in the community, they have got to do something for the people who have money, why should it just be people that live in council houses."

Shelly "Or rented property?"

Ivy: "Why should it be just down to them to volunteer to do community things?"

Shelly: "It's down to class, isn't it? It can be put down to class."
(Women's Benefit Claimant Group)

This opinion was in direct contrast to the Middle Class Charity Group who were uncompromising in their belief that the state should not try to link rights to fiscal and occupational benefits to additional communal responsibilities. It was strongly believed that the better off already made enough of a contribution to society both through the payment of "tax at a very heavy rate", and by any voluntary work that they undertook. Compulsion in this case was seen as unjust and unenforceable.

"Well why should you, why should you? Now I agree with things like windfall taxes but why should you. Here we are now, two old men who have worked dammed hard all our lives – why should you now have rules enforced where we have to pop something from what little bit we might have made to keep a scrounger who is looking for drugs, possibly?" (William, Middle Class Charity Group)

In the two other groups that gave opinions on this issue, while there was a widespread acceptance that the poor were being treated differently from the more affluent members of society and that conditionality was being differentially applied across classes, many users were unconvinced about the feasibility of such a scheme and whether it would serve any practical purpose.

"I'm all for encouraging community. My doubt is to whether that is the way to do it, through money.... Is that genuine? I don't think it is." (Peter, Lone Parents Group)

In spite of some users believing that if was unfair to selectively apply the principle of conditionality exclusively to certain sectors of social welfare, the most prevalent opinion was that any attempt to impose additional responsibilities on the recipients of fiscal and occupational benefits would be unlikely to succeed.

Conclusions

In the area of public healthcare it is apparent that the most extensively held view is that the right to treatment should remain unconditional. While accepting that personal habits or behaviour may have a negative impact on an individual's health, an overwhelming majority of those interviewed believed that an attempt to limit access to healthcare on such grounds would be inappropriate and serve neither the needs of the individuals concerned nor wider society. The users defended this view by pointing out that behaviour which potentially carries a risk to health is very much part of contemporary social life and that decisions to impose limits on some actions and not others would be largely arbitrary. They were also concerned that policies which attempted to restrict an individual's right to care on the grounds of individual behaviour took no account of wider social, cultural or environmental factors which may have an influence on individual habits or health. Although a small minority of the users opposed this view and believed that it was reasonable for the right to healthcare to be dependent on individuals adhering to certain patterns of behaviour (that somehow come to be morally defended as 'responsible'), the dominant view stressed unconditional healthcare rights above any behavioural responsibilities.

This position, in which rights dominate responsibilities, is somewhat reversed when the right to housing is considered. There are at least a couple of reasons why the users see a closer link between rights and responsibilities as more appropriate when applied to housing. First, a person has to behave in a manner so as to actively and persistently cause nuisance to somebody else before losing their right to housing. Second, the users were clear that eviction and the subsequent loss of the right to social housing should only ensue if individuals chose to ignore earlier warnings and continued to seriously misbehave. It is clear that the majority of users believe that attaching conditions, such as probationary tenancies and anti-social behaviour clauses, to the right to be housed is reasonable. Coupled with this, they were keen to stress that their continued support for such policies depended on the conditions proposed and the spirit in which such policies are implemented. Although a small number of users objected to PTPs (with the possibility of malicious complaint central to their doubts), it appears that in principle they too believed that ultimately the right to a house should be conditional on certain standards of behaviour. As previously discussed, the idea of linking the right to a house directly to the acceptance of wider communal responsibilities did, however, find some strong supporters with roughly a third of users in favour of MACs. In spite of extensive support from the users for harsh sanctions, to be applied if individuals were persistently engaged in anti-social behaviour, it should be noted, however, that many users dismiss the imposition of compulsory, communal care responsibilities via mutual aid clauses as unworkable, unnecessary and outdated.

Making the right to social security, and more particularly unemployment benefit, increasingly conditional on recipients of benefit performing additional tasks (ranging from applying for jobs to attending compulsory schemes) attracted substantial support, with more than half the users supporting the idea. Supporters of conditional unemployment benefit regimes tended to justify their stance in two ways. They were keen to stress the positive potential that training schemes could have on a claimant's chances of future employment, and they also believed that it was desirable for claimants to have specified responsibilities in return for benefit as this would help to counter the development of a body of inactive benefit recipients. In terms of the causes and solutions of unemployment, these users chose to emphasise the individual behaviour of claimants, with regular reference being made to available employment and lazy individuals who choose not to work. In contrast, the substantial minority who opposed policies that made unemployment relief increasingly conditional were highly sceptical of the motives behind their introduction. Drawing on past experiences, they were critical of the quality of government-sponsored schemes and saw them as being of little long-term value to the unemployed. They oppose the linking of benefit rights to responsibilities as they primarily view unemployment as the outcome of a set of circumstances which are often beyond the control of individual claimants, and so feel that increased conditionality and the punitive removal of benefit rights is inappropriate. That strong views were held by users both for and against conditional benefit regimes should be apparent from the preceding text; however, what must also be stressed is that those who supported conditionality in this particular context regularly qualified their support by stating that much depended on how any policy was administered and the groups to whom it was applied.

The discussion on CI appeared to raise similar concerns among the users, with the introduction of a universal unconditional benefit attracting little support. Many, including those who voiced support for some form of CI, were keen to differentiate between those who were in need but actively striving to improve their lives, and those they identified as passive idlers who choose to simply live on benefit. Many of the users remained resolute that the social security system should reward 'responsible' citizens rather than support the 'irresponsible' freeloaders. The users who discussed the uneven application of conditionality were aware that it is largely the welfare rights of the poor that are being made more conditional, and while some believe that this is unfair and that the principle of conditionality should be applied to the fiscal and occupational welfare rights that the wealthier members of British society enjoy, it became obvious that the majority believed that this was highly unlikely.

This analysis of the users' views on conditionality clearly illustrates that strong disagreements about the balance between citizens' rights and responsibilities exist. In this way their differences can be seen to resemble opposing positions taken in wider philosophical, political and policy debates. In general terms it is possible to group the users into two broad camps: those in favour of conditionality and those opposed to it. In the light of previous discussions this would be too simplistic an approach, because the degree to which the users are willing to accept the principle that welfare rights should be contingent on individuals adopting certain patterns of behaviour appears to depend extensively on the context of its imposition. Similarly, it must be stressed that although many of those interviewed supported current attempts to make the right to both social housing and unemployment benefit conditional on certain types of behaviour, they reserved their right to withdraw their support if they deemed future polices to be unjust.

Notes

[1] The respondent is referring to the DHSS (1980) report *Inequalities in health: Report of a Research Working Group*, under the chairmanship of Sir Douglas Black. More recently the government-commissioned Acheson Report (1998) re-emphasised the negative effect of poverty on individuals' health (Gordon et al, 2000).

[2] For an interesting allied debate to this issue, see Oliver and Barnes (1998, p 79) and their discussion of grassroots disabled people's organisations and the campaign for an adequate disability income in the 1970s.

SIX

Membership

Introduction

The concept of citizenship implies membership of some form of community; in turn the notion of community opens up questions about terms of inclusion and exclusion. This chapter's focus is to consider the ground rules which are seen by welfare service users as being pertinent for individuals to be included in or excluded from arrangements for the collective provision of welfare benefits and services. Throughout the research sessions, it became clear that many users saw certain people as having legitimate claims to welfare while the claims of others were often seen as invalid. A distinction between 'deserving' and 'undeserving' claims was apparent in the users' dialogue. This was a recurrent and often strongly expressed discourse that was regularly used to justify the inclusion or exclusion of certain people from public welfare. Illustrative examples of the users endorsing either an inclusionary or exclusionary approach (and the strategies that they use to justify their stance) in healthcare, housing and social security respectively are offered in the following discussions. Where relevant, comments about all social provision and welfare rights in general are included. It should be noted that in common with previous discussions on conditionality (see Chapter Five), a lack of individual contribution and/or responsibility once again appears to be of significance among those who are seeking to defend their decisions to exclude certain individuals from welfare rights.

Inclusion and exclusion from healthcare: undeserving immigrants, deserving senior citizens

Several of the questions that were put to the groups for discussion were designed to explore whether any of the users saw the exclusion of particular individuals (or groups) from access to certain welfare rights as justified. Question 5 (see Appendix) attempted to specifically address the question of access to free public healthcare in relation to two groups, immigrants/asylum seekers and senior citizens.

Excluding immigrants

When considering the claims of immigrants/asylum seekers, the most prevalent opinion (49% of users) was that the denial of free healthcare for those who had recently entered Britain could, in some instances, be justified. Users were keen to acknowledge that healthcare rights should be granted to 'genuine' immigrants, that is, those who had openly entered the country in order to seek political asylum and escape persecution in their homeland; but their comments also tended to echo a belief that a substantial number of immigrants entered Britain primarily to make use of free treatment. This was regarded as an abuse of the NHS and many users were adamant that free healthcare should not be available to such people.

> "It is a question that I'm not prepared to answer at this moment. I don't think I can answer that question. If they live in this country, fair enough, but I don't think that they should come over just to use our National Health. We have got us own to treat and we can't afford to treat us own. That's my opinion. Now, it's not a racist opinion. If they are coming over and paying, that is OK." (Molly, Lone Parents Group)

> "Immigrants, yes if they are authentic immigrants; they have come here legally. But there are a number of people who are coming to the United Kingdom just for healthcare and then going back to wherever they came from. I think people come in and have their treatment and then go away again." [General Agreement] (Darren, Middle Class Charity Group)

A perceived shortfall in the resources that are available to treat British residents was also regularly used to justify the exclusion of outsiders from rights to free healthcare. Perhaps the most surprising support for this approach came from the Asian JSA Claimants Group, whose spokesman commented,

> "It should be given to the old people because they actually live in this country, but it shouldn't be given to people that are from outside the

country, because at the end of the day we lose out. We have got difficulties as it is now. Say right that over the year there are 500 people come over and they have got treatment free, then so many of us lose out, because at the end of the day there is only so much money that will go into it." (Mohammed, Asian JSA Claimants Group)

Similarly, when on two separate occasions a respondent spontaneously voiced support for the highly publicised treatment in Britain of children who were seriously injured in the Bosnian war, on both occasions other users were quick to disagree strongly with such actions.

Roger: "But at what price? There are children in this country wait two and three years and if you have got a child in this country then you don't have much sympathy for anybody else's child, I'm afraid."

Interviewer: "So do you see limits then?"

Chris: "Yes, the thing is at the end of the day that health system was set up to help the people in this country."

Jane: "It is the British NHS." (Disabled Claimants Group)

Although at first such sentiments may seem ruthless, the following poignant dialogue illustrates that it was perceived as fair to limit access to free NHS treatment to residents of Britain if and when care provided on humanitarian grounds was believed to have a negative effect on the treatment of British citizens.

Hollie: [upset when saying this, almost crying] "I agree with you. My niece was nearly a year old and had to go down to Great Ormond Street for a heart operation. It was delayed and delayed because of children coming in from overseas for operations. My niece died and it destroyed my sister, absolutely destroyed my sister, because if she had had it done when she was well enough she would be alive now. When something like that happens to you, to your immediate family, we've paid ... for what, a child's death."

Kate: "Yes, I agree with Hollie, in the sense that there is enough suffering in our own country without having to afford from other countries. There are enough suffering children of our own without having to bring in foreign children and look after them as well. It is putting a strain on a system that is already overstretched."

Hollie: "Yes, I think you should look after your own and then, you know, let's put medals on our chests." (Benefit Claimants Group)

Hollie's comment "we've paid" is illustrative of the other main justification that, implicitly, underpins the opinions offered by those who believe it to be reasonable to exclude non-nationals, that is to say that immigrants' claims to healthcare and wider social rights are seen as invalid because of a lack of previous financial contributions towards the cost of benefits and services. (See Chapter Four for a previous discussion of the importance of contribution in relation to healthcare rights.) The idea that some people would continue to take from the welfare state while making a conscious decision not to contribute in any way towards it was particularly condemned by members of the Residents Group.

"Well you are talking about British citizenship, right, in my knowledge there is a family that live not on the immediate estate but around the estate that are Muslim. They both came over here as young adults, were married and have British citizenship through their family. They were born here but taken back to Pakistan and then come back once they were married. Now they have got a house here, they go back to Pakistan every year and every year they come back to have a child, every year. The child is born in this country with British citizenship with entitlement to a school place, to free school meals, to housing, to housing benefit, to social security benefits, to NHS, to everything. And they can go and live in Pakistan and come back. Now I'm not racist but, and I know that people start off by saying I'm not racist but, but this is definitely the case. I think that everyone, everybody, especially the elderly and children should get healthcare whether they have paid for it or not – but when you are blatantly abusing the system as this family are doing! Blatantly! And there are people in this country who might be waiting for hip replacements, or they can't go to the dentist's because they can't afford it. They are just not getting anywhere and that is why people are being penalised in this country because others are allowed to come in and take over.... I think that there should be limits.... There is enough good people in this country without more and more pouring in. We have got to draw the line at immigrants, no matter what the colour of their skin, or where they come from. They have got to draw the line." (Millie, Residents Group)

An initial consideration of the above comment may lead to the conclusion that its basis is inherently racist; however, further investigation of the data indicates that it is the "blatant abuse" of the welfare system, claiming welfare entitlements without any intent to contribute in some way to the (national) community which grants those rights, that causes Millie and her co-users most distress. This is not to deny that such views or comments may often have racist undertones and outcomes, but in this particular case it may be reasonable to argue that Millie's comments were focusing on the view (held also by her colleagues) that claims to welfare rights should to some extent include an acceptance of minimal reciprocal responsibilities. She had previously harshly condemned a member of her own family, because he

"... doesn't work a bloody day in his life, who thinks that nobody has got the right to make him work, and I'll do as I please and I'll have this money each week and it's mine and I'm entitled to it." [agitated] (Millie, Residents Group)

When discussing this issue of non-nationals having access to healthcare and other welfare rights the Residents Group concluded that visitors to Britain should be made to nominate a sponsor who agrees to meet any welfare needs/costs incurred during a stay. Interestingly, a respondent in another group had experience of this requirement when her mother-in-law came on an extended stay to Britain. Sabrina was keen to point out that such regulations existed but that they may in certain situations cause hardship.

"My husband, he had to sponsor his mum to come here. He was in full-time work then, so he was able to sponsor her to come over and we had to pay for her glasses, her teeth, doctor's care, clothes, whatever she ate, her transport backwards and forwards, while she was here. That was our responsibility for the six months that she stayed. We did it because that's our mum to bring over here, because my husband says we're wanting her to come so that's our responsibility, which it is for your own mum, isn't it? While a lot of people think is she coming to claim, is she coming to claim, they don't all come to claim. It can be all different stories. It just depends. I'm in two minds [about having to meet sponsorship requirements] because it is our mother and it is not the government's fault that she is living somewhere else. It was my husband who came to this country, of his choice. It wasn't as if he had to flee, he came of his choice, he got work. At the time we didn't see it as anything wrong, we just naturally did it. Maybe not all families can afford to bring over [relatives] and if they are on social security they may have to leave some other of their family over there and they then have to go to Pakistan so they have to keep some money back. Then some might say, 'how can they afford to go to Pakistan?', but they may eventually have to go back because someone dies. Some of us families are split sometimes." (Sabrina, Women's Benefit Claimants Group)

A minority of users (16%) opposed those who believed that healthcare (and more generally welfare) rights should be limited to legally defined 'British citizens' and/or those who were long-term residents. One respondent defended his view by drawing on universal justifications of rights and others focused on the rights of asylum seekers forced abroad because of persecution.

"Asylum seekers, prisoners, everybody has the same right to basic health. The same as we have all got other basic rights like food." (Frank, Benefit Claimants Group)

Sabrina: "They may have fled for all sorts of reasons that we don't know about."

Paula: "Do you mean when they have fled because of fighting and things like that? Well, a nice caring person wouldn't deny them money for food and a home and that." (Women's Benefit Claimants Group)

However, once again the issue of immigrants/asylum seekers contributing towards the welfare system in future was also raised.

Paula: "Well, they are going to work and pay insurance and tax, if they can get a job, that is."

Irene: "I say that they usually do work and they contribute a lot because they work long hours when they do work. I don't always agree that they get set up. I believe that they get set up with a fund when they come here at first. I can't really offer an opinion on it because we don't really know enough of how it works." (Women Benefit Claimants Group).

It would appear that for all the users contributions (past, present or future) are a central concern when making decisions about who has a legitimate claim to rights to free public healthcare. It was generally believed that those who benefited from the NHS should accept that they had a duty to help meet its financial requirements (via compulsory taxation) if they were in a position to do so.

Including senior citizens

In contrast to the differing opinions offered on the welfare rights of immigrants/asylum seekers, there was unanimous agreement among all the users that it was unacceptable to limit or deny healthcare according to the age of particular individuals. On more than one occasion discussion on this issue arose spontaneously as the groups debated. Strongly held views were expressed, with users typically stating in unequivocal terms that exclusion from treatment on grounds of age was wrong.

All: "Disgusting! Disgraceful! Outrageous!" [general agreement – exclusion on grounds of age is wrong] (Disabled Claimants Group)

"I would just like to say that one thing I disagree with in the health service at the moment is age. There is at least one hospital in England refusing to treat anybody over the age of 65, male or female, and I think that is disgraceful." (Donald, Benefit Claimants Group)

The denial or rationing of care according to age criteria was condemned for three reasons. First, echoing previous comments in support of unconditional healthcare (see Chapter Five) it was felt that everybody should have the right to treatment.

"Where there's life there's hope, and nobody should be denied treatment." (Molly, Lone Parents Group)

Second, and perhaps most importantly, the issue of older people's past contributions to society was seen as a powerful reason why the denial of treatment to senior citizens was viewed as being unjust.

> "They are the people who have put their money in for people to take it out. They have worked 50 years or gone through whatever number of wars. Sacrificed things, not just financially, and now they have been deprived. When you get to 70 you can't have a hip replacement if they are only expecting you to live another five years. It is disgusting." (James, Disabled Claimants Group)

> "My grandmother worked in the mills when she was 10 and she was deaf by the time she was 12. We are going back to the turn of the century, but she has worked all her life and paid into the NHS. When she was 60 she was told to go and see a specialist who could probably make her hear again, and he said I am sorry but you are too old. We can do children but you are not going to benefit. She lived until she was 96, she could have had 36 years of clear hearing, but she was too old and yet she had paid for all those years. So where do you draw the line?" (Jane, Disabled Claimants Group)

Third, it was pointed out that if it became generally accepted that age was a valid factor on which to base denial of care, then the possibility for all sorts of arbitrary decisions existed in the future.

> "Where do you draw the line – 70 this week because you know they have stopped producing, or when they get their pension at 65, so they don't need to take any more off the state. Oh, they have stopped working, haven't they, so we'll cut it down. Fifty five? He's had a good life, and then it gets down to 50. So where do you draw the line? Twenty-five and you're on the scrap heap. He doesn't go out playing football on a Sunday any more. He only needs his false leg or his hip replacement to prop the bar up on a Saturday night and his sex life is over with at 30. Well then." [mocking] (James, Disabled Claimants Group)

One woman related how regulations about age had acted against both her mother's interests as a patient and her own needs as a carer. Ironically, in this instance care was denied because her mother was too young.

"No, it's quite ridiculous [limiting access to care because of age]. My mum was 76 and she were dying and she were going to be 77 five days later and the GP phoned up the hospital and said, 'I want to admit an elderly patient to the geriatric ward'. It was because I hadn't had any sleep [through caring for her mum] and I were really heartbroken. They said she was too young and the doctor said, 'how do you mean she is too young to go on the geriatric ward?' She had to be 77. I was telling Fred and I bust out laughing but that was my nerves and I said, 'isn't it ridiculous that she were going to be 77 five days later'." (Paula, Women Benefit Claimants Group)

Housing rights and unwelcome neighbours: troublesome tenants, sex offenders and other criminals

The issue of troublesome tenants who behave in an anti-social manner towards their neighbours has already been discussed in some detail (see Chapter Five), so all that needs to be reiterated here is that most of the users would agree that to some extent housing rights should be contingent on individuals behaving so as not to disturb the peace of their neighbours. The purpose of this section is to look more closely at the users' views on the housing/welfare rights of certain individuals whose actions are seen as posing a threat to the communities that they inhabit. Question 11 (see Appendix) was a specific attempt to ask the users to engage in debate about which rights should prevail: an individual's right to housing, or the rights of a community to exclude certain individuals because of past or persistent criminal activity.

A substantial majority of the users (70%) believed that it was right for a local community to deny housing to certain individuals who they believed posed a threat to the well-being of other members of their community. This was particularly the case when the question of rehousing convicted paedophiles was discussed. For many, the exclusion of convicted paedophiles, from not only social rights such as housing but also basic civil rights, was unproblematic. Due to the type of offence and a fear that they would re-offend, it was widely felt that the well-being of a local community had to prevail over concerns about limiting the rights of sex offenders. Individuals who had committed such offences in the past were viewed as largely having forfeited their rights. Opinions expressed ranged from, at one extreme,

> "Well, paedophiles should be shot first of all. That would rule them out." (William, Middle Class Charity Group)

to

> "I think that depending on the offence, if it's paedophile, rape, drugs, then I believe that the neighbourhood should be informed and they should have the right to say no." (Donald, Benefit Claimants Group)

However, all these users were reluctant to have sex offenders, particularly convicted paedophiles, resident in their communities unless drastic actions were taken to identify and control them.

> "I wouldn't want one on our estate, I really wouldn't. I think that the only way that there should be anybody like that on the estate or anywhere where there is children is if, and it has been done, is if they have actually been castrated. It takes any emotions away from them and if that is the case, then yes, let them back on to the estate, but still monitor them." (Gail, Residents Group)

> Peter: "Personally I would like to see them all electronically tagged so that the authorities know where they are all the time."

> Renie: "… and tattooed on their heads so we all know who they are."

> All: "Yes, yeah! [general agreement] But it is not going to be, is it?" (Lone Parents Group)

Although some of the strongest opinions were reserved for the discussions about excluding or controlling the behaviour of paedophiles, in a number of cases serious criminal behaviour that was believed to be to the detriment of a local community was also seen as sufficient grounds for the denial of certain welfare rights. As Donald's previous comment illustrates, drug dealing was also widely frowned upon and often viewed as sufficient reason for the denial of housing. The initial response of the Pakistani Muslim Women's Group for example, was to state, in no uncertain terms, "that they [sex offenders, burglars, drug dealers] should all be thrown out!" When a woman made the point that it could (hypothetically) be a member of their own family that was made homeless, the group mellowed but only slightly. It was agreed that to "give them a chance" to reform would be reasonable, but another respondent expressed the feelings of the whole group by stating, "Just one chance, no more." It appears that the rights of a community to evict wrongdoers were held to be more important than the individual right to housing of someone who persistently offended the members of that community. "Let them all go live together" out of the way of other law abiding citizens was very much the approach endorsed. Another respondent felt that as far as drug dealing was concerned it would be unlikely that anyone would reform because of the vast sums of money that such an occupation could generate for the individual concerned. This view was later confirmed by the spokesman for the Asian JSA Claimants Group who responded on behalf of the group when a colleague, Sajid, stated that in his opinion people should be given a chance to be rehoused if they could show that they had reformed and were no longer engaged in anti-social/criminal behaviour that was detrimental to the community.

> "They should be refused, a drug dealer whatever. You said your own opinion, but would you take the risk? Say you are living in a street, right, and there is a guy, right, who is a drug dealer and he has been drug dealing for 20 years, then he stops for six months. Don't you think he will go back into it? I don't think you know how much money there is to be made in drugs. There is a fortune. You can make £80,000 to £100,000 per week, that is how much profit there is. Anybody can lay off for six months then move back into it [selling drugs]. You cannot trust anybody. I wouldn't be happy if someone like that lived around my place, my area." [nods in agreement] (Mohammed, Asian JSA Claimants Group)

Such users perceived the present criminal justice system as failing to meet the needs of individual victims and the wider community. In the absence of stricter punishments (and/or providing adequate rehabilitation and supervision of past offenders), many users believed that physical exclusion from a community through the eviction of persistent wrongdoers was justified.

Harold: "Well, I have always said in the past that certainly with these habitual burglaries that go on in my village, probably because of the heroin addiction, I am not quite sure. The police are finding these guys, arresting them, finding them with the goods and within a matter of hours they are back on the street doing it again. Now I have said in fun on a lot of occasions that it is time that we found an island like Australia and we should ship all the buggers out there. I think that there is a lot of truth in something of that nature. I don't see why we, the village, should be subject to living in fear."

James: "I know a case of one who has six children. Well, he doesn't cohabitate but he is on the birth certificate for each one, and every time he goes to court it is, 'well I've got six children to look after'. I mean, in America he would be doing life now."

Harold: "The problem with the courts and with the authorities is that they are not allowed to punish them properly. They don't get the punishment that they deserve. Fining them a couple of hundred pounds today is nothing. They can go and earn that in the next bloody half an hour."

Interviewer: "Do you think that part of the punishment should be, then, that they should be evicted if they get involved in such things?"

All: "Yes, definitely, of course." [general agreement] (Disabled Claimants Group)

Those users (16%) who were opposed to the exclusion of individuals who had past convictions for various criminal offences tended to stress that exclusion from a particular communal setting often left many important wider issues unresolved. Simply denying a criminal the right to reside in one location was viewed as merely exacerbating problems rather than attempting to solve them. Two likely outcomes of a policy based on a simplistic 'not in my back yard' approach – the creation of ghettos populated entirely by excluded miscreants and/or a large homeless criminal population – were seen as detrimental to both the rights of the other communities in which past offenders may in future reside, and also the rights of those who had committed the offences in the first instance.

"I think that everybody has a right to housing, everyone, no matter what they have done or where they have come from, no matter what their background. Most offences are offences, otherwise it would not be wrong and they should be monitored wherever they live.... But I do feel that everyone, no matter what they have done, deserves to live somewhere and you just cannot put them all together somewhere, because that is like the previous question. You are just creating an area for certain people. No, it would not prevent them from doing things, not in my opinion anyway." (Millie, Residents Group)

"If we are talking about the criminal fraternity, bad criminals who have been refused housing, I think that you have got to get them off the streets and try in some way to rehabilitate them and you are not going to do that by leaving them to live in cardboard boxes, so you have got to provide something for them, even if it is only keeping them in prison." (Darren, Middle Class Charity Group)

The notion that all individuals should continue to enjoy certain basic rights, no matter what they had done in the past, was present in these users' opinions; however, three users within this group were keen to ensure that communities were protected from certain individuals and stated that arrangements should be made which included a measure of punishment for offenders, while simultaneously maintaining a universal basic right to provision that would not see offenders become homeless in the future.

Frank: "I think you mentioned hostels though, didn't you, Barry? I agree with what Barry said about that, when I said that people should not forfeit their right to housing. They can forfeit their right to a tenancy, I agree with that, but they should have some right to a roof."

Barry: "Very basic."

Frank: "Yeah, very basic, like the old workhouse." (Benefit Claimants Group)

Social security benefits: deserving workers and carers, undeserving 'scroungers' and 'layabouts'

Previous discussions on the notion of conditionality (see Chapter Six, in particular the comments of those opposed to CI) have already implied that some users viewed certain claims for welfare as more legitimate than others. Further analysis of the data, however, indicates that a number of users (46%) were keen to make a more explicit distinction between individuals who they saw as 'deserving' or 'undeserving' of access to public welfare. There appears to be a widely held belief among these users that benefits should be reserved only for those individuals who accepted, both in principle and in practice, that (whenever possible)[1] they, as well as the state, had a part to play in the welfare deal within a particular society. These users expected that in return for benefit rights individuals had to show a measure of individual responsibility, either by striving to return to paid employment as soon as possible, so that they could resume a formal (financial) contribution to welfare, or by contributing informally to welfare needs via the provision of informal (unpaid) family or voluntary care. In each case claims to state-provided benefits were only considered as legitimate by certain users when recipients displayed an inclination towards self-help and/or the assistance (either formal or informal) of others in their community with welfare needs.

Willingness to work

Within the focus groups, some users clearly saw certain individuals as undeserving cases for the receipt of public welfare because of a perceived unwillingness to work. As the following dialogue indicates, two members of the Disabled Claimants Group in particular were keen to make a distinction between themselves as 'deserving' and certain other unemployed recipients whose claims they believed to be 'undeserving' because they were not attempting to find work, but were happy to remain idle and live on welfare.

> Harold: "I am not on JSA. I'm on incapacity benefit, but what they are saying is that all people who are unemployed because they have got to go to the DSS are uncombed hairy people, lazy people, people who won't go for a job. It is wrong for them to categorise me into that category, because I am not."

> Chris: "I think it is reasonable to ask people to do that [sign agreements, follow directives] because it is only in their interests to go to that interview, be smart and give them a better chance of getting a job. But at the end of the day I agree that we should not be stigmatised because

we are on certain benefits, to be classed as unemployed. I am not unemployable, I am employable."

Harold: "Them at DSS, all that they have got to do, you don't get nothing just by filling a form in and sending it through the post. You have got to go down and sign on. All it needs is for them to [note], scruffy/unscruffy, pleasant/unpleasant. We could all be pigeonholed then, couldn't we?"

Chris: "Yes."

Harold: "And all the people then that are slobs, if you like, and it is fairly obvious who are and who aren't, 99 per cent of them anyway. I would say then this jobseeker's allowance where you have got to go for five jobs a week, then them people, they probably should be made.... I am categorised as an 'unemployed person' which could be anything from an ex-managing director, but by and large when we are talking about the unemployed, we are talking about the yob that stands on the street corner. I don't do that." (Disabled Claimants Group)

This view, that there should be more distinctions made between individual claimants who were trying their best to help themselves and those who were unwilling to work, was repeated on a number of subsequent occasions. The Informal Mosque Group and the Asian JSA Claimants Group were in general agreement that individuals who were content to passively sit back and take benefits did not deserve to retain their right to benefits.

"You have got to get the balance between people who are genuinely in need and who are striving. The principle is this, I do believe that an individual should strive to the best of his [sic] ability to better his situation, because not only is he an individual, he is a member of his community. So yes, we should provide for all people in need as long as there is a striving of the individual as well." (Salim, Informal Mosque Group)

"Yes, they all agree with that, because if a person disagrees with doing all this, then he is not actually looking for a job, is he? He is not interested. All that he wants to do is sit on his arse." (Mohammed, Asian JSA Claimants Group)

Contributing through caring

As the previous illustrative comments suggest, a substantial number of users (46%) believes that it is justifiable to exclude certain individuals from benefit rights according to a deserving/undeserving divide. They see able-bodied claimants who they judge to have consciously chosen to remain indolent, or uninterested in doing anything to help themselves back to work, as undeserving of benefit. It is not simply the case that 'the unemployed' are seen as undeserving: only those considered lazy and irresponsible are to be punished by loss of the right to cash benefit. The same users were, however, often quick to acknowledge the legitimacy of benefit rights of people engaged in unpaid, informal care work. Mary's justification of a CI for carers or those engaged in voluntary work may be seen as evidence of this (see Chapter Five), and Millie forcefully reinforces the view that people (especially women) who accept family care responsibilities have a legitimate claim to state support.

> "As far as I'm aware, the welfare state was set up for people who really desperately needed help. It wasn't a means of support for the rest of their lives. It was just something to get them on the road to becoming independent for themselves and getting employment for themselves. Now I do understand that in this day and age that there isn't as many jobs, but I think if you really are willing to work, because you get some people who go 'no, I'm not doing that, you must be joking, I am not doing that', because they have got the welfare system to fall back on. I think it should only be a stopgap for people who need it. Like Rita has just had this young son [referring to the baby that Rita is rocking] but Rita has worked before and will work when she can work, as most people who aren't disabled would, but there are just some people who think that they are totally entitled to have their dole or their social security and that's it. They don't have to go out to work. It penalises people who do go out to work, who pay a lot out in NI and tax and things like that and it is unfair. Because when those people are out of work and they go for benefits they are getting a pittance. They are getting the same thing as somebody who hasn't worked a day in their life and I think that is totally wrong." (Millie, Residents Group)

Although the benefit claims of unpaid carers like Rita (above) are supported, again there is endorsement of the idea that individuals should, ideally, be self-supporting (through paid employment) as soon as is reasonably possible. This in turn is coupled with a strong condemnation of those who are seen as not wanting to work for a living but who continue to take from a welfare system while giving little or nothing in return. It would appear that contributing to society via unpaid care work is seen as a valid contribution to society and one that is worthy of public financial support. Indeed, one person was explicit in distinguishing between single parents who contribute to society through family care work, and irresponsible school leavers, who she believed should be compelled to go on work or training schemes or face benefit sanctions.

> "Quite easy, you don't force a single parent to go out to work when she has got children. I'm talking about kids as they are leaving school. The kids that have got no responsibility at all and they are just loafing around all day at home burgularing [*sic*] at night, a lot of them, as we all know. So that is the section that I'm talking about, not single parents. I was one myself and I know the difficulties and the hardships and everything else that a single parent goes through." (Molly, Lone Parents Group)

Conclusions

The preceding discussions appear to indicate that the notion of 'community' continues to have an important relevance for issues of welfare and citizenship. At a number of different levels – local, national and in certain instances supranational – ideas about community continue to influence the users' justifications for either including or excluding certain individuals from collective arrangements of welfare provision. The right of an individual to claim membership of a particular community is crucial if that individual is to gain access to a community's collective welfare arrangements. The above discussions serve to illustrate some of the various ways in which the users use the notion of membership in attempts to resolve dilemmas about competing claims for welfare.

Interestingly, those in favour of excluding outsiders from welfare provisions appear to use similar justifications to the users who were in favour of highly conditional welfare rights (see Chapter Five). The twin issues, of contribution and of access to collective welfare rights being conditional on individuals behaving in a manner commonly deemed as acceptable by the communities that they inhabit, were often used to explain an exclusionary stance. When discussing access to free healthcare, for example, those users who believed that immigrants should be denied access to free healthcare defended their position on the grounds that resources were limited and, therefore, argued that care should restricted to individuals who had contributed (or would be contributing in the future) to the substantial costs of public provision. The past contributions of older citizens were similarly strongly cited as a major reason why exclusion from treatment on the grounds of old age was seen as unreasonable. In the case of rights to free healthcare, it seems that certain users, however, do feel justified in combining arguments about contributions to a *national* health service with notions of a national community, in order to legitimise the exclusion from healthcare arrangements of individuals from beyond the national boundary.

A substantial number of users also appear to believe that it is reasonable that an individual should accept certain communally defined responsibilities before enjoying the benefits of any of the welfare provisions that a given community may bestow upon its members. When considering access to social security benefits, a number of users held the view that only those individuals who exhibited a willingness to contribute to the community, either by engaging (if at all possible) in paid employment or performing unpaid care work, were deserving of rights to financial assistance. An individual's claim on a community for the right to benefit is judged on their willingness to accept the corresponding ground rules as laid down by that community. The exclusion from social security arrangements of 'undeserving' individuals who refuse to accept their personal responsibility to work and/or provide some other useful contribution is viewed as relatively unproblematic; any claim to a right to welfare from a person who will not accept such rules is undermined by their previous rejection of the reciprocal principles on which many believe welfare arrangements should be based. Indeed, the identification of a total disregard for the rights and needs of other individuals appears to have informed the views of those users who believed it was acceptable to physically exclude certain criminals, particularly paedophiles, from a community. Many of the users indicated in very strong terms their support for the exclusion of certain past offenders who were popularly identified as a criminal nuisance and/or a threat to members of a neighbourhood. In spite of the fact that many welfare rights are negotiated and defined at a national level, the exclusionary potential of local communities in certain instances should not be overlooked.

In contrast, those users who outlined an inclusive vision of citizenship tended to stress universalistic justifications of a guaranteed base line of welfare provisions available to all. In such approaches, welfare rights were seen by supporting users as non-negotiable and tied explicitly to each individual as part of their status as a human being. Justifications such as these, which draw on an individual's rights rather than their responsibilities, are more likely to promote inclusive resolutions to claims for welfare. When welfare rights are intrinsically bound up with membership of a particular community (and the right to membership is itself conditional on an individual's acceptance of communally agreed and enforced rules and norms of behaviour), exclusive outcomes become both justifiable and increasingly probable. A considerable number of users, however, appear to be of the opinion that the exclusion of certain individuals who are unable or unwilling to meet communally prescribed membership rules (that often relate to issues of contribution and/or responsible behaviour) is justified. For some at least, such exclusion is a relatively unproblematic part of the bounded realities on which citizenship is based. A number of users see the imposition of certain limits to welfare provision as a legitimate part of the citizenship package.

Note

[1] Although the issue of providing benefits to people unable to work because of disablement was not explicitly explored, users' comments indicate that in principle they would support the claims to benefit of disabled people who were unable to work by reference to two justifications. First, disabled people would meet commonly held views about legitimate need for the provision of financial support and care through the public welfare system; and second, the cause of their inactivity in the paid labour market is seen by many users as being beyond their control. In short, questions about whether disabled people are lazy or not have little relevance as they are perceived as unable to work due to their impairment. Such views have been identified as disabling by disabled people's organisations and their allies. Barnes (1992), for example, discusses how disabled people are challenging such discriminatory views and demanding the eradication of disabling attitudes and environments so that they can realise the right to paid employment.

SEVEN

Citizenship and welfare: principles and practice

Introduction

This concluding chapter aims to address several issues. Initially, the major findings of the study are reiterated and the central themes of provision, conditionality and membership are reconsidered in light of the empirical findings generated in the analysis of the data. Some other relevant findings from recent studies of citizens' attitudes to welfare are also included. In this way an attempt is made to take an overview of the opinions offered by the welfare service users who took part in the research, and see what their perspectives may have to offer in terms of a more general consideration of citizenship and welfare. Next, moving beyond simply recording what the users had to say, a more explanatory approach looks at some of the major principles and moral values which the users use when legitimating their views. This considers why they choose specific policy options above other alternatives, and may also go some way towards illuminating the kind of citizenship status and welfare provision that they expect to enjoy in the future. This chapter then goes on to explore the extent to which it may be possible to account for the differing views of users by relating these to the philosophies of liberalism and communitarianism, while the penultimate section looks at some of the key findings of this study and discusses some of the implications that they may have in terms of New Labour's welfare reform agenda. Finally, a concluding comment is offered.

The state and welfare provision

A significant finding of the fieldwork that informs this book is that the users endorse a notion of citizenship which includes civil, political and social rights. It is clear that the social element (ie social rights) is seen as a valid and valued part of the citizenship package, and that the users believe that individuals who properly enjoy the status of 'citizen' should have a right to call on the state to provide an extensive range of services to meet their welfare needs. This is in line with evidence from other studies (Dean, 1999; Dean with Melrose, 1999; Dean and Melrose, 1996; Conover et al, 1991; Taylor-Gooby, 1991). Dean and Melrose (1996) report that for many, social rights are regarded as being as much a part of citizenship as civil and political rights, while a comparative study concerned with conceptions of citizenship rights in the United States and Britain goes a step further and notes that the majority of its British users had "no hesitation in according *primacy* to social rights" (Conover et al, 1991, p 808; author's emphasis). It is perhaps not surprising, therefore, that the view overwhelmingly endorsed by users in the present study was that the state should continue to have a centrally important role in meeting future welfare needs. This was particularly clear when healthcare and social security were being discussed; by contrast, when users were considering the state provision of housing, support was weaker and the range of responses offered by the users more diverse.

Partington (1994) may provide a valuable insight as to why this difference occurs. Healthcare and social security are areas of welfare that continue to be dominated by the direct provisions of the state. The financial costs of private services (or the required insurance premiums) effectively bar many of the users from the major alternative of purchasing provisions on the open market. The overwhelming majority of users, drawing largely on contributory or universalistic principles, looked, therefore, primarily to the state and its agents to directly meet their social security and healthcare needs. In contrast, an essential feature of housing provision is its "complexity and lack of homogeneity. Partly it is directly provided by the state, but predominately it is provided by private or quasi-public bodies subject to a wide variety of legislative measures" (Partington, 1994, p 126). One outcome of this situation is that there are, potentially at least, a variety of options which people in need of shelter can pursue. The varied opinions expressed in response to the question about which agency should take the lead in providing housing may be a reflection of the diverse characteristics of contemporary provision. More generally, the users' views seem to reflect not only some preference for extensive state involvement in the direct provision of welfare, but also the realities of how provision is differently organised in discrete areas of welfare and the real options open to people when trying to address their particular needs. This perhaps suggests that people's understandings and beliefs are likely to be confirmed or negotiated in the context of their daily experience.

Although the research found strong support for the state to maintain a leading role in the direct provision of welfare, this should not be taken as an indication of widespread satisfaction in the benefits and services currently offered. Much present state-led welfare provision is seen as inadequate. The users' accounts about this issue (many of which draw on personal experience) suggest that the present public provisions often fail to meet even essential needs. Similar findings are well documented elsewhere (Beresford et al, 1999; Beresford and Turner, 1997; Kempson, 1996; Cohen et al, 1992). The 'civilised life' that Marshall (1992) hoped social rights would help to facilitate remains for many a distant promise. Allied to these apparent deficiencies, the stigmatisation of social security claimants as 'scroungers' by both the workers in government agencies and elements of wider society remains a persistent concern. Such findings are reiterated in Dean and Melrose's (1999, pp 95-9) overview of the British Social Attitudes Survey (BSAS) data: a project that has been running annually since 1983. Dean and Melrose note that while approximately 50% of the population are supportive of a welfare state organised around redistributive principles (and that there is similar agreement about the potential stigma attached to claiming social security), they also point out that simultaneously approximately one third of the population may hold contrary views and are openly hostile to both the payment of public welfare benefits and claimants of those benefits. The most recent set of survey figures available (Bryson, 1997) appears to confirm the above.

In spite of the fact that the state has assumed a major role in providing welfare for the past 50 years, the private sector has also continued to flourish. Certainly raising the profile of private welfare, as an alternative to state welfare provision, has been an important aspect of the policies of recent governments. Attempts to reduce the amount of public revenue spent on the various aspects of welfare provision have often been accompanied by tax incentives for those who sought to make greater use of privately provided services (tax relief on private pensions, healthcare schemes and so on). The introduction of 'quasi-markets' (Le Grand and Bartlett, 1993) was partially justified as a means of introducing an element of fiscal responsibility to publicly provided welfare, while simultaneously enforcing some competition between providers in order to force down costs. In Britain, welfare has never been a simple question of exclusively either state or privately purchased provision, the relationship between the two sectors being more complex.

The users' opinions on privately purchased welfare seem to reflect this element of entanglement between public and private provision. In general, they are antagonistic towards moves to establish a welfare system in which individually purchased private provisions increasingly play a part, often to the detriment of collectively financed services. Attempts to impose a market mentality on the welfare state are regarded by the majority as having a detrimental effect on social rights. In healthcare, the imposition of internal markets was widely viewed as leading to increased bureaucracy while contributing little or nothing to the standard of care. When contemplating private welfare insurance and social security schemes, aside from the obvious question of cost, many feared that they would be excluded from such schemes as they would be deemed a 'bad risk' because of a lack of long-term secure employment and/or poor health. Recent research (Burchardt and Hills, 1997) appears to substantiate such views. When discussing housing, the denial of access to private rented property if in receipt of benefit was also a familiar occurrence for many of those users who had previously looked to private landlords to meet their housing needs. The majority strongly believe that private provision has inherently exclusive tendencies, and that it will not adequately serve their welfare needs or those of many other disadvantaged individuals and groups. It should be noted, however, that the users were not against private welfare *per se* (compare Dean with Melrose, 1999, p 96); indeed some had used it in the past and many hoped to be able to afford it in the future. What they objected to were the principles and practices of the market being imposed on public welfare provision. These are seen as being incompatible with both the substantive social rights and the notions of social justice that the users view as integral to their vision(s) of citizenship.

Conditional citizens?

Discussions concerning conditionality take us to one of the central issues of competing accounts of citizenship: the relationship between rights and responsibilities. When reconsidering the users' views on linking welfare rights to certain behavioural responsibilities, it is clear that strong disagreements exist. However, when comparing the three areas of welfare that are under scrutiny in this study (healthcare, housing, and social security), it is apparent that the degree to which the users are willing to accept the principle of conditional welfare rights depends extensively on the context of their imposition. In the area of healthcare the users overwhelmingly endorsed unconditional rights to treatment. Although they accept that individual behaviour may indeed be a contributory factor in certain cases of ill health, the majority, for two important reasons, view any attempt to deny care on the basis of individual lifestyle or habit as unacceptable. First, they view social, cultural and environmental conditions as relevant contributory factors in causing ill health. Second, it would appear from some of the users' comments that for doctors or other healthcare professionals to impose care sanctions on some types of behaviour but not others would be unfair, as such decisions would be based on largely arbitrary moral judgements rather than agreed clinical practices.

An unconditional right to healthcare on demand has, of course, never entirely been a constituent part of status of citizenship in Britain. Political rhetoric aside, the reality of finite financial resources means that doctors routinely take into account non-clinical factors when reaching decisions about the allocation of care to particular patients (Brazier, 1994). The ethical code of the General Medical Council notes,

> You must not allow your views about a patient's lifestyle, culture, beliefs, race, colour, sex, sexuality, age, social status, or perceived economic worth to prejudice the treatment you give or arrange.

And also,

> You must not refuse or delay treatment because you believe that patients' actions have contributed to their condition. (General Medical Council, 1995, p 5)

As Langan (1998a) points out, however, 'discrete rationing' decisions based on principles other than individual need (which include the denial of treatment because of individual behaviour or habit) that are contrary to the above ethical statement continue to be routinely made by some doctors and healthcare managers: an example perhaps of practice not reflecting adopted principles. Only a small minority of users condone such actions. For the majority, an unconditional right to treatment is one of the foundational principles on which they believe citizenship should be built. They would certainly strongly oppose Selbourne's (1994) view that individuals who engage in harmful activities should not be eligible for treatment.

Recently (1996), the BSAS has started to explore such issues and the initial findings make interesting reading. Judge et al (1997, p 64) report that significant numbers believe rationing and denial of treatment according to lifestyle/behaviour and/or age to already be established practice within the NHS. It should be noted, however, that the numbers who support such practice are considerably lower, and support varies according to the criteria which applied: some 39% believe that non-smokers should get priority over smokers. These findings obviously run counter to views expressed by the majority of users interviewed for this book; however, Judge et al's data also indicate that across the board a majority believe that healthcare decisions should not be made according to lifestyle criteria.

With reference the housing sector, in contrast to the above, the dominant view is that a closer link between welfare rights and responsibilities is appropriate. Users were unanimous in agreeing that individuals had a basic responsibility to behave in a reasonable manner towards their neighbours, and a clear majority believed that linking the right to housing to conditions such as PTPs and anti-social behaviour clauses was reasonable. Interestingly, support for conditionality in housing was significantly more widespread when it was linked to 'irresponsible behaviour' in what may loosely be termed a negative sense. That is, users felt that if a person repeatedly chose to ignore an agreement, and any subsequent warnings stating they could not engage in certain types of specified behaviour deemed to be anti-social, then it was justifiable to evict such persons. When the users were asked to consider if they thought it was reasonable to link the right to housing to a positive requirement that individuals agree to accept additional responsibilities, as is the case with MACs, support for conditionality was much less widespread. Roughly two thirds of the users dismissed MACs as unworkable, unnecessary and outdated. Young and Lemos' (1997) view that, at a local level, a sense of community could be regained via the introduction of such mutual aid agreements attracted only limited support.

Policies that linked the right to unemployment benefit to specified responsibilities attracted substantial support among the users, with more than half of those who took part in the study voicing their approval. These users stressed the positive potential of a conditional benefit regime in two ways. First, they believed that compulsory work/training could enhance the employment prospects of many individuals. Second, they believed that in return for a right to benefit it was reasonable, indeed desirable, that a community should expect a benefit claimant to accept specified training/work responsibilities; that is, that able-bodied individuals who received benefit should be expected to contribute in some positive way to the needs of the wider community. It was thought that this would help to counter the possibility of benefit provision creating a body of passive welfare dependants. The users who supported these views tended to see the causes of unemployment as being primarily related to the individual failings of claimants; consequently they supported conditionality in this context largely because they believed it would address those failings. Lazy individuals would effectively be forced into activity by benefit sanctions, while those 'genuine' claimants lacking the necessary skills for the jobs that were available would willingly accept a chance of retraining. The substantial minority who opposed conditional benefit regimes believed unemployment to be primarily the result of failings within the wider economy rather than failings of individual claimants. Such users, therefore, viewed the linking of unemployment benefit rights to specified responsibilities as being both punitive and inappropriate.

Three further issues that relate to conditionality are also worthy of comment in this conclusion. The first is the lack of extensive support for the introduction of a universal, unconditional Citizen's Income (CI) in place of current benefit arrangements. The idea of CI was generally rejected because it was seen as severing any link between rights and responsibilities. The users preferred that a form of Participation Income (PI) should be given only to those individuals who accepted that the right to PI carried with it certain reciprocal responsibilities. This suggests that the majority of users endorse a notion of citizenship in which access to social security payments is linked to an agreed concept of need (defined by some form of means test) and/or some generally accepted notion of desert. It would then be possible to take into account an individual's attempts to strive to better themselves or meet the needs of others in society, by contributing either financially or through unpaid voluntary or care work before granting entitlement to PI. Smith (1999) is in favour of this approach. He believes that PI has the potential to challenge the centrality of paid employment in underpinning current claims to many welfare benefits. Smith goes on to outline a strong philosophical justification for PI to be paid to lone parents on grounds of desert due first, to their acceptance of parenting/care responsibilities in often disadvantaged circumstances; and second because of lone parents'"valuable contribution to both economic and social sustainability" (Smith, 1999, p 325). His view that a "participation income [would] be paid to all those who participate in activities deemed to be socially useful – which would necessarily include caring for children" (Smith, 1999, p 328) appears to fit well with the users' outlook on this kind of benefit.

The second point to note is that the majority of those users who were asked about the possibility of extending a principle of conditionality to include the 'fiscal' and 'occupational' (Titmuss, 1958) welfare rights of the more affluent supported such moves. The only exception to this were the Middle Class Charity Group, who believed that in paying taxes and engaging in voluntary activities they already did enough to be counted as responsible citizens worthy of the fiscal and occupational welfare rights that the state endorses for more affluent citizens. At present the application of conditionality is, to borrow Deacon and Bradshaw's (1983) terminology, reserved for 'the poor'. Many of those users asked to consider this issue felt that it was unfair to selectively apply a principle of conditionality only within certain sectors of social welfare.

Third, financial conditionality (ie limiting public welfare entitlement according to some form of means test) was unpopular with an overwhelming majority of users. Respondents in the fieldwork believed that such tests were unfair in that they tended to penalise those who had previously met their responsibilities to wider society through past financial and social contributions. Research commissioned by the present government similarly notes, "[people] appeared to be uncomfortable with the idea of means-testing social security benefits in general and contributory benefits in particular" (Williams et al, 1999, p 2). In spite of such findings, it appears that the government continues to see means testing as an appropriate strategy

In drawing this discussion on conditionality to a close, it is worth restating the important point made earlier: that the degree to which the users are willing to endorse a principle of conditionality in the provision of welfare depends extensively on the context of its imposition. It should also be noted that while some users strongly support current policies which make the right to social housing and unemployment benefit highly conditional, they reserve the right to revoke their support if they consider future policies to be unjust.

Membership of the welfare community: legitimising exclusion, claiming inclusion

The distinction between undeserving/deserving recipients of social welfare has long exerted an influence throughout the development of social welfare in Britain (see Morris, 1998, 1994; Mann, 1992). It would appear that such distinctions remain a powerful contemporary theme for many of the users. When making judgements about the inclusion or exclusion of certain individuals from communal welfare arrangements, users' decisions often revolved round the contentious notion of desert.

When seeking to justify the exclusion of certain individuals from welfare rights (while simultaneously endorsing their own claims for inclusion), users resorted to the now familiar dialogues of contribution and individual behaviour. In many ways the arguments advanced are similar to those used by supporters of highly conditional welfare regimes.

This should not be surprising, as central to the whole conditionality issue is debate about whether or not it becomes justifiable to exclude those individuals deemed to have acted 'irresponsibly' from public welfare (Hewitt, 1997). Exclusion from a right to welfare was regularly justified in two ways: either because individuals engaged in what was considered by the users to be 'unacceptable' behaviour, or because of a lack of contribution to a community's welfare needs.

For example, in healthcare, the claims of immigrants and asylum seekers to a right to treatment are often rejected because, as outsiders from beyond the boundary of the nation state, they are perceived as having made no contribution to either the financial costs of the NHS or the wider needs of the nation. A recent opinion poll in *The Guardian* focusing on asylum seekers' rights to claim social security appears to confirm this exclusive approach: a majority of those polled believed the withdrawal of benefit rights to be appropriate (Travis and Ward, 1999). Conversely, it was widely viewed as unfair to exclude senior citizens from health services precisely because they are seen as having earned a right to care through previous contributions of both money and service[1]. Given that much public welfare is regarded as inadequate and the widely held view that resources are scarce, a substantial number of users argue that welfare rights should be limited to the individuals and families of those who had previously paid their dues, or were willing to contribute in the future. Such views may at first appear to be contradictory to the unequivocal endorsement of unconditional healthcare rights noted above. A consistency of argument can, however, be traced between these two apparently opposed positions. Support for the exclusion of certain groups or individuals from healthcare rights is consistent with the view that citizenship (welfare) rights should be limited to fellow citizens, that is, individuals who meet formal and/or informal 'rules' of membership. A large number of users, therefore, believe it to be perfectly acceptable to endorse unconditional healthcare rights for 'citizens', while simultaneously denying such rights to those whose claims were dismissed as invalid either because they could not or would not contribute. Similar views were expressed when social security and housing were discussed.

The belief that it was acceptable in both principle and practice to deny welfare rights to those who failed to show a measure of personal and communal responsibility was also a strong feature when users justified the exclusion of some people from rights to housing and social security. Those identified as unwilling to contribute in some way to the wider welfare needs of the community (ie through paid employment, taxes or unpaid care work) were deemed to be undeserving of social security.

Similarly, it was popularly believed that those who threatened the physical and mental security of their neighbours, or who disturbed the peace in a community, should have their right to housing within that community revoked.

In contrast, the minority of users who outlined a more expansive view of 'citizenship' drew on universalistic justifications to defend their more inclusive approach. Significantly, they tended to use arguments that stressed a guaranteed non-negotiable base line of welfare provisions available to all, rights rather than attendant responsibilities being the primary focus. The concept of universal needs rather than membership of a particular 'community of welfare' (and the acceptance of its specified rules) informed this outlook. They also believed that in many cases the exclusion of individuals from communal welfare arrangements because of past misdemeanours failed to solve any underlying problems and often created new ones. The 'outing' of convicted paedophiles is a good example with which to illustrate the conflicting views of the users on this issue. In the past, community disclosure about certain individuals has lead to communities resorting to violent vigilante behaviour in order to enforce what they hold to be a collective right to ensure their children's safety; indeed such actions are sometimes regarded as acceptable, given the type of offending that is involved. In reality, the forceful exclusion of paedophiles may create more problem than it solves. Individuals may 'go underground' or assume false identities, making them difficult to monitor in the future, and non-offenders may be mistakenly targeted; therefore a policy of outing certain offenders, which effectively removes a right to housing, may be counterproductive (Chartered Institute of Housing, 1998). It must be stated, however, that even those users who took a more universalistic approach generally accepted that individuals should be expected to behave in a responsible manner, not least by living within the law and contributing to the society in which they live, as and when they are able.

It seems that even among individuals who are heavily reliant on public welfare services a substantial number seek to endorse their own claims, or even sense of self-worth, by utilising discourses that attack other welfare recipients as undeserving. The exclusion of certain groups both within and beyond national boundaries has long been a principle on which the notion of citizenship is built (Lister, 1998a, 1997a; Twine, 1994). Significantly, it would appear that many of those who took part in the research are aware of this exclusionary dimension of citizenship, but they do not see such exclusion as problematic. A substantial number of users see the imposition of certain limits to welfare provision, and the exclusion that this implies, as a legitimate part of the citizenship package.

Liberals and communitarians: competing visions of citizenship

Walzer (1989) believes that normative accounts of citizenship can be divided into two distinct camps.

> "The first [communitarianism] describes citizenship as an office, a responsibility, a burden proudly assumed; the second [liberalism] describes citizenship as a status, an entitlement, a right or set of rights passively enjoyed. The first makes citizenship the core of our life; the second its outer frame. The first assumes a closely knit body of citizens, its members committed to one another; the second assumes a diverse and loosely connected body, its members (mostly) committed elsewhere." (Walzer, 1989, p 216)

The early chapters of this book looked at the competing communitarian and liberal philosophies and how they related to citizenship: five perspectives on citizenship and welfare were also then explored. It has been argued that the social component of citizenship in Britain is effectively undergoing a redefinition so that the state's role in meeting the welfare needs of its citizens is being reduced, while simultaneously ideas of individual and mutual responsibility are being emphasised. Consequently, individuals who fail to meet their defined responsibilities by behaving in a certain manner are excluded from collectively organised welfare provisions. At the level of competing ideologies about citizenship, links can be drawn between conditional welfare and a communitarian outlook, and unconditional welfare and an essentially liberal predisposition. An interpretation of the users' accounts of rights may help to generate an understanding of whether or not an essentially liberal (rights-based) or a communitarian (with an emphasis on responsibility) philosophy underpins their visions of welfare citizenship.

Throughout the research, the users' thinking can be interpreted as regularly invoking three differing principles in order to justify their right to welfare: these can be identified as a *universal* principle, a *contributory* principle and a *social assistance* principle. Let us take as an example discussions on a right to healthcare. Primarily, this was justified according to the first two principles, namely universalism and contribution. The former, as David's comment cited below illustrates, has at its core a universal right to treatment in which the needs of an individual override the issue of past contribution.

> "I was brought up to believe that the Health Service should be a universal service. It should be available to those who require those services, not dependant on their income. It should be dependant upon need." (David, Benefit Claimants Group)

When invoking a contributory principle, the users emphasised the previous payment of financial contributions and an understanding that in agreeing to fund collective health provision individuals then had a right to access such services as and when they required. Linda, for example, argues that she has a right to healthcare because,

> "I have worked all my life so I have paid in all my life." (Linda, Women's Benefit Claimants Group)

When considering whether or not it was reasonable for the state to levy a charge on individuals to offset the costs of dental work, prescriptions and so on, the users divided roughly into two camps: those who stated that all NHS treatments should to be free at point of service with contributions set at a level to ensure a universal right to 'free' treatment; and those who approved of selectively limiting the right to free (or subsidised) services to financially disadvantaged individuals. This indicates that a number of users approved of a social assistance principle and the application of a means test in certain areas of public health provision. For example,

> "Sorry, but I have to say this before I explode. I am supposed to have glasses, I have to pay £5.50 for my prescriptions and I cannot afford to go to the dentist and I cannot afford to go to the optician's for the simple reason that they do not take into account that some people's wages are just on the borderline, some are just living on the borderline.... I don't mind having to pay but there should be a grading system and I think that £5.50 for somebody on £20,000 a year is all right but we as people who are on a minimum wage should pay something like £2.50.... Have a certificate printed out by your employer saying this is their wage and so they only have to pay half the amount. It is not graded. It is just a set thing without consideration for other people. We are not all on the same pay but they seem to think that everybody has to pay exactly the same, and it is wrong." (Millie, Residents Group)

It should come as no surprise that the users made regular references which can be seen to reflect these three differing principles when discussing welfare, as much current public provision is organised according to these principles.

An emergent fourth principle, a principle of conditionality (effectively allied to the contributory principle already identified) in which eligibility to welfare rights is contingent on the acceptance of certain responsibilities, is of course a central focus of this book. As an organising principle of welfare it is one that sits happily alongside new communitarian concerns about the imbalance between rights and responsibilities and the detrimental moral effect that this is believed to have. In the areas of housing and social security provision it was a principle that attracted substantial support from the users. At first glance this support could be interpreted as the users embracing the communitarian concerns outlined by Etzioni (1997, 1995) and Selbourne (1994, 1993); however, this endorsement of conditionality can be more properly understood in many cases by reference to the users drawing on essentially liberal conceptions of citizenship.

Supporting the exclusion of anti-social or criminal individuals from local neighbourhoods might seem to be the most obvious example of illiberal behaviour by a community, but a closer look at the users' comments indicates that they often invoke the language of rights rather than responsibilities: an individual's right to live in peace, or a community's right to ensure the physical security of its members. Conditional housing rights can also be seen as an area where social rights are linked explicitly to the liberal notion of contract more usually associated with civil rights. Anti-social behaviour clauses, PTP and MACs are in fact legally binding contracts between landlords and tenants in which both parties ultimately have recourse to the courts. The exclusion of certain types of offenders from particular neighbourhoods is, of course, an example of communal rights dominating individual rights, but once again the users are quick to point out that it is the inadequacies of the criminal justice system in tackling persistent and/or dangerous offenders that forces issues of criminality, disorder and punishment (via the loss of a right to housing) into the realm of welfare.

The discussions on conditionality and exclusion further highlight the extent to which users tend to see rights in individualistic terms. To a great extent public welfare is viewed as a contract between the individual citizen and the state, in which individuals who keep their side of the bargain by making recognised contributions to a nation state's collectively organised welfare arrangements in return have a right to demand access to extensive provisions when required. Throughout the study individual contribution is the most prevalent principle used to justify the inclusion or exclusion of individuals from publicly provided welfare. It is particularly strong among those users who endorsed a highly conditional and exclusive view of welfare citizenship. Those in favour of conditionality believe that individuals who they deem to be unwilling or in certain cases unable to contribute to the common good should be denied access to welfare rights: the indolent because they will not contribute via paid work, and those beyond the nation's boundaries because they have not contributed. It should also be noted that those who outlined universalistic justifications of welfare rights (eg healthcare) regularly used the language of contribution to support their assertions. Evidence gathered in this study tends to support the claim (Dean, 1999, 1997; Dean and Melrose, 1998, Dean with Melrose, 1999; Dean, 1997; Conover et al, 1991) that while people continue to value and support the state led, collectively organised welfare provisions of the post war settlement, they tend to justify social rights by utilising a framework that is "contractual, individualistic, and closer to a liberal rather than a communitarian vision of citizenship" (Conover et al, 1991, p 811).

As previously noted, all the users believe that the state should be extensively involved in the provision of welfare. By endorsing extensive state welfare the users largely reject the libertarian liberal assertion (Nozick, 1995; Friedman, 1962; Hayek, 1960, 1944) that the state should play only a minor role in welfare provision. Although the discussions on financial conditionality and private provision illustrate that the users believe that the justice of the market has its place, that place is clearly not in public welfare. Indeed, many believe that individuals should be able to accumulate private property and assets to the best of their ability, and that the institutions of the welfare state should continue to extensively meet their welfare needs (eg long-term residential care for elderly citizens), even if individuals privately hold what amount to quite substantial financial assets (compare Williams et al, 1999). Again, users cite past contribution as the major factor that gives them a right to claim access to public services and provisions. As Millie's quote below emphasises, attempts to curtail those provisions are widely viewed as the state reneging on its side of the welfare deal.

"I think that it is wrong because they have worked all their lives, God, 60 or 70 years some of them and have paid to be in that home, state run homes for the elderly. The state should pay for it. Those people

have gone through wars and kept this country afloat through jobs.....
I think it is disgraceful, absolutely diabolical." (Millie, Residents Group)

The rejection of some ideas associated with libertarian liberalism begs the question of whether or not the users can be seen as supportive of the more egalitarian liberal/social democratic approaches that have previously been outlined (Miller, 1995; Rawls, 1995, 1971; Marshall, 1992; Plant, 1990). When stressing universalistic justifications for welfare rights, users can, to a large extent, be seen as endorsing an unconditional right to welfare and an expansive, inclusive notion of citizenship that gives priority to the meeting of basic universal human needs of citizens. Similarly, a social assistance principle again uses a notion of need (albeit a much more constrained understanding of need, usually tied to a means test) to judge specific claims to welfare. Support for both these principles can be seen as essentially egalitarian as they stress extensive and universality held rights that recognise a right to physical survival and a measure of individual agency (compare Doyal and Gough, 1991; Parry 1991).

A shift in emphasis occurs when users stress support for a contributory principle and/or a principle of conditionality. Issues of contribution, reciprocity and virtue (see the quotations from Plant [1998] in the conclusions to Chapter Three and Walzer [1989] at the beginning of this section) rather than needs become the overriding concern: an individual's rights in effect become contingent on their acceptance of additional responsibilities. These responsibilities may vary from an agreement to behave in a civil manner or accepting that individuals have a general duty to make a recognised contribution to wider society, to more specific responsibilities that tie access to specific social rights to certain specified tasks or forms of behaviour. It has already been argued that the widespread support for a contributory principle may be understood in terms of liberal ideas of contract; however, the endorsement of a principle of conditionality, and the exclusion that it implies, may more properly be seen as an assertion by some users that the communitarian project (with its emphasis on responsibilities rather than rights and its tacit acceptance of highly conditional welfare) has an important role to play in redefining the social element of citizenship.

An additional and related issue of concern for many social science accounts of citizenship from across the liberal and communitarian perspectives (eg Etzioni, 1995; Selbourne, 1994; Giddens, 1994; Roche, 1992) is the contested and ambiguous nature of the idea of 'responsibility'. The problems of perspectives of citizenship that place great emphasis on individual responsibility are best illustrated by a comment given by a lone parent during a focus group session.

> "Well, how can you be responsible on a low income. You have got to dodge and be a deviant to survive, haven't you? [laughter etc] I have been in the past, to survive, yes, and I think the biggest majority have to survive. I mean, there is deviants in all walks of life. Look at your millionaires, your tax evaders. We just try it on to know that we can put food in the kids' mouths, put clothes on their backs. Personally I would say with children – because I've had them and I've been there – my money would never stretch out from Monday to Monday. It would never ever stretch out so I was one of those that was deviant to survive. I'm not saying everybody is but a lot are. I would get a little job here, get a little job there, or do a bit of shoplifting – it's survival, isn't it?" (Molly, Lone Parents Group)

Molly argues that some lone parents, including herself, have effectively been forced to behave in what many would deem to be an 'irresponsible' manner because of inadequate benefits; interestingly she also draws a parallel with the tax evasion of the extremely wealthy, a type of irresponsible behaviour that is often judged to be less damaging than shoplifting or benefit fraud. It could also be argued that although Molly is acting illegally she is essentially acting in a responsible manner; as a mother she is using the only means at her disposal in order to ensure that her children are fed and clothed. Whether we view Molly's behaviour as responsible or irresponsible depends on the particular moral perspective we bring to bear in judging her behaviour. Accounts of citizenship that stress 'responsibility' do not offer the straightforward answers that some authors highlight. Dean with Melrose (1999, 1998) note that people make use of a complex mixture of competing moral repertoires as they try to make sense of the rights and responsibilities that citizenship entails. Similarly, Conover et al (1991) conclude that citizens draw on both liberal and communitarian frameworks in giving meaning to their accounts of citizenship. This study further illustrates the complex ways in which ordinary people construct their accounts of citizenship.

On the right track? New Labour and welfare citizenship

Within its broad remit to investigate citizenship and welfare, this research investigated three themes: provision, conditionality, and membership. Three key findings from the study that relate to these themes are listed as follows.

- There is a view that the state should continue to play a direct role in future welfare provision.
- The degree to which individuals are willing to accept the principle of conditional welfare rights depends substantially on the context of its imposition.
- A substantial number of citizens see the imposition of certain limits to welfare provision and, therefore, the exclusion of certain individuals, as a legitimate part of the citizenship package.

The New Labour government continues with its reform of the welfare state (see Chapters One and Three). Powell and Hewitt (1998) have noted that while in some areas the present government's social policies appear to be a continuation of its Conservative predecessors, in others New Labour have reversed or challenged the Conservative agenda. For example, New Labour appears generally comfortable with the idea of allowing the private or charitable sectors to take on some of the welfare provisions that were previously financed or provided directly by the state; at the same time, however, it has scrapped the nursery vouchers scheme, and released the money raised from council house sales to provide finance for social housing. In some other areas (the private finance initiative, the imposition of fees in higher education) it is noted that New Labour has "out-Toried the Tories" (Powell and Hewitt, 1998, p 8). Other commentators (Dean, 1999; Dean with Melrose, 1999; Heron and Dwyer, 1999; Lund, 1999; Driver and Martell, 1998; Dwyer, 1998; Lister, 1998a, b) have noted New Labour's comfortableness with the notion of conditionality: in several areas access to welfare rights is increasingly becoming dependent on citizens first accepting specified responsibilities. Recent statements from the Prime Minister indicate that he is happy to extend this conditional approach to welfare; moves are currently being considered to deprive young offenders who are in receipt of social security of 40% of their benefit if they fail to obey court orders (Brindle, 1999). It has previously been argued that, contrary to New Labour's assertions, such conditionality can lead to exclusive rather than inclusive outcomes. The revised rules for asylum seekers in regard to entry into Britain and access to welfare provisions, announced in the newly ratified 1999 Immigration and Asylum Act (Home Office, 1999a, b) further limit the potential for persecuted individuals from countries beyond Britain's borders to claim full social citizenship rights and, therefore, such rules promote exclusion rather than inclusion.

A comparison of the research's three key findings and New Labour's present welfare reform agenda provides some interesting insights. In terms of provision, New Labour's comfortableness with a reduced role for the state in the provision of welfare sits uncomfortably beside the users' endorsement of a dominant role for the state in the provision of welfare. When considering conditionality, the loudest voices within the focus groups could possibly be seen as a confirmation of the government's approach. In healthcare, access to most services remains, theoretically at least, unconditional; this strongly reflects the almost unanimous opinion of the users in this study. In housing, New Labour's view that a right to social housing should be linked to certain responsibilities on the part of the citizen closely mirrors the views of the majority of those interviewed. When considering social benefits (unemployment benefits in particular) conditionality proved to be a more contentious issue. As previously noted, a substantial minority of the users were deeply unhappy about the implementation of workfare type schemes; however, a small majority of users effectively welcomed the idea of New Labour's New Deal, with its emphasis on defined citizen responsibilities as well as rights[2]. It should be remembered, however, that for many users their support for a principle of conditionality was dependent on how it was applied in relation to particular groups and specific policies. With regard to the imposition of certain barriers in order to limit access to welfare, New Labour's approach could also be viewed as being in step with those users who believe that it is legitimate to restrict citizenship rights according to national boundaries. In common with those users who support conditional welfare rights, a lack of contribution is often highlighted as sufficient reason to exclude certain individuals (compare van Oorschot, 2000)[3]. The above discussion draws on some strong voices from within the welfare users' accounts presented in this research, but it should be stressed that other more expansive views of citizenship, based on principles of universalism and common entitlement, were also represented: a point emphasised by Dean and Melrose, who note,

> ... people have not necessarily rejected the idea of citizenship based
> on social rights and may feel betrayed by the extent to which
> conditionality and means testing have been replacing contributory

and universal principles of entitlement. (Dean with Melrose, 1999, p 99)

Certain of the above findings, most notably that outlining strong support (in some instances) for an exclusive notion of citizenship, could be seen as surprising, given that many users were themselves reliant on public welfare at the time of interview. The exclusive tendencies noted may also be indicative, however, of their personal experiences of welfare state institutions within recent years. It remains within the capabilities of governments, nevertheless, to influence thinking in more constructive directions via their policy agendas. It would be disappointing if New Labour's reform of the welfare state fails to grasp the more positive possibilities that such change may bring for both public welfare and citizenship. Brah (1992) has noted that,

> Structures of class, racism and gender and sexuality cannot be treated as independent variables because the oppression of each is inscribed within the other – it is constituted by and is constitutive of the other. (Brah, 1992, p 137)[4]

If citizenship is to be of future use in challenging such oppressions a more ambitious welfare project than the one being mapped out by New Labour will be required. It has been argued elsewhere (Lister, 1997a; Harrison, 1995) that an inclusive vision of citizenship, that attempts to combine an identification of different needs and voices under an umbrella that recognises the claims of individuals to universalistic treatment, may provide a more positive way forward.

Where New Labour can be accused of duplicity is in their claim to being involved in the construction of an inherently new and inclusive social policy. Rather than being a radical renewal of social democracy, as some (Giddens, 1998) would have us believe, the mythical Third Way has more in common with the politics of the right (Levitas, 1998). Many of New Labour's welfare reforms combine the paternalistic politics of what George and Wilding (1994) have labelled the 'Middle Way', with elements of New Right thinking and social policies.

As Mouffe (1988) indicates, the ways in which we define citizenship are indicative of the kind of society we aspire to and the values that underpin that vision. New Labour has made it clear that responsibilities rather than rights are central to their vision for social citizenship. For welfare service users, however, responsibility appears to cut both ways. Although many are comfortable, in certain circumstances, with the operation of a principle of conditionality (and it needs to be re-emphasised that the context of its application is an important factor in the respondents' approval/disapproval), this is accompanied by a strong belief that the state should not forget its own responsibility to take the lead in adequately meeting the welfare needs of its citizens. It should be noted, however, that the type of social citizenship currently being promoted by New Labour (which is apparently endorsed by many of those who took part in the study) is built largely on notions of conditional contract rather than universal entitlement: it is likely, therefore, to promote exclusion rather than inclusion. If the present New Labour government is serious about ensuring an inclusive system of public welfare that meets the diverse needs of all its citizens in the future, then it may need to rethink its current approach.

Concluding comment

The issues addressed in this study are complex and the voices represented diverse. The research draws on the experience of various groups of individuals, experiences that may be influenced by differing social locations and issues of gender, ethnicity, disability and age; however, two points need to be emphasised. First, is not claimed that the views presented are representative of all women, all disabled people and so on; such a claim lies beyond the remit of qualitative research and would ignore the real differences that often exist within such crude categories. Second, as indicated in the introduction, this book does not attempt to explore in detail how differences of gender, ethnicity, disability, and age may influence accounts of citizenship; each dimension warrants further study in its own right and should form the basis of future work.

The new welfare settlement currently being mapped out in Britain has both a reduced direct role for the state in the provision of welfare and a principle of conditionality at its core. The increasing application of a principle of conditionality once again marks the formal acceptance and approval of a deserving/undeserving distinction within public welfare arrangements. The view that the state should continue to have a major role in the direct provision of welfare is strongly endorsed by the overwhelming majority of the users who took part in this study. The question as to which values should underpin that role remains contested and highly controversial, but it is likely that welfare organised according to a principle of conditionality will promote exclusive rather than inclusive outcomes.

If the notion of social citizenship is to be developed beyond merely a formalised philosophical or political ideal into a substantive reality for all of Britain's citizens, then issues concerning the right to welfare need to be addressed. In this context, the twin questions of first, who provides welfare, and second, what are the terms and conditions attached to that provision, are of central importance. As the relationship between the individual citizen and the state is renegotiated, particularly within the welfare arena, this book attempts to allow a service user dimension to enter these debates about citizenship and welfare: debates which continue to be dominated by other powerful voices. It is not intended that this study should provide a definitive statement on how citizens view the notion of citizenship and its important welfare dimension; however, it is hoped that it goes some way to filling the "empirical void" (Conover et al, 1991) in which many of the sociological, political and philosophical discussions about citizenship and welfare continue to be conducted. Although the research involved a limited number of users, in one specific location, it is not too great a leap of faith to suggest that their insights may be of wider relevance in understanding how ordinary (British) citizens, particularly those who rely heavily on publicly provided welfare, make sense of both the relationships that are central to social citizenship and the competing values on which those relationships are built.

Notes

[1] For a further discussion of this point and wider concerns about senior citizens being denied health and long-term care, see the Age Concern report by Gilchrist (1999) and coverage in *The Daily Telegraph* by Laville and Hall (1999a, b).

[2] Disagreement among users about the principles behind (and the overall worth) of workfare type schemes in tackling unemployment are mirrored in academic debates. For example, Prideaux (1999) and Tonge (1999) are highly sceptical about their value in tackling social exclusion and unemployment. For more optimistic accounts of New Labour's New Deal refer to Oppenheim (1999) and Toynbee (1999).

[3] A recent Dutch survey into deservingness criteria and conditionality in public welfare notes,

> That when confronted with somebody asking for their support the Dutch public is likely to ask first: 'Why are you needy?', 'Are you one of us?', and 'What have you done or can you do for us?' (van Oorschot, 2000, p 43)

Van Oorschot (2000) also states that factors of 'control, identity and reciprocity' are central to how people make decisions about whether individuals deserve to

Bibliography

Acheson, D. (1998) *Independent Inquiry into Inequalities in Health*, London: The Stationery Office.

Ackers, L. (1998) *Shifting spaces: Women, citizenship and migration within the European Union*, Bristol: The Policy Press.

Adair-Toteff, C. (1995) 'Ferdinand Tonnies: utopian visionary', *Sociological Theory*, vol 13, no 1, pp 59-65.

Ahmad, K. (ed) (1982) 'Editors preface', in I. Taymiya [Translated by M. Holland] *Public duties in Islam: The institution of the hisba*, London: The Islamic Foundation, pp 5-11.

Ahmad, W.I. and Husbands, C. (1993) 'Religious identity, citizenship and welfare: the case of Muslims in Britain', *American Journal of Islamic Social Science*, vol 10, no 2, pp 217-33.

Alcock, P. (1985) 'Socialist security: where should we be going and why', *Critical Social Policy,* vol 5, no 1, pp 29-48.

Alcock, P. (1989) 'Why citizenship and welfare rights offer new hope for new welfare in Britain', *Critical Social Policy,* vol 19, no 2, pp 32-43.

Alder, J. and Handy, C. (1997) *Housing associations: The law of social landlords*, London: Sweet and Maxwell.

Allen, S. (1989) 'Women and citizenship: the British experience', Paper to the international conference, 'Women and Politics', Institute of Contemporary Living, Istanbul.

Andrews, G. (ed) (1991) *Citizenship*, London: Lawrence and Wishart.

Avineri, S. and de Shalit, A. (eds) (1995) *Communitarianism and individualism*, Oxford: Oxford University Press.

Bagguley, P. and Mann, K. (1992) 'Idle thieving bastards? Scholarly representations of the underclass', *Work, Employment and Society*, vol 6, no 1, pp 113-26.

Barbalet, J.M. (1988) *Citizenship*, Milton Keynes: Open University Press.

Barnes, C. (1991) *Disabled people in Britain and discrimination: A case for anti-discrimination legislation*, London: Hurst/BCODP.

Barnes, C. (1992) 'Institutional discrimination against disabled people and the campaign for anti-discrimination legislation', *Critical Social Policy*, vol 12, no 1, pp 5-22.

Barnes, C. and Mercer, G. (eds) (1997a) *Exploring the divide: Illness and disability*, Leeds: The Disability Press.

Barnes, C. and Oliver, M. (1995) 'Disability rights: rhetoric and reality in the UK', *Disability and Society*, vol 10, no 1, pp 111-16.

Barry, N. (1990) 'Markets, citizenship and the welfare state: some critical reflections', Part 2 of R. Plant and N. Barry, *Citizenship rights in Thatcher's Britain: Two views*, London: IEA.

Barton, L. (1993) 'The struggle for citizenship: the case of disabled people', *Disability, Handicap and Society*, vol 8, no 3, pp 235-48.

Bell, D. (1995) *Communitarianism and its critics*, Oxford: Clarendon Press.

Bell, C. and Newby, H. (eds) (1974) *The sociology of community*, London: Frank Cass and Co.

Bellamy, R. and Greenaway, J. (1995) 'The new right conception of citizenship and the citizen's charter', *Government and Opposition*, vol 30, no 4, pp 467-91.

Beresford, P. and Croft, S. (1986) *Whose welfare: Private care or public services*, Brighton: Lewis Cohen Urban Studies Centre Brighton Polytechnic.

Beresford, P. and Croft, S. (1995) 'It's our problem too! Challenging the exclusion of poor people from the poverty discourse', *Critical Social Policy*, vol 15, no 2/3, pp 75-96.

Beresford, P. and Turner, M. (1997) *It's our welfare: Report of the citizens' commission on the future of the welfare state*, London: NISW.

Beresford, P. and Wallcraft, J. (1997) 'Psychiatric system survivors and emancipatory research: issues, overlaps and differences', in C. Barnes and G. Mercer (eds) *Doing disability research*, Leeds: The Disability Press, pp 67-87.

Beresford, P., Green, D., Lister, R. and Woodard, K. (1999) *Poverty first hand: Poor people speak for themselves*, London: CPAG.

Bin Hamzah, M. and Harrison, M. (2000) 'Islamic housing values and perspectives: issues for influentials in Malaysia', RAPP Working Paper 1, *Islamic values, human agency, and social policies*, Leeds: Race and Public Policy Research Unit, Department of Sociology and Social Policy, University of Leeds.

Black, D., Morris, J., Smith, C. and Townsend, P. (1980) *Inequalities in health*, London: HMSO.

Blaikie, N. (1992) 'The relationship between ordinary language and sociological discourse', Paper to the International Conference of Social Science Method, University of Trento, Italy, 22-26 June.

Blaikie, N. (1993) *Approaches to social enquiry*, Cambridge: Polity Press.

Blair, T. (1995a) *Let us face the future*, 1945 anniversary lecture, Fabian Society Pamphlet No 51, London: The Fabian Society.

Blair, T. (1995b) 'The rights we enjoy reflect the duties we owe', Spectator lecture, Queen Elizabeth Conference Centre, Labour Party Press Release, 22 March, London: Labour Party.

Blair, T. (1996a) *New Britain: My vision of a young country*, London: Fourth Estate.

Blair. T (1996b) Speech to Singapore Business Community, 8 January, London: Labour Party.

Blair, T. (1997) Speech to Labour Party Conference, London: Labour Party.

Blair, T. (1998a) *The third way: New politics for a new century*, Fabian Society Pamphlet No 588, London: The Fabian Society.

Blair, T. (1998b) Speech to the Labour Party Conference, Blackpool, 29 September, London: Labour Party.

Blair, T. (1999a) *Beveridge lecture*, 18 March, London: Labour Party.

Blair, T. (1999b) 'Should the welfare state be reformed? The case for', *Guardian Unlimited on line*, 11 April.

Blunkett, D. (1998) 'New year, new deal, new hope', DfEE Press Release, 3 January, London: DfEE.

Bottomore, T. (1992) 'Citizenship and social class forty years on', Part 2, in T.H. Marshall and T. Bottomore, *Citizenship and social class*, London: Pluto Press, pp 55-93.

Bradford MDC (Metropolitan District Council) (1997) *Bradford in brief,* Bradford: Directorate of Corporate Services Research Services.

Brah, A. (1992) 'Difference, diversity and differentiation', in J. Donald and A. Rattansi (eds) *'Race', culture and difference,* London: Sage Publications/Open University Press, pp 126-45.

Brazier, M. (1994) 'Rights and healthcare', in R. Blackburn (ed) *Rights of citizenship,* London: Mansell, pp 56-74.

Brindle, D. (1999) 'Court order defaulters face 40% cut in benefits', *The Guardian,* 18 November.

Brown. G (1997) 'Responsibility in public finance', Speech by Shadow Chancellor of the Exchequer, London: Labour Party, 20 January.

Brubaker, W. (1989) *Immigration and the politics of citizenship in North America and Europe,* New York, NY: University Press of America.

Bryson C. (1997) 'Benefit claimants: villains or victims?', in R. Jowell, J. Curtice, A. Park, L. Brook, K. Thompson and C. Bryson (eds) *British social attitudes. 14 Report: The end of Conservative values?,* Aldershot: Ashgate/ Social and Community Planning Research, pp 73-85.

Buchanan, J.M. and Tullock, G. (1962) *The calculus of consent,* Michigan, MI: Michigan University Press.

Bulmer, M. and Rees, A.M. (eds) (1996) *Citizenship today,* London: UCL Press.

Burchardt, T. and Hills, J. (1997) 'Private welfare insurance and social security', *Social Policy Research Findings,* No 111, York: Joseph Rowntree Foundation.

Burkitt, B. and Ashton, F. (1996) 'The British stakeholder society', *Critical Social Policy,* vol 16, no 4, pp 3-16.

Byneo, I., Oliver, M. and Barnes, C. (1991) *Equal opportunities for disabled people: The case for a new law,* London: IPPR.

Cabinet Office (1999) 'What's it all about: Frequently asked questions', http://www.cabinet-office.gov.uk/seu/index/faqs.html, London: Cabinet Office.

Chartered Institute of Housing (1998) *Rehousing sex offenders: A summary of the legal and operational issues,* Coventry: Chartered Institute of Housing.

Clark, D.B. (1973) 'The concept of community: a re-examination', *Sociological Review*, vol 21, pp 403-4.

Clarke, C.M. and Kavanagh, C. (1996) 'Basic income, inequality and unemployment: rethinking the linkage between work and welfare', *Journal of Economic Issues*, vol 30, no 2, pp 399-406.

Clarke, J. (1996) 'The problem of the state after the welfare state', *Social Policy Review 8*, London: Social Policy Association, pp 13-39.

Clarke, J. and Langan, M. (1998) 'Review', in M. Langan (ed) *Welfare, needs, rights and risks*, London: Routledge/Open University Press, pp 259-71.

Cohen, R., Coxall, J., Craig, G. and Sadiq-Sangster, A. (1992) *Hardship Britain: Being poor in the 1990's*, London: CPAG.

CSJ (Commission on Social Justice) (1994) *Social justice: Strategies for national renewal*, London: Vantage/IPPR.

CSJ (1998) 'The UK in a changing world', in J. Franklin (ed) *Social policy and social justice*, London: IPPR/Polity Press, pp 11-36.

Conover, P.J., Crewe, I.M. and Searing, D.D. (1991) 'The nature of citizenship in the United States and Great Britain: empirical comments on theoretical themes', *Journal of Politics*, vol 53, no 3, pp 800-32.

Conservative Party (1996) 'Housing the nation', *Politics Today*, no 2.

Cook, D. (1998) 'Between a rock and a hard place: the realities of working on the side', *Benefits*, Issue 21, pp 11-15.

CPAG (Child Poverty Action Group) (1996) 'The Jobseeker's Act: its main provisions', *Welfare Rights Bulletin*, no 129, pp 6-9, London: CPAG.

Croft, S. and Beresford, P. (1989) 'User involvement, citizenship and social policy', *Critical Social Policy*, vol 15, no 2/3, pp 5-17.

Dahrendorf, R. (1994) 'The changing quality of citizenship', in B. Van Steenbergen (ed) *The condition of citizenship*, London: Sage Publications, pp 10-19.

Daly, G. (1997) 'Participatory citizenship and public accountability', Paper to the 'Citizenship for the 21st Century' Conference, University of Central Lancashire, 29 October.

Darling, A. (1998) 'Modernising the welfare state for the next millennium', DSS Press Release, London: DSS.

Darling, A. (1999) 'Opportunity for all', Speech at the launch of the government's first annual report on tackling poverty, Tower Hamlets, London, http://www.dss.gov/hq/press/1999/sep99/povspeech.htm.

Deacon, A. (1994) 'Justifying workfare: the historical context of the workfare debates', in M. White (ed) *Unemployment and public policy in a changing labour market*, London: PSI, pp 53-63.

Deacon. A (1996) (ed) *Stakeholder welfare*, Health and Welfare Unit, No 32, London: IEA.

Deacon, A. (ed) (1997a) *From welfare to work: Lessons from America*, Health and Welfare Unit, No 39, London: IEA.

Deacon, A. (1997b) 'Benefit sanctions for the jobless: "tough love" or rough treatment?', *Economic Report*, vol 11, no 7, Southbank House, London: Employment Policy Institute.

Deacon, A. (1998) 'The Green Paper on welfare reform: a case for enlightened self interest?', *Political Quarterly*, vol 69, no 3, pp 306-11.

Deacon, A. and Bradshaw, J. (1983) *Reserved for the poor: The means test in British social policy*, Oxford: Blackwell.

Deacon, A. and Mann, K. (1999) 'Agency, modernity and social policy', *Journal of Social Policy*, vol 28, no 3, pp 413-36.

Dean, H. (1996) *Welfare, law and citizenship*, London: Prentice Hall/Harvester Wheatsheaf.

Dean, H. (1997) 'Poverty, wealth and citizenship: popular paradigms and welfare values', Paper to the 'Citizenship and Welfare Fifty Years of Progress?' Conference, Ruskin College, Oxford, 18-19 December.

Dean, H. (1999) 'Citizenship', in M. Powell (ed) *New Labour, new welfare state? The 'third way' in British social policy*, Bristol: The Policy Press, pp 213-33.

Dean, H. and Khan, Z. (1997) 'Muslim perspectives on welfare', *Journal of Social Policy*, vol 26, no 2, pp 193-211.

Dean, H. and Melrose, M. (1996) 'Unravelling citizenship', *Critical Social Policy*, vol 16, no 3, pp 3-31.

Dean, H. and Melrose, M. (1998) 'Perceptions of poverty, wealth and citizenship', *Benefits*, January, issue 21, p 27.

Dean, H. with Melrose, M. (1999) *Poverty, riches and social citizenship*, Basingstoke: Macmillan.

Dean, H. and Shah, A. (1999) 'Muslim identity and welfare citizenship', Paper to the Social Policy Association Conference, London: Roehampton Institute, 19-21 July.

DoH (Department of Health) (1999) *Long term care: The government's response to the health committee's report on long term care*, Cm 4414, London: The Stationery Office.

Dolowitz, D. (1997a) 'British employment policy in the 1980s: learning from the American experience', *Governance: An International Journal of Policy and Administration*, vol 10, no 1, pp 23-42.

Dolowitz, D. (1997b) 'Reflections on the UK workfare system', *Review of Policy Studies*, vol 3, no 1, pp 3-15.

Doyal, L. and Gough, I. (1991) *A theory of human need*, London: Macmillan.

Driver, S. and Martell, L. (1997) 'New Labour's communitarianisms', *Critical Social Policy*, vol 17, no 3, pp 27-47.

Driver, S. and Martell, L. (1998) *New Labour: Politics after Thatcherism*, Cambridge: Polity Press.

DSS (Department of Social Security) (1998a) *Welfare reform focus files: The case for welfare reform*, London: DSS.

DSS (1998b) *New ambitions for our country: A new contract for welfare*, Green Paper, Cmd 3805, London: DSS.

DSS (1998c) 'A new contract for welfare', Statement to Parliament on the Welfare Reform Green Paper by the Minister for Welfare Reform, 26 March, London: DSS.

DSS (1998d) 'Darling reaffirms government commitment to helping pensioners', DSS Press Release, 25 September, London: DSS.

DSS (1999a) *Opportunity for all: Tackling poverty and social exclusion. Indicators of success: Definitions, data and baseline indicators*, London: DSS.

DSS (1999b) *Welfare Reform and Pensions Act: Chapter 30*, London: The Stationery Office.

DSS (1999c) *Long term illness and disability*, Fact sheet no 6, London: DSS.

Dworkin, L. (1995) 'Liberal community', in S. Avineri and A. de Shalit (eds) *Communitarianism and individualism*, Oxford: Oxford University Press, pp 205-23.

Dwyer, P. (1998) 'Conditional citizens? Welfare rights and responsibilities in the late 1990s', *Critical Social Policy*, vol 18, no 4, pp 519-43.

Dwyer, P. (2000) 'British Muslims, welfare citizenship and conditionality: some empirical findings', RAPP Working Paper No 2, *Islamic values, human agency, and social policies*, Leeds: Race and Public Policy Research Unit, Department of Sociology and Social Policy, University of Leeds.

ERAS (Employment Rights Advice Service) (1996) *News Brief No 41*, September/October, London: ERAS.

Etzioni, A. (1995) *The spirit of community: Rights and responsibilities and the communitarian agenda*, London: Harper and Collins.

Etzioni, A. (1997) *The new golden rule*, London: Profile Books.

Faulks, K. (1998) *Citizenship in modern Britain*, Edinburgh: Edinburgh University Press.

Ferge, Z. (1979) *A society in the making: Hungarian social and societal policy 1945-75*, Hammondsworth: Penguin.

Fido, J. (1977) 'The COS and social casework in London', in A. Donajgrodzki (ed) *Social control in 19th century Britain*, London: Croom Helm, pp 207-30.

Field, F. (1996) 'Making welfare work: the underlying principles', in A. Deacon (ed) *Stakeholder welfare*, Health and Welfare Unit No 32, London: IEA, pp 8-43.

Field, F. (1997) 'Consolidated financial insurance', Speech given to the Victoria and Albert Museum, DSS Press Release, 24 September, London: DSS.

Field, F. (1998) Personal statement to the House of Commons, 29 July, *Hansard*, London: The Stationery Office, 29 July.

Finch, J. (1993) 'It's great to have someone to talk to: ethics and politics of interviewing women', in M. Hammersley (ed) *Social research: Philosophy, politics and practice*: London: Sage Publications.

Finn, D. (1998) 'Welfare to work: a new deal for the unemployed', *Benefits*, Issue 21, pp 32-3, January.

Franklin. J. (ed) (1998) *Social policy and social justice*, London: IPPR/Polity Press.

Friedman, M. (1962) *Capitalism and freedom*, Chicago, IL: University of Chicago Press.

Furbey, R., Wishart, B. and Grayson, J. (1996) 'Training for tenants: citizens and the enterprise culture', *Housing Studies*, vol 11, no 2, pp 251-69.

General Medical Council (1995) *Duties of a doctor*, London: British Medical Association.

George, V. and Miller, S. (1996) *Social policy towards 2000*, London: Routledge.

George, V. and Wilding, P. (1994) *Welfare and ideology*, London: Harvester and Wheatsheaf.

Giddens, A. (1994) *Beyond left and right: The future of radical politics*, Cambridge: Polity Press.

Giddens, A. (1998) *The third way: The renewal of social democracy*, Cambridge: Polity Press.

Gilchrist, C. (1999) *Turning your back on us. Older people and the NHS*, London: Age Concern England.

Gilroy, P. (1992) 'The end of anti-racism', in J. Donald and A. Rattansi (eds) *'Race', culture and difference*, London: Sage/Open University Press, pp 49-61.

Glaser, B.G. and Strauss, A.L. (1970) 'Theoretical sampling', in N.K. Denzin (ed) *Sociological methods: A source book*, London: Butterworths, pp 105-14.

Gordon, D., Shaw, M., Dorling, D. and Davey-Smith, G. (eds) (1999) *Inequalities in health: The evidence presented to the Independent Inquiry into Inequalities in Health, chaired by Sir Donald Acheson*, Bristol: The Policy Press.

Gordon, P. (1989) *Citizenship for some? Race and government policy 1979-89*, Commentary no 2, London: Runnymeade Trust.

Green, D.G. (1996) *Reinventing civil society: The rediscovery of welfare without politics*, Health and Welfare no 17, London: IEA.

Gutmann, A. (1995) 'Communitarian critics of liberalism', in S. Avineri and A. de Shalit (eds) *Communitarianism and individualism*, Oxford: Oxford University Press, pp 120-36.

Hakim, K. (1987) *Research design: Strategies and choices in the design of research*, London: Routledge.

Harman, H. (1997) Speech at the launch of the Centre for Analysis of Social Exclusion, LSE, 12 November, DSS Press Release, London: DSS.

Harrison, M.L. (1995) *Housing, 'race', social policy and empowerment*, Aldershot: Avebury.

Hay, C. (1997) 'Blaijorism: towards a one-vision polity?', *Political Quarterly*, vol 68, no 4, pp 372-8.

Hay, C. (1998) 'That was then, this is now: the revision of policy in the modernisation of the British labour party, 1992-97', *New Political Science*, no 36, January.

Hayek, A. (1944) *The road to serfdom*, London: Routledge/Keegan Paul.

Hayek, A. (1960) *The constitution of liberty*, London: Routledge/Keegan Paul.

Heron, E. and Dwyer P. (1999) '"Doing the right thing": Labour's attempt to forge a new welfare deal between the individual and the state', *Social Policy and Administration*, vol 33, no 1, pp 91-104.

Hewitt, M. (1999) 'New Labour and social security', in M. Powell (ed) *New Labour, new welfare state? The 'third way' in British social policy*, Bristol: The Policy Press, pp 149-70.

Hill, D.M. (1992) 'The American philosophy of welfare: citizenship and the politics of conduct', *Social Policy and Administration*, vol 26, no 2, pp 117-28.

Hill, D.M. (1994) *Citizens and cities: Urban policy in the 1990s*, London: Harvester Wheatsheaf.

Hills, J. (1998) *Thatcherism, New Labour and the welfare state*, Paper 13, London: Centre for the Study of Social Exclusion.

Hobsbawm, E.J. and Ranger, T. (1983) *The invention of tradition*, Cambridge: Cambridge University Press.

Home Office (1997) *Crime and Disorder Act*, London: The Stationery Office.

Home Office (1997) 'New bill will deliver government's promise to tackle crime and disorder', Press Release, 3 December, London: Home Office.

Home Office (1999a) *Immigration and Asylum Act*, London: The Stationery Office.

Home Office (1999b) 'Immigration and asylum bill receives royal assent', Press Release, No 353/99, London: Home Office.

Hurd, D. (1988) 'Citizenship in Tory democracy', *New Statesman and Society*, 29 April.

Hutton, W. (1996) *The state we're in*, London: Vintage.

Hutton, W. (1997a) 'An overview of stakeholding', in G. Kelly, D. Kelly and A. Gamble (eds) *Stakeholder capitalism*, Basingstoke: Macmillan.

Hutton, W. (1997b) *The state to come*, London: Vintage.

Inland Revenue (1999) *Working Families Tax Credit: Better deal for working parents: Pass it on*, London: Inland Revenue.

Johnson, A. (1996) 'It's good to talk: the focus group and the sociological imagination', *Sociological Review*, vol 144, no 3, pp 517-38.

Jones Finer, C. (1997) 'The new social policy in Britain', *Social Policy and Administration*, vol 31, no 5, pp 154-70.

Jordan, B. (1988) 'The prospects for a basic income', *Social Policy and Administration*, vol 22, no 2, pp 115-23.

Jordan, B. (1998) *The new politics of welfare: Social justice in a global context*, London: Sage Publications.

Judge, K., Mulligan, J. and New, B. (1997) 'The NHS: new prescriptions needed?', in R. Jowell, J. Curtice, A. Park, L. Brook, K. Thompson and C. Bryson (eds) *British social attitudes. 14th report: The end of Conservative values?*, Aldershot: Ashgate/Social and Community Planning Research, pp 49-71.

Kearns, A.J. (1992) 'Active citizenship and urban governance', *Transactions of the Institute of British Geographers*, vol 17, no 1, pp 20-34.

Kemp, P.A. (1999) 'Housing policy under New Labour', in M. Powell (ed) *New Labour, new welfare state? The 'third way' in British social policy*, Bristol: The Policy Press, pp 123-48.

Kempson, E. (1996) *Life on a low income*, York: York Publishing Services/Joseph Rowntree Foundation.

Kennedy, H. (1992) 'Time for too many women', *The Independent*, 11 October.

Khan, M.A. (1982) 'Al-hisba and the Islamic economy', appendix in I. Taymiya (transl M. Holland) *Public duties in Islam: The institution of the hisba*, London: The Islamic Foundation, pp 135-48.

Khan, M.E., Anker, M., Patel., B.C., Barge, S., Sadhwani, H. and Kohle, R. (1991) 'The use of focus groups in social and behavioural research: some methodological issues', *World Health Statistics Quarterly*, vol 44, pp 145-9.

King, D.S. (1987) *The New Right: Politics, markets and citizenship*, Basingstoke: Macmillan.

Krueger, R.A. (1993) 'Quality control in focus group research', in D.L. Morgan (ed) *Successful focus groups: Advancing the state of the art*, London: Sage Publications, pp 65-85.

Krueger, R.A. (1994) *Focus groups: A practical guide for applied research*, London: Sage Publications.

Kymlicka, W. (1992) *Contemporary political philosophy: An introduction*, Oxford: Oxford University Press.

Kymlicka, W. (1995) 'Liberal individualism and liberal neutrality', in S. Avineri and A. de Shalit (eds) *Communitarianism and individualism*, Oxford: Oxford University Press, pp 165-85.

Labour Party (1994) *Jobs and social justice*, London: Labour Party.

Labour Party (1996) *Protecting our communities*, London: Labour Party.

Labour Party (1997) *Leading Britain into the future*, London: Labour Party.

Langan, M. (1998a) 'Rationing healthcare', in M. Langan (ed) *Welfare, needs, rights and risks*, London: Routledge/Open University Press, pp 35-79.

Langan, M. (ed) (1998b) *Welfare, needs, rights and risks*, London: Routledge/Open University Press.

Laville, S. and Hall, C. (1999a) 'Elderly patients left starving to death on the NHS', *The Daily Telegraph*, 6 December, p 1.

Laville, S and Hall, C. (1999b) 'NHS and the elderly', *The Daily Telegraph*, 6 December, pp 10-11.

Law, I., Hylton, C., Karmani, A. and Deacon, A. (1994) *Racial equality and social security service delivery: A study of the perceptions and experiences of black minority ethnic people eligible for benefit in Leeds*, Working Paper 10, Leeds: Department of Sociology and Social Policy, University of Leeds/ Joseph Rowntree Foundation.

Le Grand, J. (1997) 'Knights, knaves or pawns? Human behaviour and social policy', *Journal of Social Policy*, vol 26, no 2, pp 149-69.

Le Grand, J. and Bartlett, W. (eds) (1993) *Quasi-markets and social policy*, Basingstoke: Macmillan.

Lewis, G. (1998) 'Citizenship', in G. Hughes (ed) *Imagining welfare futures*, London: Routledge/Open University, pp 103-50.

Levitas, R. (ed) (1986) *The ideology of the new right*, Cambridge: Polity Press.

Levitas, R. (1996) 'The concept of social exclusion and the new Durkheimian hegemony', *Critical Social Policy*, vol 16, no 1, pp 5-20.

Levitas, R. (1998) *The inclusive society? Social exclusion and New Labour*, Basingstoke: Macmillan.

Lister, R. (1990a) *The exclusive society: Citizenship and the poor*, London: CPAG.

Lister, R. (1990b) 'Women, economic dependency and citizenship', *Journal of Social Policy*, vol 19, no 4, pp 445-67.

Lister, R. (1993) 'Welfare rights and the constitution', in A. Barnett et al (eds) *Debating the constitution*, London: Charter 88/Polity Press.

Lister, R. (1997a) *Citizenship: Feminist perspectives*, Basingstoke: Macmillan.

Lister, R. (1997b) 'Citizenship: towards a feminist synthesis', *Feminist Review*, vol 57, pp 28-48.

Lister, R. (1997c) 'From fractured Britain to one nation? The policy options of welfare reform', Paper to Annual Conference of the Social Policy Association, University of Lincolnshire and Humberside, Lincoln, 15 July.

Lister, R. (1998a) 'Vocabularies of citizenship and gender: the UK', *Critical Social Policy*, vol 18, no 3, pp 309-33.

Lister, R. (1998b) 'From equality to social exclusion: New Labour and the welfare state', *Critical Social Policy*, vol 18, no 2, pp 215-25.

Lister, R. (1998c) 'Principle of welfare', in P. Alcock, A. Erskine and M. May (eds) *The student's companion to social policy*, Oxford: Blackwell Publishers Limited, pp 214-20.

Lukes, S. (1973) *Individualism*, Oxford: Basil Blackwell.

Lund, B. (1999) 'Ask not what the community can do for you: obligations, New Labour and welfare reform', *Critical Social Policy*, vol 19, no 4, pp 447-62.

MacIntyre, A. (1995) 'Justice as a virtue', in S. Avineri and A. de Shalit (eds) *Communitarianism and individualism*, Oxford: Oxford University Press, pp 51-64.

MacKain, S. (1998) 'The citizen's new clothes: care in a Welsh community', *Critical Social Policy*, vol 18, no 1, pp 27-50.

Major, J. (1991) *Citizen's charter: Raising the standard*, Cm 1599, London: HMSO.

Mandelson, P. (1997) *Labour's next steps: Tackling social exclusion*, Fabian Society Pamphlet No 581, London: The Fabian Society.

Mann, K. (1992) *The making of an English 'underclass'*, Buckingham: Open University Press.

Mann, M. (1987) 'Ruling class strategies and citizenship', *Sociology*, vol 21, no 3, pp 339-54.

Marshall, T.H. (1965) *Social policy*, London: Hutchinson University Library.

Marshall, T.H. (1985) *The right to welfare*, London: Heinemann Educational Books.

Marshall, T.H. (1992) 'Citizenship and social class', Part 1 in T.H. Marshall and T. Bottomore, *Citizenship and social class*, London: Pluto Press, pp 3-51.

Marsland, D. (1992) 'The roots and consequences of paternalistic collectivism: Beveridge and his influence', *Social Policy and Administration*, vol 26, no 2, pp 144-51.

Marsland, D. (ed) (1995) *Self reliance: Reforming welfare in advanced societies*, London: Transaction Publishers.

Marsland, D. (1996) *Welfare or welfare state?*, London: Macmillan.

Mason, D. (1995) *Race and ethnicity in Britain*, Oxford: Oxford University Press.

Mason, J. (1996) *Qualitative researching*, London: Sage Publications.

Mead, L.M. (1982) 'Social programs and social obligations', *Public Interest*, no 69, Fall, pp 17-39.

Mead, L.M. (1986) *Beyond entitlement*, New York, NY: Free Press.

Mead, L.M. (1997a) 'From welfare to work: lessons from America', in A. Deacon (ed) *From welfare to work: Lessons from America*, London: IEA, pp 1-55.

Mead, L.M. (1997b) 'Citizenship and social policy: T.H. Marshall and poverty', *Social Philosophy and Social Policy*, vol 14, no 2, pp 197-230.

Mead, L.M. (ed) (1997c) *The new paternalism: Supervisory approaches to poverty*, Washington, DC: The Brookings Institute.

Meikle, J. (1994) 'Patten castigates young for apathy to country and community', *The Guardian*, 6 May.

Miles, M.B. and Hubermann, M. (1994) *Qualitative data analysis: An expanded sourcebook*, London: Sage Publications.

Miller, D. (1995) 'Community and citizenship', in S. Avineri and A. de Shalit (eds) *Communitarianism and individualism*, Oxford: Oxford University Press, pp 85-100.

Milne, S. and Thomas, R. (1997) 'Welfare to work sets tough terms', *The Guardian*, 6 April.

Modood, T. (1998) 'Racial equality: colour, culture and difference', in J. Franklin (ed) *Social policy and social justice*, London: IPPR/Polity Press, pp 167-81.

Modood, T. (1992) *Not easy being British: Colour, culture and citizenship*, London: R.T. Trentham.

Morgan, D.L. (1988) *Focus groups as qualitative research*, London: Sage Publications.

Morgan, D.L. (ed) (1993) *Successful focus groups, advancing the state of the art*, London: Sage Publications.

Morris, L. (1994) *Dangerous classes: The underclass and social citizenship*, London: Routledge.

Morris, L. (1998) 'Legitimate membership of the welfare community', in M. Langan (ed) *Welfare, needs, rights and risks*, London: Routledge/Open University Press, pp 215-57.

Mouffe, C. (1988) 'The civics lesson', *New Statesman and Society*, no 1, pp 28-31.

Mullard, C. (1979) *Black Britain*, London: Allen and Unwin.

Murray, C. (1984) *Loosing ground*, New York, NY: Basic Books.

Murray, C. (1996) 'The emerging British underclass', and 'Underclass: the crisis deepens', in R. Lister (ed) *Charles Murray and the underclass: The developing debate*, London: IEA, pp 22-53, 99-135.

Murray, C. (1999) *The underclass revisited*, Washington, DC: American Institute for Public Policy Research, http://www.aei.org/ps/psmurray.htm.

NHF (National Housing Federation) (1996) *A guide to the Housing Act 1996*, London: NHF.

Novak, T. (1997) 'Hounding delinquents: the introduction of the jobseeker's allowance', *Critical Social Policy*, vol 17, no 1, pp 99-111.

Nozick, R. (1995) 'Distributive justice', in S. Avineri and A. de Shalit (eds) *Communitarianism and individualism*, Oxford: Oxford University Press, pp 137-50.

Oakshott, M. (1975) *On human conduct*, Oxford: Oxford University Press.

Oliver, D. (1991) 'Active citizenship in the 1990s', *Parliamentary Affairs*, vol 44, no 2, pp 157-72.

Oliver, D. and Heater, D. (1994) *The foundations of citizenship*, London: Harvester Wheatsheaf.

Oliver, M. (1996) *Understanding disability: From theory to practice*, Basingstoke: Macmillan.

Oliver, M. and Barnes, C. (1991) 'Discrimination, disability and welfare: from needs to rights', in I. Byneo, M. Oliver and C. Barnes, *Equal opportunity for disabled people: The case for a new law*, London: IPPR, pp 7-16.

Oliver, M. and Barnes, C. (1998) *Disabled people and social policy: From exclusion to inclusion*, London: Longman.

ONS (1998) *Social Trends 28* (1998) London: The Stationery Office.

Oppenheim, C. (1999) 'Welfare reform and the labour market – a third way?', *Benefits*, issue 25 April/May, pp 1-5.

Page, R. (1997) 'Caring for strangers: can the altruistic welfare state survive?', Paper presented at 'Citizenship and the Welfare State: Fifty Years of Progress?' Conference, Ruskin College, Oxford, 18-19 December.

Parry, G. (1991) 'The paths to citizenship', in U. Vogel and M. Moran (eds) *The frontiers of citizenship*, Basingstoke: Macmillan.

Partington, M. (1994) 'Citizenship and housing', in R. Blackburn (ed) *Rights of citizenship*, London: Mansell, pp 124-38.

Pateman, C. (1992) 'Patriarchal welfare state', Article 6.2 in L. McDowell and R. Pringle (eds) *Defining women: Social institutions and gender difference*, Cambridge: Polity Press/Open University Press, pp 223-45.

Paton, C. (1999) 'New Labour's health policy: the new healthcare state', in M. Powell (ed) *New Labour, new welfare state? The 'third way' in British social policy*, Bristol: The Policy Press, pp 51-76.

Plant, R. (1978) 'Community: concept, conception and ideology', *Politics and Society*, no 8, pp 50-107.

Plant, R. (1988) *Citizenship, rights and socialism*, London: The Fabian Society.

Plant, R. (1990) 'Citizenship and rights', Part 1 in R. Plant and N. Barry, *Citizenship rights in Thatcher's Britain: Two views*, London: IEA.

Plant, R. (1992) 'Citizenship rights and welfare', in A. Coote (ed) *The welfare of citizens: Developing social rights*, London: IPPR, pp 15-30.

Plant, R. (1998) 'So you want to be a citizen?', *New Statesman*, 6 February, pp 30-2.

Powell, M. (ed) (1999) *New Labour, new welfare state? The 'third way' in British social policy*, Bristol: The Policy Press.

Powell, M. and Hewitt, M. (1997) 'Towards measuring social citizenship', Paper to the 'Citizenship and Welfare: Fifty Years of Progress?' Conference, Ruskin College, Oxford, 18-19 December.

Powell, M. and Hewitt, M. (1998) 'The end of the welfare State?', *Social Policy and Administration*, vol 32, no 1, pp 1-13.

Prideaux, S. (1999) 'New Labour: the Trojan horse of functionalism and North American social policy', Unpublished dissertation, Leeds: Department of Sociology and Social Policy, University of Leeds.

Purdy, D. (1994) 'Citizenship, basic income and the state', *New Left Review*, no 208, pp 30-48.

Rawls, J. (1971) *A theory of justice*, London: Oxford University Press.

Rawls, J. (1995) 'Justice as fairness: political not metaphysical', in S. Avineri and A. de Shalit (eds) *Communitarianism and individualism*, Oxford: Oxford University Press, pp 186-204.

Rees, A.M. (1995a) 'The promise of social citizenship', *Policy & Politics*, vol 23, no 4, pp 313-25.

Rees, A.M. (1995b) 'The other T.H. Marshall', *Journal of Social Policy*, vol 24, no 3, pp 341-62.

Roche, M. (1987) 'Citizenship, social theory and social change', *Theory and Society*, vol 16, pp 363-99.

Roche, M. (1992) *Rethinking citizenship: Welfare, ideology and change in modern society*, Cambridge: Polity Press.

Roseneil, S. and Mann, K. (1994) 'Some mothers do 'ave 'em: backlash and gender politics of the underclass debate', *Journal of Gender Studies*, vol 3, no 3, pp 317-31.

Sacks, J. (1997) *The politics of hope*, London: Jonathan Cape.

Sandel, M. (1995) 'The procedural republic and the unencumbered self', in S. Avineri and A. de Shalit (eds) *Communitarianism and individualism*, Oxford: Oxford University Press, pp 12-18.

Selbourne, D. (1993) 'Civic duty first or we drown', *The Independent*, 25 November.

Selbourne, D. (1994) *The principle of duty*, London: Sinclair Stevenson.

Shelter (1998) 'Fast facts: the comprehensive spending review', *Roof*, July/August.

Smith, A. (1776) *An enquiry into the nature and causes of the wealth of nations*, Edinburgh: Adam and Charles Black.

Smith, S.R. (1999) 'Arguing against cuts in lone parent benefits: reclaiming the desert ground in the UK', *Critical Social Policy*, vol 19, no 3, pp 313-34.

Spencer, I.R.G. (1997) *British immigration policy since 1939: The making of multiracial Britain*, London: Routledge.

Stacey, J. (1998) 'The right family values', in C. Yo and M. Schwarz (eds) *Social policy and the conservative agenda*, London: Blackwell.

Stanton, A. (1989) *Invitation to self-management*, Middlesex: Dab Hand Press.

Stepney, P., Lynch, R. and Jordon, B. (1999) 'Poverty, social exclusion and New Labour', *Critical Social Policy*, vol 19, no 1, pp 109-27.

Stewart, D. W. and Shamdasani, P.N. (1990) *Focus groups: Theory and practice*, London: Sage Publications.

Stone, E. and Priestly, M. (1996) 'Parasites, pawns and partners: disability research and the role of researchers', *British Journal of Sociology*, vol 47, no 4, pp 699-716.

Tam, H. (1998) *Communitarianism: A new agenda for politics and citizenship*, Basingstoke: Macmillan.

Taylor, D. (1989) 'Citizenship and social power', *Critical Social Policy*, vol 15, no 2/3, pp 19-30.

Taylor, C. (1995) 'Atomism', in S. Avineri and A. de Shalit (eds) *Communitarianism and individualism*, Oxford: Oxford University Press, pp 29-50.

Taylor-Gooby, P. (1991) 'Attachment to the welfare state', in R. Jowell et al (eds) *British social attitudes: 8th report*, Aldershot: Social and Community Planning Research/Dartmouth Publishing Group, pp 23-42.

Taymiya, I. (1982) (transl by M. Holland) *Public duties in Islam: The institution of the hisba*, London: The Islamic Foundation.

Teles, S.M. (1996) *Whose welfare? The AFDC and elite politics*, Kansas, MO: University of Kansas Press.

Thatcher, M. (1988) Speech to the Church of Scotland, in J. Raban (1989) *God, man and Mrs Thatcher*, London: Chatto and Windus, May.

Theodore, N. and Peck, J. (1999) 'Welfare-to-work: national problems, local solutions?', *Critical Social Policy*, vol 19, no 4, pp 485-510.

Thomas, R. and Wintour, P. (1998) 'Labour to means-test the disabled', *The Observer*, 4 October.

Titmuss, R.M. (1958) 'The social division of welfare', in R.M. Titmuss, *Essays on the welfare state*, London: Allen and Unwin, pp 34-55.

Tonge, J. (1999) 'New packaging, old deal? New Labour and employment policy innovation', *Critical Social Policy*, vol 19, no 2, pp 217-32.

Tonnies, F. (1955) *Community and association*, London: Routledge and Paul.

Toynbee, P. (1999) 'A very good deal', *The Guardian*, 26 November, p 23.

Travis, A. and Ward, L. (1999) 'Backing to end benefits for asylum seekers', *The Guardian*, 9 February.

Turner, B.S. (1986) *Equality*, London: Tavistock.

Twine, F. (1994) *Citizenship and social rights: The interdependence of self and society*, London: Sage Publications.

van Oorschot, W. (2000) 'Who should get what and why? On deservingness criteria and the conditionality of solidarity among the public', *Policy & Politics*, vol 28, no 1, pp 33-48.

Vogel, U. (1991) 'Is citizenship gender-specific?', in U. Vogel and M. Moran (eds) *The frontiers of citizenship*, Basingstoke: Macmillan, pp 8-85.

Vogel, U. and Moran, M. (eds) (1991) 'Introduction', in U. Vogel and M. Moran, *The frontiers of citizenship*, London: Macmillan.

Walby, S. (1994) 'Is citizenship gendered?', *Sociology*, vol 28, no 3, pp 379-95.

Walker, D. (1999) 'Rationing: calling the shots on health', *The Guardian*, 26 January, pp 13-14.

Walzer, M. (1989) 'Citizenship', in T. Ball, J. Farr and R.L. Hanson (eds) *Political innovation and conceptual change*, Cambridge: Cambridge University Press, pp 211-20.

Walzer, M. (1995) 'Membership', in S. Avineri and A. de Shalit (eds) *Communitarianism and individualism*, Oxford: Oxford University Press, pp 65-84.

Wetherly, P. (1996) 'Basic needs and social policies', *Critical Social Policy*, vol 16, no 1, pp 45-65.

White, M. (1999) 'PM's deadline to end child poverty', *The Guardian*, 19 March.

White, S. (1998) 'Interpreting the "third way": not one road but many', *Renewal*, vol 6, no 2, pp 17-30.

Wilding, P. (1997) 'The welfare state and the Conservatives', *Political Studies*, vol 45, no 4, pp 716-26.

Wilkinson, M. (1999) 'Lots of carrot and a bit of stick', *Disability Now*, November edition, p 12.

Williams, F. (1992) 'Somewhere over the rainbow: universalism and diversity in social policy', in N. Manning and R. Page, *Social Review 4*, London: Social Policy Association.

Williams, F. (1996) 'New thinking on social policy research into inequality, poverty and social exclusion', Unpublished manuscript.

Williams, L. (1995) 'Rights not charity', Chapter 14, in H. McConchie and P. Zinkin (eds) *Disability programmes in the community: Disabled children in developing countries*, London: Mackeith Press, pp 214-18.

Williams, T., Hill, M. and Davies, R. (1999) *Attitudes to the welfare state and response to reform*, Research Report No 88, London: DSS.

Wilson, M. (1997) 'Citizenship and welfare', in M. Lavalette and A. Pratt (eds) *Social policy: A conceptual and theoretical introduction*, London: Sage Publications, pp 182-95.

Young, M. and Lemos, G. (1997) *The communities we have lost and can regain*, London: Lemos and Crane.

Appendix: Methods and methodology

Methodological considerations: an abductive approach

An important aim of the research was to gain insight into the views of some 'ordinary citizens' and to allow their opinions to become part of ongoing social science and political debates about the reform of the welfare element of British citizenship. An abductive research strategy (see Mason, 1996; Blaikie, 1993, 1992) within what may broadly be defined as an interpretative/qualitative research approach was, therefore, particularly relevant to the study. The abductive approach, defined as,

> ... the process used to produce social science accounts of social life by drawing on the concepts and meanings used by social actors and the activities in which they engage. (Blaikie, 1993 p 176)

offers the possibility of moving backwards and forwards between lay and social science accounts. It begins by seeking to discover and describe the way the social world is experienced and perceived from the 'inside' by developing an understanding of the insider views, moves across to social science ('outsider') accounts, and aims ultimately to form a more comprehensive understanding of the social world by developing or amending social science accounts that take lay explanations seriously. It is a layered process that Blaikie (1993, p 177) summarises as follows:

> *Every day concepts and meanings*
> provide the basis for
> *Social action/interaction*
> about which
> *Social actors can give accounts*
> from which
> *Social science descriptions can be made*
> from which
> OR
> and understood in terms of
> *Social theories can be generated Social theories and perspectives*

It is in the process of moving from lay descriptions of social life, to technical descriptions of social life, that the notion of abduction is applied. (Blaikie, 1993 p 177)

Ontological and epistemological concerns

The research is fundamentally geared towards getting at 'lay' (ie welfare service user) accounts of experiences and attitudes to citizenship and welfare and relating them to the understandings generated by social science. The ontological position on which the research is based is, therefore, one which recognises that the differing experiences, attitudes, perceptions and accounts of various groups are relevant and meaningful constituent elements of social reality that are suitable for further investigation. Epistemological concerns about how the research could then go on to gain insights into the social worlds of citizens' guided the choice of method that was utilised in the field work. As Hakim (1987) has stated, qualitative research is "concerned with people's own accounts of situations and events, with reporting their perspectives and feelings", (1987, p 8); this fits well with the intended field investigations which seek to explore such accounts. It should be noted that the respondents used terms such as 'citizenship' and 'citizen' on very few occasions during the discussions; however, the integrated research strategy and the fieldwork questions were designed to allow the researcher to interpret their responses and relate them to the issues of citizenship and welfare under investigation.

Ethics

As both Mason (1996) and Miles and Hubermann (1994) stress, ethical considerations are an important aspect of qualitative research. From the outset an awareness of this aspect of the research process informed the study. Several ethical dilemmas were identified and it was decided that the two basic principles of informed consent and confidentiality would underpin the approach to the fieldwork (see Miles and Hubermann, 1994, pp 291-3). In practical terms this led to the development of a short introductory session that preceded every focus group. After initially thanking everybody for attending the interview, time was taken to personally introduce both the moderator and his assistant (when present) and a full explanation of the research was offered. It was explained that the fieldwork was part of a PhD project, that it was concerned with three areas of welfare provision, and that it was interested in getting at service user views on the provision of services, the fit between rights and responsibilities, and issues about inclusion and exclusion from welfare rights. The respondents were then given the opportunity to pose any questions or queries that they might have, and it was stressed that people were free to leave at that point or at any time during the session if they felt uncomfortable or they had other commitments[1]. It was then explained that they would shortly be asked for some basic autobiographical background information, but that if they did not want to offer certain personal details to either the researchers and/or the group it was perfectly acceptable to withhold them. The issue of confidentiality was then raised and it was explained that first names only were required and that respondents were free to use an assumed name if they wished.

An emancipatory approach?

In recent years much has been written on participatory and emancipatory research methods (Beresford and Turner, 1997; Stone and Priestly, 1996; Oliver, 1996; Stanton, 1989) in which the notions of empowerment and reciprocity are seen as fundamental to the act of research (Oliver, 1996). In several ways the ethical decisions about the aims of the study and the method of enquiry were influenced by the above approaches. The focus group method was chosen in part because of its relatively informal style, and because the numbers involved were seen as a potential challenge to the social/power relationships that are part of the research process; and similarly, the respondents were encouraged to view themselves as important participants rather than mere subjects of research.

Johnson takes the view that (radical) focus groups offer the potential to "blend different kinds of expert knowledge – tacit and everyday with scientific and theoretical – [with the ability] to empower and foster social change" (Johnson, 1996 p 536). It is perhaps his former claim about different kinds of knowledge that is most appropriate to this study. In spite of a research strategy that holds that the opinions of ordinary citizens are a fundamentally important, if often overlooked, part of contemporary citizenship and welfare debates, it is realistic to emphasise the study's limited emancipatory potential. Given the small amount of contact time between the researcher and the respondents and the probable limited future impact of the research on policy, any claim to 'empower and foster social change' on a significant level is, in this instance, too grandiose.

The focus group method

Beyond Johnson's (1996) positive appraisal, others (Kruegar, 1994; Morgan, 1993, 1988; Khan et al, 1991; Stewart and Shamdasani, 1990; Hakim, 1987) have listed both the advantages and limitations of focus group interviews. These can be summarised as follows:

Advantages

- They can offer a wealth of insights into attitudes, perceptions and experiences that it is hard to get from a quantitative approach.
- It is a socially orientated approach to research that takes into account that people develop opinions of, and experience the social world through, interactions with others.
- A group setting may be more informal than a one-on-one interview; participants may feel more at ease and supportive of one another. This could be beneficial in encouraging people to speak.
- Focus groups have high face validity.
- The use of focus groups allows the researcher to increase the sample size within a qualitative study without major increases in time and financial cost.

Limitations

- The interviewer has less control of a group when compared to an individual interview. It is important therefore to be aware of detours in discussion and attempt to keep the discussion focused.
- The data generated can be more difficult to analyse.
- The successful negotiation of focus group interviews is often dependent on the skills of the moderator.
- Groups can be difficult to assemble.
- Focus groups are said to suffer from a lack of generalisability because samples are small and purposively selected.

In spite of any of the potential drawbacks that have been noted, it was believed that the use of the focus group method would best provide the research with the qualitative data required for a subsequent analysis. Specialist texts (Kruegar, 1994, 1993; Morgan, 1993, 1988; Stewart and Shamdasani, 1990) which provide discussions of how best to set up and conduct focus groups were consulted to ensure good practice in the field[2].

The discussions which followed were recorded on audio tape and field notes were taken throughout either by the moderator, or more usually his assistant. A copy of the full transcript was also sent to the groups along with a letter of thanks, a summary of the session and a request for any comments or criticisms that they might have[3]. Because the research attempted to study a range of similar themes with different groups, it was necessary to impose a fair amount of structure on the sessions and this was done by putting the same basic questions to every group (refer to the list of questions and prompts below). The questions were carefully structured to ensure that people had the space to develop their own approach in answering, and similarly a full range of prompts was included that could be utilised as necessary. A degree of flexibility was also encouraged, in that if an issue that related to later questions arose spontaneously, it would be explored at that point in the session. The question list was not used to impose a rigid framework on the respondents; rather it was used to ensure that the sessions remained focused. Language was also an issue in each of the three groups that were made up of Asian respondents. In each of these three sessions the moderator (due to his own lack of linguistic abilities) had to rely on some group members translating the replies of their non-English speaking colleagues.

The fieldwork: generating data

The fieldwork that informs this book took place within the boundaries of the metropolitan district of Bradford. Bradford is a northern city situated in West Yorkshire with a total population of some 483,400 residents[4]. The population is ethnically diverse, the majority (390,600) being classified as white; however, approximately 68,000 residents are of Pakistani or Bangladeshi origin, and Bradford has a thriving Muslim community. Purposive (theoretical) non-random sampling techniques (Finch and Mason, 1990; Glaser and Strauss, 1970) were used to identify and select potential respondents who would be able and willing to provide insights into their experiences, attitudes and perceptions on the central themes chosen for investigation.

A series of semi-structured interviews with 10 separate focus groups was carried out. These varied in size from 4 to 10 respondents and they were selected on the basis of the previously outlined predetermined criteria. In all a total of 69 respondents took part in the sessions between March 18 and October 6, 1997. An outline of the basic characteristics of the various groups and their members is detailed in Table 1 (pp 240 or below?). The length of the sessions varied from 50 minutes to 2 hours 45 minutes, with the average being approximately 2 hours.

Handling and analysis of data

The 10 focus groups generated approximately 280 pages of transcript, plus summaries and field notes. All the interviews were transcribed verbatim. The transcripts were then analysed in three different but complementary ways: that is, by group (summaries), by question (grid analysis), and according to selected themes (thematic codes). It was believed that by connecting with the transcripts in this way a rigorous and systematic analysis would be facilitated. Following on from this, the data was further coded using NUD*IST so that it could then be retrieved in any combination according to various base characteristics, specific questions or individual focus group. The use of three approaches also enabled the researcher to cross check each set of findings against two other views of the data. Any inconsistencies that this may have thrown up could then be investigated further to see if the cause was a simple error or, more importantly, an indication of a previous oversight in the analysis.

List of fieldwork questions and prompts

Healthcare

Q1.   Given that everybody has healthcare needs at some time, who do you think should be responsible for meeting those needs? (Prompt: the individual by going private, charitable organisations, or the state through the NHS, volunteers, individual carers in the family; do children have a duty to care?)

Q2.   Should some people have to pay for healthcare, or should it be available free of charge to everybody?   (Prompt: who should have to pay then?)

Q3.   Do you think all health provision should be available free of charge to everyone? (Prompt: what about dentistry, opticians or prescriptions?)

Q4.   In Britain the NHS is funded mainly (there are also donations and charges) by individuals' contributions in taxes. Should you have to contribute in this way before getting access to free healthcare or should treatment be available to everybody regardless of their personal contribution? (Prompt: what about children? What about disabled people, home carers or others who may be unable to contribute financially because they are unable to gain access to paid employment?)

Q5.   Are there any situations when you think it might be reasonable to deny access to healthcare provision for certain groups of people? (Prompt: older people, immigrants, asylum seekers?)

Q6.   In order to receive healthcare provision, do we have a responsibility to look after ourselves? Is an unhealthy lifestyle sufficient grounds for a provider of healthcare (the state) to deny treatment? (Prompt: should a smoker, overweight person, drug abuser, heavy drinker have as much right to treatment as someone who has a healthy lifestyle and generally keeps themselves fit?)

Housing

Q7.   If people need somewhere to live, does it matter who provides the required accommodation? If so, who should take the lead – family and friends, the public sector (the local authority backed by government money for council houses), housing associations, or private landlords?

Q8.   If you are housed, do you have a responsibility to behave in such a manner so as not to annoy your neighbours?

Q9.   What do you think of the idea of probationary tenancy periods where the agency which houses you, say the council or housing association, does so initially for a trial period and ultimately has the right to evict you if your neighbours complain that your behaviour is anti-social or a nuisance?

Q10.   In Bradford a scheme is being proposed by a housing association whereby people who wish to rent or buy a house in a certain area will be under obligation to give something back to the local community. Some local people will be trained to staff a nursery and to meet other local welfare needs; but the housing association also expects all residents to accept a measure of responsibility for the care of older people, disabled people and children within their community. Anybody who refuses to sign a formal agreement to meet such measures in their deeds or tenancy agreement will be refused housing. What do you think of this idea of linking your right to housing with such Mutual Aid Clauses?

Q11.   Do some people ultimately forfeit their right to be housed? When, if ever, would it be reasonable to refuse to house certain people? (Prompt: criminal/anti-social activity, eg drug dealing, sex offenders?)

Social security

Q12.   What do you think of the argument that the role of the state in the provision of social security payments should be reduced and that wherever possible people should be encouraged to be responsible for meeting their own needs through private insurance schemes?

Q13. Do you think that a system of social security that targets certain individuals and groups via 'means testing' is a satisfactory way to decide who should receive benefits? (Prompt: what about people's savings – should they be taken into account when calculating an individual's right to social benefits? Should their right to receive help be dependant on them spending any savings that they had previously managed to acquire? How strongly do you agree/disagree that it is fair to demand that an old person who is a homeowner must sell their house to finance any long-term residential care if and when it becomes appropriate?

NB Q14. On what grounds then should individuals be denied or granted access to social security payments? (Prompt: fraud/homelessness/asylum seekers?) was dropped before the start of the field work and never put to the respondents.

Q15. In October last year unemployment benefit was replaced by Jobseeker's Allowance. Now in order to receive benefit you have to sign what is called a jobseeker's agreement to say that you will actively seek work. If you do not sign such an agreement your money can be suspended for up to 26 weeks. If you don't act on the advice of your client adviser at the benefit office, for example if they tell you to get your hair cut, there are also penalties and suspensions that can be applied. Again, for up to six weeks, your money can be suspended. What do you think about the idea of tying your right to unemployment benefit to conditions like that?

Q16. In the past year both major political parties have announced that in the future the long-term unemployed will have to agree to go on compulsory community work or training schemes (for approximately £10 increase in benefit) or they will face a substantial reduction in benefit. How do you feel about linking the right to full employment benefit (JSA) to such additional conditions?

Q17.   At present certain social security benefits are means tested (eg Income Support, Family Credit, Housing Benefit); others such as the state pension and the JSA are only available to those who have previously made certain contributions to the state system. What do you think of the idea of replacing them with a single basic income payable to everyone regardless of their need?

Q18.   We have been speaking about issues of rights and responsibilities with regards to social welfare issues that often relate directly to some of the more disadvantaged members of our society. What about the better off who benefit from fiscal and occupational welfare rights (tax relief, mortgage tax relief, tax relief on occupational pension schemes) – should we as a society demand more of them? Douglas Hurd, for example, has talked about just paying your tax not being enough anymore. Should the welfare that the more wealthy members of society receive be conditional on them recognising further responsibilities?

Notes

[1] Throughout the series of focus group sessions only one respondent left due to unease; however, on a couple of occasions respondents left-mid session because of other commitments.

[2] Kreuger's (1993) discussion of 'Quality control in focus group research' proved to be particularly useful in this respect.

[3] With the Muslim/Pakistani Women's Group the researcher was advised not to circulate an English language summary as the respondents would not be able to respond to it. However, it became possible to verify the women's views verbally on a subsequent visit that was arranged in order to complete the research.

[4] All figures quoted from *Bradford in brief* (Bradford MDC, 1997).

Table 1: Focus groups: basic information

No	Organisation	Name given	Sex M	F	Ethnic status	Age range
FG1	Training/ED1	Benefit claimants and one worker	6	3	White	23-54
FG2	Local residents	Residents Association	1	5	White	30-57
FG3	Training/ED 2	Disabled benefit claimants	6	2	White	21-58
FG4	Pensioners association	Senior citizens	4	2	White	71-80+
FG5	Lone parents	Lone parents	1	4	3 White 2 African-Caribbean	25-63
FG6	Local charity	Middle Class Charity	3	1	White	34-77
FG7	Training/ED 1	Women benefit claimants	0	8	1 Asian 7 White	31-52
FG8	Muslim men	Informal Mosque Group	5	0	1 African 4 Asian	27-56
FG9	Job club	Asian JSA claimants	10	0	10 Asian	19-40
FG10	ESOL	Muslim/Pakistani women	0	8	8 Asian	19-40
			36	33		

Total number of respondents = 69

Index

state 103-8, 116, 192, 208
waiting times 110, 116
Heater, D. 2, 54-5, 57
Hewitt, M. 207
Hobsbawm, E.J. 38
homelessness 117, 139
Housing Act (1996) 70-1, 129
housing associations 11, 106
housing provision 5
  adequacy 117
  anti-social behaviour: exclusive
    measures 11-12, 70-1, 88-9
  service users' views 137, 138, 167,
    179, 196, 203
  conditionality 136-43, 165-6,
    167-8, 196, 203, 208
  membership 179-83, 199-200
  New Labour perspective 88-9
  New Right perspective 11-12,
    70-1
  provision
    private sector 112-13, 194
    state 105-6, 115, 117, 192
Huberman, M. 237
Hutton, Will 81, 82

I

immigrants
  healthcare eligibility 172-7, 188,
    199
  legislation on immigration 59, 96*n*,
    207-8
  see also Muslim perspective on
    welfare
incapacity benefit 9, 84
inclusion in welfare provision *see*
  membership
individualism 13
  communitarian context 27-34,
    74-6
  and concept of community 39-41
  contributory principle 201, 202,
    204, 205
  liberal context 20-7, 28, 39-41, 44
Inequalities in health 169*n*
Informal Mosque Group (focus
  group) 127, 245
  healthcare 104, 105, 135-6

housing 137, 142-3
social security 120-1, 145, 153,
  154, 162, 185
insurance contributions 82-3, 107,
  194
Islam *see* Muslim perspective on
  welfare

J

Jobseeker's Act/agreements 70, 129,
  144-8, 184-5
Johnson, A. 238
Judge, K. 195-6
justice *see* distributive justice; social
  justice

K

Kemp, P.A. 11-12
Khan, M.A. 92
Khan, Z. 91, 94
King, D.S. 22
Kurwille 35
Kymlicka, W. 20, 34

L

Labour party *see* New Labour
laissez-faire economics 22-3
Langan, M. 195
Law, I. 100
Lemos, G. 196
Levitas, R. 8, 10
liberalism 13, 15, 19, 20-7, 201-6
  citizenship theories 41, 42-3, 44,
    46, 201, 204-5
  communitarian critiques 27-34
  community concept 39-41
  social justice theories 29-30, 31-4
  see also 'libertarian' liberalism
'libertarian' liberalism 13, 20, 21-3,
  25-6, 27, 42, 46, 204-5
  see also New Right
lifestyle: conditionality applied to
  130-43, 167, 195-6
Lister, R. 3, 56
lone parents
  care responsibilities 187, 197

political rights 51, 54, 63, 191, 192
poverty
conditionality differentials 164-5, 198
deserving/undeserving poor 64
effect on welfare rights 133, 165, 169
New Labour policies on 7-8, 9, 10
New Right perspective on types of 64
see also social exclusion
Powell, M. 7, 207
primacy of rights theory 30-1
private sector welfare provision 68-9, 125-6, 127, 193-4, 207
healthcare 108-12, 194
housing 112-13, 194
social security 107-8, 113-14, 119, 194
'stakeholder welfare' 82-3
see also market system
Probationary Tenancy Periods (PTPs)
Conservatives introduce 70-1
service users' accounts 137-9, 165, 167-8, 196, 203
provision of welfare 4, 5, 13, 14
family/charitable provision 115-16
Muslim perspective 91-2
new communitarian perspective 76-8
New Labour perspective 86-7
New Right perspective 63, 68-70
rights-based perspective 56-7, 193
service users' accounts 103-28, 191-4
see also healthcare provision; housing provision; private sector welfare provision; social security provision; state: welfare provision role
psychiatric system survivors 96*n*
'psychological communities' 38
PTPs *see* Probationary Tenancy Periods

Q

qualitative research framework 2, 14, 99-101, 235-45
quasi-markets 108, 193

R

Ranger, T. 38
Rawls, John 20, 23-4, 27, 29-30, 32, 33, 46
redistributive welfare economics 22, 26, 32, 81
research framework 2, 14, 99-101, 235-45
residential care *see* long-term residential care
Residents Group (focus group)
healthcare 109, 112, 130-1, 134, 174-5, 202, 245
housing 137, 139-40, 140-1, 141-2, 180, 182-3
social security 114, 118-19, 121-2, 124-5, 146, 186
Citizen's Income 162, 163
financial conditionality 156, 159, 204-5
responsibilities *see* conditionality

S

Sandel, M. 27, 29-30, 34, 42, 43
savings *see* personal savings
school-time working drawbacks 119
Selbourne, D. 36, 73, 76, 78, 195, 203
senior citizens *see* older citizens
Senior Citizens Group (focus group)
healthcare 111-12, 130, 133, 245
housing 117, 139
social security 126, 150, 153, 155, 156, 162
service users *see* welfare service users
sex offenders 179-80, 188, 200, 203
Shah, A. 93-4
single parents *see* lone parents
Smith, Adam 22
Smith, S.R. 197
social assistance principle of welfare 201, 202, 205